Developments in Economics & Public Policy

Editors

Manoj Sharma, Yogesh Gupta & Aman Sharma

Copyright © 2018 Manoj Sharma

All rights reserved.

Disclaimer: The view expressed in the articles/papers/chapters are those of the Authors/contributors and not necessarily of the editors and publisher. Author/Contributors are themselves responsible for any kind of plagiarism found in their articles/papers/chapters.

Email: manoj.nith@gmail.com

ISBN: 1979460752
ISBN-13: 978-1979460750

DEDICATION

To Academicians, Scholars and Researchers

CONTENTS

Contributors   *viii*

Preface   *x*

1. The Impact of Foreign Direct Investment on the Economic Growth of India   1
   Mohd. Fayaz and Sandeep Kaur
2. Growth Rates of India's Mountainous States: Testing Economic Performance and Spillover Effects   21
   Susheel Kumar
3. A Comparative Analysis of Small Scale Industries: Pre- and Post Era of Globalization   36
   Bishwajeet Prakash and Rakesh Kumar Gautam
4. Mahatma Gandhi National Rural Employment Guarantee Scheme (MGNREGS): A Literature Review   49
   Monika Devi and Aman Sharma
5. Growth and Structure of Organized Manufacturing Sector of Himachal Pradesh   78
   Sanjeev Kumar and Falguni Pattanaik
6. Healthcare Service Quality in Public Hospitals from the Perspective of Outpatients-An Empirical Assessment from Jammu City of India   94
   Shahid Hamid Raina, Khursheed Hussain Dar and Waseem Hassan Khan
7. Rural Tourism as a Source of Rural Development in Mawlynnong Village in Meghalaya: A Case Study of the Cleanest Village of Asia   106
   Elwin Kro Nihang
8. Development of Rural Area and Human Resource: Real Overview   113
   Praveen Prakash
9. FIIs & DIIs and its Impact on Indian Stock Market   125
   Sahil Mahajan
10. Demonetisation: A Move Towards Cashless Economy   139
    Dharuv Pal Singh
11. Transforming of Higher Education for Sustainable Development   157

	Vibha Thakur	
12	Role of Pradhan Mantri Jan Dhan Yojana in Financial Inclusion: An Evaluation Study *Baljeet Jamwal*	168
13	Foreign Direct Investment in India: A Study of Growth and Instability in Telecommunications Sector *Manoj Sharma and Ritu Rana*	176
14	Microfinance in India: A Succinct Literature Review *Aman Sharma*	192

CONTRIBUTORS

Aman Sharma, Lecturer, Department of Management & Humanities, National Institute of Technology, Hamirpur, Himachal Pradesh, India.

Baljeet Jamwal, Associate Professor, Government College Dhaneta, Hamirpur, Himachal Pradesh, India.

Bishwajeet Prakash, Research Scholar, Centre for Economic Studies, Central University of Punjab, Bathinda, India.

Dharuv Pal Singh, Associate Professor, Department of Commerce, Government Degree College, Chowki Maniar, Una, Himachal Pradesh, India.

Elwin Kro Nihang, Research Scholar, Banaras Hindu University, India

Falguni Pattanaik,, Assistant Professor, Department of Humanities and Social Sciences, Indian Institute of Technology Roorkee, Uttarakhand, India.

Khursheed Hussain Dar, PhD Scholar, Department of Economics, Central University of Jammu, India.

Manoj Sharma, Assistant Professor, Department of Management and Humanities, National Institute of Technology Hamirpur, Himachal Pradesh, India.

Mohd. Fayaz, Research Scholar, Central University of Punjab, Bathinda, India.

Monika Devi, Research Scholar, Department of Economics, Himachal Pradesh University, Shimla, India.

Praveen Prakash, Assistant Professor, Department of Economics, Government College Jwalaji, Kangra, Himachal Pradesh, India.

Rakesh Kumar Gautam, Research Scholar, Centre for Economic Studies, Central University of Punjab, Bathinda, India.

Ritu Rana, PhD Scholar, Department of Management and Humanities, National Institute of Technology Hamirpur, Himachal Pradesh, India.

Sahil Mahajan, Assistant Professor (Commerce), Government College Baroh, Kangra, Himachal Pradesh, India.

Sandeep Kaur, Assistant Professor, Central University of Punjab, Bathinda, India.

Sanjeev Kumar, Junior Research Fellow, Department of Humanities and Social Sciences, Indian Institute of Technology Roorkee, Uttarakhand, India.

Shahid Hamid Raina, PhD Scholar, Department of Economics, Central University of Jammu, India.

Susheel Kumar, Research Scholar, Department of Economics and Public Policy, Central University of Himachal Pradesh, Dharamshala, India.

Vibha Thakur, Associate Professor, Government College Sujanpur, Hamirpur, Himachal Pradesh, India.

Waseem Hassan Khan, PhD Scholar, Department of Economics, Central University of Jammu, India.

PREFACE

Research in Economics and Public Policy generate understanding and disseminate knowledge about the different issues and aspects pertaining to Economics and Public Policy amongst its stakeholders. It requires placing the results and outcome of these research exercises. The placing of results and outcome can be done through seminars and conferences. Hence, it is in this background the Department of management & Humanities, NIT Hamirpur organized a National Conference on Management, Economics and Social Sciences (NCMESS 2017) on July 14-15, 2017. The conference covered a whole range of issues of concern to Foreign Direct Investment, Small Scale Industries, Manufacturing Sector, Health Care Services, Rural Tourism, Microfinance etc.

The present book is a collection of select research papers/articles presented in NCMESS 2017. It is expected that this book will provide sensible and useful guidance to the budding researchers, practitioners and analyst in these fields. Due care has been taken by the editorial board to shortlist papers/articles having innovation, depth of thoughtful and workability in application, nevertheless, the Authors have the ultimate responsibility with respect to the novelty.

The editors duly acknowledge the support and help provided by the advisory committee, experts and authorities of National Institute of Technology, Hamirpur, Himachal Pradesh, India.

Editors

CHAPTER: 1
THE IMPACT OF FOREIGN DIRECT INVESTMENT ON THE ECONOMIC GROWTH OF INDIA

Mohd. Fayaz and Sandeep Kaur

Abstract

Though FDI has been argued and observed as an important determinant of economic growth especially for developing countries and is expected to have positive outcomes, it may generate negative effects. The positive effects of FDI in Developed countries are largely undisputed among the policy makers. But, in developing countries, the growth increasing effect of FDI varies from country to country depending on various country-specific factors. The liberalizing trade and investment regimes, deregulation and privatization of markets, especially after the 1980s, led to a rapid expansion of FDI in many countries including India. But the FDI inflows to India, as compared to that of other Asian economies, are modest, with a bulk of investment going to the financial and non-financial service sector. Further, the present study analyzed the growth equation capturing the impact of capital formation, FDI, exports of goods and services, and merchandise trade on the GDP of India using Johansen cointegration and VECM, over the period 1981 to 2015. The study found a negative relationship between FDI and GDP of India. The FDI in India is may be diverted more towards the import substitution industries because then only the magnitude of FDI is limited to the domestic market and the gains from it become negative.

1.1. Introduction

Foreign Direct Investment (FDI) inflows play a multidimensional role in the development of the host country. As it brings non-debt creating foreign capital resources, skills improvement, and technology, and thereby generate new employment. After the financial and currency crisis during the late 1990s, in Asia and Latin America, the newly industrialized and developing countries were advised to rely mainly on FDI to add-on capital inflows and boost their economic development (Nunnenkamp, 2002). Because, FDI has been argued and observed as an important determinant of economic growth and is expected to have positive outcomes, especially for developing countries. As FDI is a significant way of transferring modern technology, creating new jobs, increasing productivity and competition and above all helps in filling the saving and investment gap (Saqib *et al*, 2013). The positive effects of FDI in developed countries are largely undisputed among the policy makers. But, in developing countries, the growth increasing effect of FDI varies from country to country depending on various country-specific factors and can even adversely impact the process of growth (Balasubramanyam *et al*, 1996; De Mello, 1999). The nature of trade policy regime of the host country is one such factor. Bhagwati (1978) had hypothesized that the efficacy of FDI inflows differs from country to country based on their strategy of trade, i.e. whether Export Promotion (EP) or the Import Substitution (IS). Because, the magnitude of EP oriented FDI would be larger as compared to that of IS-induced FDI. As later would be limited to host country's market but former promotes growth efficiently as it allows operating in a free environment. For low-income countries, FDI is considered as a major source through which they may access advanced technologies. But, the rate of growth reckons on the extent to which this low-income country adopts and applies the advanced technologies (Findlay, 1978). Similarly, knowledge and managerial expertise may spill out to the local companies in the host countries. This combined with relaxed human capital constraints may promote the growth of host country and further help to strengthen the competitiveness of its export sector (Chakraborty & Nunnenkamp, 2008). Conceiving the contiguous effects of FDI and its ability to enhance the exports via spillovers, in the long-run its impact on the balance of payments (BoP) has also been assumed positive. However, owing to high import and other foreign exchange expenses, a significant negative impact of FDI on the current account of the host country is noted by many studies (for survey see Verma, 2015).

In the context of Indian economy, the liberalization of capital account has led to an upsurge in both FDI and foreign portfolio investment (FPI). However, the policy planners of India have looked for FDI mainly for enhancing the productivity of the economy through technological advancement.

1.2. Literature Review

According to Adams (2009), the theoretical link between FDI and economic growth can be determined in the theories of modernization and dependency. Where, the former suggests that economic growth demands capital investment, and FDI could serve the purpose. As it increases total factor productivity and contributes to the capital formation (Al-Mamun & Nath, 2005). However, the dependency theory suggests the opposite, that the economic growth of a country would confront negative impacts if it depends on foreign investment (Adams, 2009). Since there is a mixed theoretical framework regarding the impact of foreign investment on economic growth, the present study leads towards the empirical studies. Balasubramanyam (1996) examined the role of FDI in the growth process of 46 developing countries and found that FDI exerts a significant influence on the growth process of the countries which are following export promotion (EP) and has no significant influence in the growth process of import substitution (IS) countries. De Mello (1999) estimated the impact of FDI on the output and total factor productivity (TFP) of OECD and non-OECD countries for the period of 1970-90 using the panel data estimations. The study found a positive impact of FDI on TFP of OECD countries while in a panel of non-OECD countries found a negative relationship between FDI and TFP. However, Archanum (2002) examined the impact of FDI on the economic performance of Thailand for the period 1970-99. The result of the study supports the Bhagwati Hypothesis that the growth impact of FDI, under an export promotion trade regime, tends to be greater. Carkovic & Levine (2002) found no independent influence of FDI on the economic growth of developing countries. Nunnenkamp (2002) analyzed the FDI and income growth correlation for 55 developing countries from Africa, Asia and Latin America covering the period 1970-1999. For Africa, the study found no relationship between FDI and growth because the investment was concentrated in the resource-based activities. For Asia also, the study found a weak correlation due to their late openness to FDI, and in the case of Latin America, a relationship between FDI and growth proved insignificant. Further, Alfaro (2003) after analyzing the effects of FDI on the sectorial growth of 47 countries over the period 1980-99, also confirmed that FDI in manufacturing sectors has a positive effect on growth while in primary sector has a negative effect and for services sector the results are ambiguous.

In the case of EU countries, Mencinger, (2003) by using causality test for the period 1994-2001, found that FDI inflows have a negative impact on their economic growth. Ciftcioglu *et al*, (2007) also investigated the effects of net FDI on economic growth, unemployment rate and openness of nine Central and East European countries using panel data analysis over the period 1995-2003. The study found that an increase in net FDI adversely affected the economic growth and the rate of unemployment. While Saqib *et al.* (2013) in the case of Pakistan, using least square method over the period 1981 to 2010, found that the economic performance of Pakistan is negatively related to the foreign direct investment. Kunle *et al* (2014) found a positive impact of FDI on the economic growth of Nigeria, using ordinary least square (OLS) over the period 1999-2013. Sakyi *et al.* (2015), in the case of Ghana, found that interaction of FDI and exports has been essential in fostering growth.

Chakraborty & Basu (2002) analyzed the two- way linkage between FDI and growth in case of India using cointegration and VECM. The study found that FDI does not cause GDP. However, causality runs from GDP to FDI. Aggarwal (2002) showed that the high-tech intensive industries are not attracting efficiency seeking FDI in India. The study found technological capacities as a crucial determinant of the exports performance of firms and suggested to upgrade the competitiveness of resources and capabilities to attract efficiency-seeking FDI. While, Aggarwal (2005) investigated the influence of Labour markets on FDI in the case of India for the period 1991-2001 and found that rigid Labour markets discourage FDI. The study suggests concentrating on export sector reforms to exploit its comparative advantage in Labour-intensive sectors. Because, FDI in Labour-intensive sectors (such as food processing, leather and leather products, light machine tools and textiles and readymade garments, etc.) would tend to have relatively high employment generating potential. Chakraborty & Nunnenkamp (2008) analyzed the industry specific FDI and output data of India by applying a panel cointegration framework. The study found that causation is mainly running from output to FDI. At the sector level analysis, the study found favorable growth effects of FDI on the manufacturing sector while that of in primary sector no causal relationship is found. From the literature above, it can be concluded that the empirical studies also exerts mixed impact of FDI on the economic growth.

1.3. Trends of FDI in Indian

Inward FDI is comprehended basically as a means of gaining industrial technology that is inaccessible through licensing and capital goods imports. However, in India, foreign investment was allowed only in designated industries and on certain conditions. Foreign Exchange and Regulation Act (FERA) 1974 specified that foreign firms could hold equity up to 40% and forbid the use of foreign brand (Nagaraj, 2003). Such a restrictive investment policy in less developed countries usually results in poor quality products and also the loss of export opportunity. However, understanding the role of FDI in the economic development of many East Asian economies, India has brought in policy reforms to attract it. Starting with a partial liberalization policy in 1980, the FDI increased to US$ 973.2 million in 1994 from a low of US$ 91.9 million in 1981 (see Figure 1). Comparing to other industrializing economies, India adopted a restrictive foreign investment regime until 1991. However, the process of liberalization and numerous policy changes, including industrial licensing and trade regime, promoted the confidence of investors to invest. Following the reforms, FDI reasonably increased from a low of US$ 2.14 billion in 1995 to US$ 44 billion in 2015. FDI (as a percentage of GDP) has increased from 0.04% in 1981 to 2.1% in 2015. However, was highest ever in 2008, i.e. 3.7%, but following the global financial crisis, it declined to 1.5% in 2013 (see Figure 1). FDI inflows to India increased significantly after the 1990s, but in comparison to other countries from Asia, it is modest. As, China is on the first rank with an FDI inflow of US$ 1741 billion over the period 1981-2015, followed by China, Hong Kong with an investment of US$ 1097 billion (see Figure 2). With FDI of US$ 687 billion, Singapore is at third rank followed by India with an investment of US$ 372 billion, far less than other top three countries. While Saudi Arabia got US$ 246 billion, followed by Korea (US$ 188 billion), Turkey (US$ 179 billion), Thailand (US$ 166 billion), Malaysia (US$ 163 billion), and then by Indonesia (US$ 144 billion) over the same period.

Figure 1: *FDI Net Inflows to India (US$ Billion) and FDI (% of GDP), Over the Period 1981 to 2015*

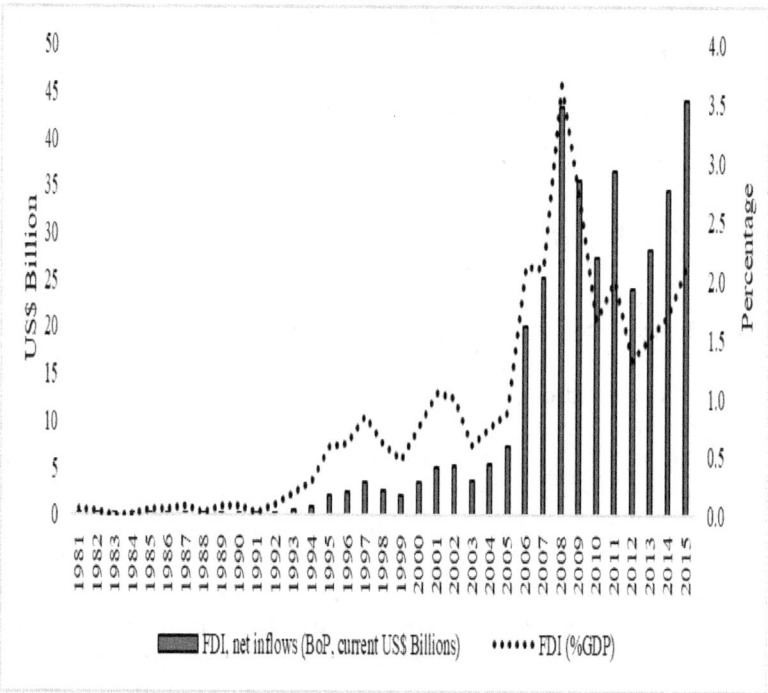

Source: *the World Bank, 2016*

Up to the recent past, FDI in India was coming to a limited number of sectors with an upper limit and certain other terms and conditions. As, the financial and non-financial service sector, which exclusively falls under the realm of the service sector, is the largest recipient of FDI in India with a share of 17.6% for the period April 2000 to March 2016 (see Table, 1). Followed by the construction development with 8.4% of share and then by computer software &

hardware with a share of 7.3% over the same period. Telecommunication sector received 6.4% of total FDI while 5.2% of total FDI gone to the automobile industry. The other sectors like drug & pharmaceuticals, chemicals (other than fertilizers), and trading received around 4% of FDI. While power, hotel & tourism, and metallurgical industries received around 3% of FDI. Construction (Infrastructure) activities, food processing industries, and Petroleum & Natural Gas received 2.8, 2.4 and 2.3% of total FDI, respectively over the same period.

Figure 2: *FDI Inflows of Top Ten Asian Countries over the Period 1981 to 2015*

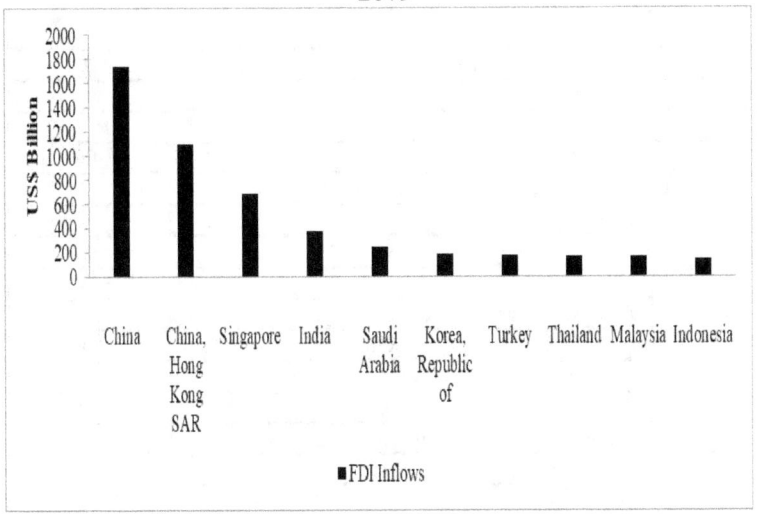

Source: UNCTAD, 2016

Less than 2% of total FDI gone to the sectors like Information & Broadcasting (Including Print Media), Non-conventional Energy, Electrical Equipment, Industrial Machinery, Cement and Gypsum Product, Miscellaneous Mechanical & Engineering and less than 1% gone to Industries, Fermentation Industries, Mining, Textiles (Including Dyed, Printed), Ports, Machine Tools, Railway Related Components, Leather, Leather Goods and Pickers, Timber Products, Industrial Instruments, and Coal Production. It is evident that high-tech intensive industries like telecommunication, automobile industry and drug and pharmaceuticals are attracting a minuscule share of total FDI inflows in India. In the development of East Asian countries technological up-gradation, in the export-oriented regions, has played a crucial role (Petri, 2012). Because, these products are high income elastic, substitute older products, create new demands, and tend to grow faster in trade (Industrial development Report, 2016).

Table 1: Sector-wise FDI Inflows in India (April 2000 to March 2016)

Rank	Sector	%age of total FDI Inflows
1.	Services sector (Financial and Non-Financial)	17.6
2.	Construction Development (Townships, Housing, Built-up, Infrastructure and Construction-Development Projects)	8.4
3.	Computer Software & Hardware	7.3
4.	Telecommunications	6.4
5.	Automobile Industry	5.2
6.	Drugs & Pharmaceuticals	4.8
7.	Chemicals (Other Than Fertilizers)	4.1
8.	Trading	4.1
9.	Power	3.6
10.	Hotel & Tourism	3.2
11.	Metallurgical Industries	3.1
12.	Construction (Infrastructure) Activities	2.8
13.	Food Processing Industries	2.4
14.	Petroleum & Natural Gas	2.3
15.	Information & Broadcasting (Including Print Media)	1.7
16.	Non-conventional Energy	1.5
17.	Electrical Equipment	1.5
18.	Industrial Machinery	1.4
19.	Cement and Gypsum Product	1.1
20.	Miscellaneous Mechanical & Engineering Industries	1.1
21.	Fermentation Industries	0.8
22.	Mining	0.8
23.	Textiles (Including Dyed, Printed)	0.6
24.	Ports	0.6
25.	Machine Tools	0.3
26.	Railway Related Components	0.3
27.	Leather, Leather Goods and Pickers	0.06
28.	Timber Products	0.05
29.	Industrial Instruments	0.03
30.	Coal Production	0.01

Source: *Ministry of Commerce and Industry, Govt. of India, (2016).*

It is also evident from the Table 1 that a very little FDI in India gone to the Labour-intensive manufacturing sector like food processing industries, leather products, timber products, etc. However, FDI in Labour-intensive sectors would tend to have relatively high employment generating potential, as found by Aggarwal (2005). In the recent years, the government has taken some initiatives like relaxing FDI norms in sectors such as PSU oil refineries, defense, power exchange and the stock exchange to reap the positive benefits of FDI.

1.4. Data Source and Methodology

Further, the study employed the empirical approach to analyze the growth effects of capital formation, exports of goods and services, FDI, and merchandise trade on the GDP of India by using annual secondary data for the period 1981 to 2015. Where, GDP is dependent variable and capital formation (CF), exports of goods and services (EGS), FDI and merchandise trade (ME) are explanatory variables. The detailed methodology is explained in the following subsequent sections.

1.4.1. Unit root and Stationary testing procedures

The aim of the study is to comprehend the impact of above-said variables in the long-run and short-run. For this purpose cointegration and error correction regression among the time series, data will be applied. However, Johansen cointegration has some special properties i.e. data must be integrated in the same order (Johansen, 1991). For this reason, firstly the Augmented Dickey-Fuller (ADF) test, proposed by Dickey and Fuller (1979), is applied. The general framework of ADF test consists of the following equation.

$$\Delta Y_t = \alpha_0 + \beta_{1,t} + \gamma Y_{t-1} + \sum_{j=i}^{m} \beta_j \Delta Y_{t-j} + \varepsilon_t \quad \ldots \ldots (1)$$

Where, $\Delta Y_t = Y_t - Y_{t-1}$ and ε_t is a white noise error term and $\Delta Y_{t-1} = (Y_{t-1} - Y_{t-2}), \Delta Y_{t-2} = (Y_{t-2} - Y_{t-3})$, etc. The number of lagged differences is determined empirically. Lagged differences are included so that error term will be serially uncorrelated and we can obtain an unbiased estimate of γ, the coefficient of lagged Y_{t-1}. The hypotheses are:

$H_0: \delta = 0$ (i.e., the time series is non-stationary)
$H_1: \delta < 0$ (i.e., the time series is stationary).

1.4.2. Cointegration procedure

The Johansen co-integration is the most appropriate and useful technique in day to day economic literature. Johansen test simultaneously determines the numbers of long run co-integrated equations in the system and provide coefficients of the long run causality (Gujarati et al. 2012). Johansen (1991) multivariate cointegration test is used in this study to find the long-run relationship among the concerned variables. The starting point in the vector auto-regression (VAR) of order p is given by

$$Y_t = \mu + \prod_1 Y_{t-1} + \prod_2 Y_{t-2} + \ldots\ldots + \prod_p Y_{t-p} + \varepsilon_t \ldots\ldots(2)$$

In equation (2) $Y_t = CF_t, EGS_t, FDI_t, ME_t$, is a 5×1 vector of variables and are integrated of order one i.e. I(1) and ε_t is a 5×1 vector of innovations. While $\prod_1$ through $\prod_p$ are 5×5 coefficient matrices. The equation (2) contains unit root and can be parameterized by subtracting Y_{t-1} on both sides and the equation will be

$$\Delta Y_t = \mu + \Gamma_1 \Delta Y_{t-1} + \Gamma_2 \Delta Y_{t-2} + \ldots\ldots + \Gamma_p \Delta Y_{t-p} - \prod_p Y_{t-p} + \varepsilon_t \ldots\ldots(3)$$

Where, $\Gamma_1 = \prod_1 - I, \Gamma_2 = \prod_1 - \Gamma_1, \Gamma_3 = \prod_2 - \Gamma_2$ and $\prod = I - \prod_1 - \prod_2 - \ldots\ldots - \prod_p$. The matrix $\prod$ is called the impact matrix which determines the extent of cointegration. The above equation is rearranged as

$$\Delta Y_t = \mu + \prod_{t-p} Y_{t-p} + \sum_{i=1}^{m-1} \Gamma_i \Delta Y_{t-i} + \beta \mu_t + \varepsilon_t \ldots\ldots(4)$$

Where Y is a p-dimensional process, while μ_t contains constant, a linear trend and seasonal dummies which are deterministic terms, $\Gamma i's$ are $p \times p$ parametric matrices and β contain the parameters associated with μ_t (Johansen, 1991). The cointegrating vectors are given by β matrix and cointegrating vector entering each equation of the VECM, also known as the 'adjustment parameter' are given by α. This test utilizes two likelihood ratios (LR) test statistics for the number of cointegrating vectors. The two statistics are Trace test (J_{trace}) and Maximum eigenvalue (λ_{max}) test.

$$J_{trace} = -T \sum_{i=r+1}^{N} In(1 - \hat{\lambda}_i) \dots \dots (5)$$

$$\lambda_{max} = TIn(1 - \hat{\lambda}_{r+1}) \dots \dots (6)$$

Where $\hat{\lambda}_i$ the estimated value for the ith is ordered eigenvalue from the matrix $\prod$ and T is the number of effective observations. The standard approach to the procedure of Johansen ML is to calculate first the Trace and Maximum Eigenvalue statistics and then compare these to the appropriate critical values. If a model consists of n different variables (like five in case of the present study), we start by testing if we have one, two, three, four or five cointegrating vectors.

1.4.3. Vector Error Correction Model

The error correction mechanism (ECM) is firstly used by Sargan (1984) however popularized by Engle and Granger (1987). The model states that, if the presence of cointegration(s) is detected then, in the vector error correction model (VECM), the Granger causality must be conducted to examine the short-run relationship of all explanatory variables on GDP. If at least one cointegration vector is found among the number of variables, then there always exists an equating error correction representation which entails that change in the dependent variable can be formulated as a function of the fluctuations occur in other explanatory variables (Yang, 2011). Under these circumstances the basic structure of an error correction model system as follows:

$$\Delta Y_t = \alpha + \beta_0 \Delta X_{t-1} + \beta_1 ECT_{t-1} + \varepsilon_t \dots \dots (7)$$

Where Δ denotes first difference, ε_t is random error and ECT is the error correction term of the model which measures the speed of adjusting prior deviations from equilibrium.
Where,

$$ECT_{t-1} = GDP_{t-1} - \beta_1 GDP - \beta_2 CF - \beta_3 EGS - \beta_4 FDI - \beta_5 ME \dots \dots (8)$$

ECT_{t-1} is the error correction term which is derived from the cointegration equation of the long-run.

1.4.4. Diagnostic Statistics

Imperative diagnostic statistics, to ascertain the normality, autocorrelation, and heteroscedasticity of the model, have been applied, and a brief discussion of them is given below.

i) Jarque-Bera test of Normality

Jarque and Bera have developed the test for normality, using the LaGrange multiplier or score test on the Pearson distribution for the normality of observations and regression disturbances.

$$JB = n\left[\frac{skewness^2}{6} + \frac{(kurtosis-3)^2}{24}\right] \ldots\ldots (9)$$

Where n is sample size. For a normal distribution, skewness must be equal to zero and kurtosis equal to three (Gujarati *et al.* 2012). The hypotheses are;

H_0 = residual are normally distributed
H_1 = residual are not normally distributed

ii) Breusch-Godfrey Test

Breusch and Godfrey test of autocorrelation is also known as LM test and is used to check the presence of serial dependence that has not been included in a proposed model structure which leads to incorrect results drawn from other tests (Belsley, 1997; Godfrey, 1994). To perform this test, the residuals from regression analysis are used to derive the test statistics, and it schemes as below;

$$GDP_t = \alpha + \beta_1 CF + \beta_2 EGS + \beta_3 FDI + \beta_4 ME + \varepsilon_t \ldots\ldots (10)$$

Presume that ε_t follows the pth-order autoregressive AR(p), outlines as follows:

$$\varepsilon_t = \alpha + \mu_1 \varepsilon_{t-1} + \mu_2 \varepsilon_{t-2} + \ldots\ldots + \mu_p \varepsilon_{t-p} + v_t \ldots\ldots (11)$$

Substituting the above formula of ε_t into the equation (10), we get

$$GDP_t = \alpha + \beta_1 CF + \beta_2 EGS + \beta_3 FDI + \beta_4 ME + \mu_1 \varepsilon_{t-1} + \mu_2 \varepsilon_{t-2} + \ldots\ldots + \mu_p \varepsilon_{t-p} + v_t \ldots\ldots (12)$$

iii) ARCH Test

Autoregressive Conditional Heteroscedasticity (ARCH) test has been devised by Engle (1982). This is a residual based test, used to detect heteroscedasticity (i.e. the variance of residuals are not constant).

$$\varepsilon_t = \beta_1 \varepsilon_{t-1} + \beta_2 \varepsilon_{t-2} + \ldots\ldots + \beta_m \varepsilon_{t-m} \ldots\ldots (13)$$

The residual from the model is ε_t with including m lags. This test tests the null hypothesis that the variance of disturbances is constant against the alternative that the variances of disturbances are not constant across observations.

1.5. Empirical Estimates

The study draws the theoretical framework provided in Archanum (2002), which estimated the nexus between the foreign trade regime and FDI-growth in a case of Thailand. Firstly, to assess the stationarity of the variables, ADF test is used and the results reported in Table 2 shows that all the said variables are non-stationary at the level, however, are stationary after first difference. As the variables are I(1), we further executed Johansen cointegration tests. The results of both Trace and Max-Eigen Statistic, reported in Table 3 and 4 show that there are three cointegrating equations.

Table 2: ADF Test Results (At Level)

Variables	t-statistic	Critical value	Prob.
GDP	1.028684	-2.951125	0.9960
CAPITAL	-1.182882	-2.951125	0.6704
EGS	-0.703746	-2.951125	0.8325
FDI	-1.329135	-2.951125	0.6046
ME	-0.976648	-2.951125	0.7504
ADF Test Results (After First Difference)			
Variables	t-statistic	Critical value	Prob.
GDP	-5.287924	-2.954021	**0.0001**
CAPITAL	-7.195609	-2.954021	**0.0000**
EGS	-5.688658	-2.954021	**0.0000**
FDI	-6.432223	-2.954021	**0.0000**
ME	-6.744953	-2.954021	**0.0000**

Table 3: Johansen Cointegration Test Results (Trace statistic)

No. of Cointegrated Equations		Eigen Value	Trace Statistic	Critical Value	Prob.**
Null Hypothesis	Alternate Hypothesis				
r =0*	r ≥ 1	0.900591	155.3145	69.81889	**0.0000**
r ≤ 1*	r ≥ 2	0.735610	83.75073	47.85613	**0.0000**
r ≤ 2*	r ≥ 3	0.644074	42.51046	29.79707	**0.0010**
r ≤ 3	r ≥ 4	0.244981	10.48644	15.49471	0.2452
r ≤ 4	r = 5	0.055651	1.775053	3.841466	0.1828

Note: * indicates rejection of the Null-hypothesis at the 5% level and ** indicates MacKinnon-Haug-Michelis (1999) p-values.

Table 4: Johansen Cointegration Test Results (Max Eigen statistics)

No. of Cointegrated Equations		Eigen Value	Max Eigen Statistic	Critical Value	Prob.**
Null Hypothesis	Alternate Hypothesis				
r =0*	r ≥ 1	0.900591	71.56381	33.87687	**0.0000**
r ≤ 1*	r ≥ 2	0.735610	41.24027	27.58434	**0.0005**
r ≤ 2*	r ≥ 3	0.644074	32.02402	21.13162	**0.0010**
r ≤ 3	r ≥ 4	0.244981	8.711385	14.26460	0.3110
r ≤ 4	r = 5	0.055651	1.775053	3.841466	0.1828

Note: * indicates rejection of the Null-hypothesis at the 5% level and ** indicates MacKinnon-Haug-Michelis (1999) p-values.

The normalized cointegrating vectors which represent the long-run relationship among the variables are reported in Table 5. While normalizing the estimated coefficients, the signs need to be reversed however that of the variable normalized remains same.

The cointegration equation is expressed as;

$$GDP = 10.79 - 0.35FDI + .05ME \ldots \ldots \ldots (14)$$

Where ME in equation (14) is merchandise exports. The

normalized equation (14) shows a positive and significant relationship between merchandise trade and GDP while a negative relationship between GDP and FDI. Similar results were shown by Chakraborty & Basu (2002) in the case of India. Carkovic & Lavine (2002), Nunnenkamp (2002) and Mencinger (2003) also found FDI negatively related to the economic growth of developing countries. Saqib *et al.* (2013) found a negative relationship between GDP and FDI in the case of Pakistan. Bhagwati presented the theory of the effect of trade policy regime on the gains from FDI (Bhagwati, 1978).

Table 5: Parameters in Normalized Cointegrating Vectors

Variables	Cointegrating Equation-1	Cointegrating Equation-2	Cointegrating Equation-3
GDP	1.000000	0.000000	0.000000
CAPITAL	0.000000	1.000000	0.000000
EGS	0.000000	0.000000	1.000000
FDI	0.353715 (0.09741) [3.63111]*	16.40983 (6.18296) [2.65404]*	-1.717471 (0.76120) [-2.25625]*
ME	-0.056350 (0.00878) [-6.41782]*	-1.664522 (0.55729) [-2.98679]*	-0.542753 (0.06861) [-7.91065]*
Constant	-10.79692	-5.900110	-0.062984

Note: * *indicates significant at 5% level, Standard error in () & t-statistics in [].*

The theory postulates that FDI in a given host country can restrict growth in the context of import substitution (IS) regime and promotes growth under export promotion (EP) regime. Because in an IS regime usually, the FDI takes place in sectors characterized by high capital intensity where the host country does not have a comparative advantage. However, under EP regime foreign investors operate in a free environment without any distortions and thus increase the output and international competitiveness of the host country (Archanum, 2002). The effects of FDI on the GDP of India are found negative by the present study which supports the Bhagwati hypothesis, i.e. the effect of FDI are likely to be negligible or even negative under an IS regime. However, the effect of FDI can become positive if India makes the policies that attract investment in export promotion industries.

The residuals of the cointegrating equations or Error Correction Terms (ECT) are used for short-run dynamics in the VECM, and the results of the same are presented in Table 6. The coefficient of the ECTs in VECM should be negative, as it measures the speed of adjustment to its long-run equilibrium and a negative sign implies a decrease in the value of the variables to reestablish equilibrium. The results reported in Table 6 shows that only ECT-1 is having a negative sign and statistically significant, which further confirms the long-run cointegration in the GDP equation. However the coefficient of ECT, in capital formation equation and exports of goods and services equation, are not statistically significant. Further, to check whether the data is normally distributed or not and to check for serial correlation and heteroscedasticity, various diagnostic tests (explained in section 4.4) have been used in this study. The results given in Table 7 shows that the data is normally distributed and there is no problem of serial correlation and heteroscedasticity.

Table 6: Short-Run Results

Variables	Coefficient	St. error	t-statistic	Probability
ECT-1	-0.365194	0.170990	-2.135758	**0.0540**
ECT-1	0.006628	0.005377	1.232557	0.2413
ECT-1	0.028437	0.038055	0.747263	0.4693
D(CF)	-0.011502	0.006619	-1.737892	0.1078
D(EGS)	-0.004688	0.053277	-0.087992	0.9313
D (FDI)	0.073149	0.036132	2.024498	**0.0658**
D (ME)	-0.011340	0.024293	-0.466800	0.6490

Table 7: Diagnostic Test Results

Test	F-statistic	Prob.
Normality Test Jarque-Bera	4.085480	0.129673
Breusch-Godfrey Serial Correlation LM Test	0.365404	0.7798
Heteroskedasticity Test ARCH Test	0.835671	0.4875

Conclusion

The FDI inflows to India, as compared to that of other Asian economies, are modest with a bulk of investment is going to the financial and non-financial service sector and a minuscule share of it go to manufacturers and Labour-intensive sectors. However, FDI in manufacturing and Labour-intensive sectors would tend to have relatively high employment generating potential and will contribute more to long-run growth as India is a Labour abundant country. Further, the investment in manufacturers and Labour-intensive sectors will help in maintaining the quality of product, efficiency and increasing productivity. The present study also empirically estimated the growth equation for capturing the impact of capital formation, FDI, exports of goods and services and merchandise trade on the GDP of India, using Johansen cointegration test and VECM. The study found a positive relationship between merchandise trade and GDP, however, a significant and negative relationship between FDI and GDP. The FDI inflows in India may be diverted more towards the import substitution industries because only then the magnitude of FDI is limited to the domestic market and the gains from it become negative. Thus, India needs to attract outward-oriented and efficiency seeking FDI to reap its positive growth effects. Because, the magnitude of outward-oriented FDI would be larger as it allows operating in a free environment and would promote growth efficiently.

References

Adams, S. (2009). Foreign direct investment, domestic investment, and economic growth in Sub-Saharan Africa. *Journal of Policy Modeling, 31*(6), 939-949.

Aggarwal, A. (2002). Liberalisation, multinational enterprises and export performance: evidence from Indian manufacturing. *Journal of Development Studies, 38*(3), 119-137.

Aggarwal, A. (2005). The influence of labour markets on FDI: Some empirical explorations in export oriented and domestic market seeking FDI across Indian states. *University of Delhi (http://knowledgeforum.tifac.org.in/IndexServer/tifac/article/22.doc).*

Al-Mamun, K. A., & Nath, H. K. (2005). Export-led growth in Bangladesh: a time series analysis. *Applied Economics Letters, 12*(6), 361-364.

Alfaro, L. (2003). Foreign direct investment and growth: Does the sector matter. *Harvard Business School, 2003*, 1-31.

Archanum, K. (2002). *Foreign Trade Regime and FDI-growth Nexus: A Case Study.* Economics Division, Research School of Pacific and Asian Studies & Asia Pacific School of Economics and Management, Australian National University.

Balasubramanyam, V. N., Salisu, M., & Sapsford, D. (1996). Foreign direct investment and growth in EP and IS countries. *The Economic Journal*, *106*(434), 92-105.

Belsley, D. A. (1997). A small-sample correction for testing for gth-order serial correlation with artificial regressions. *Computational Economics*, *10*(3), 197-229.

Bhagwati, J. N. (1978). Anatomy and consequences of exchange control regimes. *NBER Books*.

Carkovic, M. V., & Levine, R. (2002). Does foreign direct investment accelerate economic growth?. *University of Minnesota Department of Finance Working Paper*.

Chakraborty, C., & Basu, P. (2002). Foreign direct investment and growth in India: A cointegration approach. *Applied Economics*, *34*(9), 1061-1073.

Chakraborty, C., & Nunnenkamp, P. (2008). Economic reforms, FDI, and economic growth in India: a sector level analysis. *World Development*, *36*(7), 1192-1212.

Ciftcioglu, S., Fethi, S., & Begovic, N. (2007). The impact of net inflows of foreign direct investment on economic growth, unemployment and openness: A panel data analysis of nine central and east European countries. *The Journal of Global Business Management*, *3*(2), 89-94.

De Mello, L. R. (1999). Foreign direct investment-led growth: evidence from time series and panel data. *Oxford Economic Papers*, *51*(1), 133-151.

Dickey, A. & Fuller, W. (1979). Distribution of the estimates for autoregressive time series with a unit root. *Journal of the American Statistical Association*, *74*(366), 427-431.

Engle, R. F. (1982). Autoregressive conditional heteroscedasticity with estimates of the variance of United Kingdom inflation. *Econometrica: Journal of the Econometric Society*, *50*(4), 987-1007.

Engle, R. F. & Granger, C. W. J. (1987). Co-integration and error correction: representation, estimation, and testing. *Econometrica*, vol. 55(2), 251-276.

Findlay, R. (1978). Relative backwardness, direct foreign investment, and the transfer of technology: a simple dynamic model. *The Quarterly Journal of Economics*, *92*(1), 1-16.

Godfrey, L. G. (1994). Testing for serial correlation by variable addition in dynamic models estimated by instrumental variables. *The Review of Economics and Statistics, 76*(3), 550-559.

Gujarati, D. N., Porter, D. C. & Gunasekar, S. (2012). *Basic Econometrics (5thed.)*. New Delhi: McGraw Hill Education Pvt. Ltd.

Industrial Development Report (2016). The Role of Technology and Innovation in Inclusive and Sustainable Industrial Development. *United Nations Industrial Development Organization.*

Johansen, S. (1991). Estimation and hypothesis testing of cointegration vectors in Gaussian vector autoregressive models. *Econometrica Journal of the Econometric Society, 59*(6), 1551-1580.

Kunle, A. M., Olowe, S. O., & Oluwafolakemi, F. O. (2014). Impact of Foreign Direct Investment on Nigeria Economic Growth. *International Journal of Academic Research in Business and Social Sciences, 4*(8), 234.

Mencinger, J. (2003). Does foreign direct investment always enhance economic growth?. *Kyklos, 56*(4), 491-508.

Ministry of Commerce and Industry, Govt. of India, (2016). Accessed on 27th of December 2016, http://www.commerce.gov.in/DOC/index.aspx

Nagaraj, R. (2003). Foreign direct investment in India in the 1990s: Trends and issues. *Economic and Political Weekly, 38*(17), 1701-1712.

Nunnenkamp, P. (2002). FDI and Economic Growth in developing Countries. *J. World Investment, 13*(3), 595.

Petri, P. A. (2012). The determinants of bilateral FDI: Is Asia different?. *Journal of Asian Economics, 23*(3), 201-209.

Sakyi, D., Commodore, R., & Opoku, E. E. O. (2015). Foreign direct investment, trade openness and economic growth in Ghana: An empirical investigation. *Journal of African Business, 16*(1-2), 1-15.

Saqib, D., Masnoon, M., & Rafique, N. (2013). Impact of foreign direct investment on economic growth of Pakistan. *Advances in Management & Applied Economics, 3*(1), 35-45.

The World Bank (2016). Accessed on 20th December 2016 from http://databank.worldbank.org/data/home.aspx

United Nations Conference on Trade and Development

(UNCTAD) (2016). Accessed on 27th December 2016 from http://unctadstat.unctad.org/wds/TableViewer/tableView.aspx

Verma, S. (2015). Current Account Fallout of FDI in Post-Reform India. *Economic & Political Weekly*, *50*(39), 45.

Yang, L. (2011). An empirical analysis of current account determinants in emerging Asian economies. *Cardiff Economics Working Paper*, Cardiff University.

CHAPTER: 2
GROWTH RATES OF INDIA'S MOUNTAINOUS STATES: TESTING ECONOMIC PERFORMANCE AND SPILLOVER EFFECTS

Susheel Kumar

Abstract

The term spillover effect is the basic key for to achieve the goal of balanced development in the regional level and also nations. Spillover effect presents to the impact that apparently unconnected events in one state can have on the economies of other states. It means, when the state changed in any economic terms, namely, growth and economic development, how to effect other states or neighbouring states around them undergo. The objective of this paper is to test whether there are any important spillover effects or trickling down effects of economic growth in the mountainous states. The study also investigates to analyse the growth performance and growth story of NSDP in the mountainous states. The study results have shown that there was variation in the growth performance and mountainous states growing faster than the regional average level. The average growth rate of NSDP accelerated both at the all India level and growth rate of all mountainous states during 1980-81 and 1996-97 to 1997-98 and 2014-15. The result of spillover effect indicates that raising the potential and effects of major economic growth among the mountainous states. It also indicated in spillover effects that very less interdependency among the mountainous states in terms of the growth rate of NSDP.

There is an urgent requirement to reinforce the investment of infrastructure and increase public investment in basic core sectors, namely, agriculture and micro small scales industries. Unneeded to say that, while above issues are critical to achieving the goal of high growth of NSDP; efficient implementation and scrutinising of growth policy changes will be of extreme importance.

2.1. Introduction

The main targets of the economy and five-year plan are to uplift the economic growth in the various terms of "Inclusive Growth" and "Sustained and More Inclusive Growth". Inclusive growth has always been one of the confirmed objectives for development and well-being of the underprivileged society of the people. It creates regionally balanced growth performance and provides a smooth path for the economic growth and regional development. Most of the researchers found that there were divergence and differences between the growth performances in the Indian states during previous two decades (Ahluwalia, 2002; Shetty, 2003 and Cherodian & Thirlwall, 2013). They also indicated that there was enlarge disparities and inequalities in the states and regions of our country. Whereas, policymakers adopted the term of "balanced growth" performance; it affected from region to region by the spillover effect and trickling down effect. In the previous literature, most of the studies have been tested these hypotheses in various ways, however, these hypotheses have not been subjected to analyse the growth performance in the mountainous states. These hypotheses are spillover effects, trickling down, polarisation and spread-backwash (Gaile, 1980 and Debnath & Roy, 2012). When one mountainous state increases in the growth rate of NSDP among the mountainous states; we want to know that how the effects in the growth rate of NSDP among the others mountainous states or regions. It can be calculated and analysed by the way and in term of "spillover effects".

The "Balanced Growth" is the economic model that might be created equilibrium in the level of economic growth in different regions by the way of trickle-down hypotheses. The hypothesis of trickling down effects would hold if income and growth of a region cause income and growth of the other region with positive coefficients (Debnath & Roy, 2012). In the causality test, negative coefficients would maintain the divergence in the economic growth and concentration hypotheses. The polarisation and concentration are also known by the growing up economic development in one factor in the regions and how much the cause or effect in other regions. In the previous literature, the concept has used by the various school of economists since physiocrats. However, the trickle-down theory is the basic idea in the entrepreneurs by encouraging production in the overall economy, which escorts to economic growth and capital conception that reimbursement everyone. These theories are helping and investigating the effects and causes of one region to other regions by the way of economic development factors. Regarding Indian economy, the economic growth rate of NSDP was dissimilar in the Indian states and major states as exposed by the literature and NSSO reports. However, it may be effects and causes of one region to other regions in the mountainous states.

This study has been attempted to empirically investigate the spill-over effects in the mountainous states or regions in their growth rate of NSDP. The study also investigates the NSDP growth performance in mountainous states or regions. The study is purely based on the secondary data in annual NSDP and covering a more recent period of 1980-81 to 2014-15 with constant prices of 2011-12. The study is limited to mountainous states namely Arunachal Pradesh, Assam, Himachal Pradesh, Jammu & Kashmir, Manipur, Meghalaya, Mizoram, Nagaland, Sikkim, Tripura and Uttarakhand. The study has been divided into three folds: first fold provides to the previous literature, followed by the discussion of the mountainous states growth rates; second fold discovers to reckon the growth of NSDP in acceleration or deceleration in the mountainous states during 1980-81 and 1996-97 and 1997-98 and 2014-15. And in the third fold, the empirical results of the spill-over effects of NSDP growth are presented. Lastly, the conclusion is offered.

2.2. Some Important Facts in the Literature

In Indian economy, the disparities have widened in recent decades, however disparity among countries is a temporary phenomenon suggests by the neoclassical growth model. In the long run, many countries or regions should not diverge; still, they rise at the similar steady-state levels. The spillover effects across regions may not be the significant always; but insignificant spillover effects across the region is relatively higher in the developing countries not in poorer countries (Higgins, 1983). Bhide et al. (2006) observed spillover effects (trickling down effect) of growth rates in the states over the other states. They also found dispersion of growth across the states during 1971 to 1998. Dholakia (2009) in his study exposed unidirectional causality of changes in the GSDP rate from better states to worse states. The study found positive coefficient and showed an increase in the growth rates of NSDP of the better states to worse states. This study clearly supported the trickle-down effect, rather than polarisation effect.

Some researchers have argued that knowledge of the rapidly developing Asian NICs demonstrates a positive connection between outward orientation and GDP growth; while others are more caution regarding the causal effects (Kokko, Zejan, & Tansini, 2001). Debnath & Roy (2012) found disparities in the states and also recorded Assam rise at lower rates as compared to the others in average North-eastern regions. This study also recorded that except Assam all others states have progressed at a high rate than an aggregate of the India level. The study results have proven that no co-integrated in NSDP pairs of states and clearly exposed poor growth interdependence among North-eastern states with bidirectional growth causality. Zhang & Felmingham (2002) analysed the development process and found that uneven growth among different regions expected and often occurs. The various regions interact with each other through input and output linkages. Input demand and output supply effects are important interaction across various regions. Technological, market demand and income remittances are important mechanisms through which interactive impacts between regions are achieved. They found that Centre and West regions have benefitted from the rapid growth of the Eastern provinces through spillover effect in the China. They also suggested that importance of incorporating spill-over tests in this analyst of the noticeable differences in individual rates of regional development. The main gap in the literature is interstate linkages of NSDP growth and not many studies to give the importance of spillover effect among the mountainous state's economy.

2.3. Growth Rates of NSDP and Performance both at all India Level and in the Mountainous States

The mountainous states are unique in terms of culture, geographical, natural resources and investment criteria. Most of the people live in the rural areas at the subsistence level; some geography areas are untouched for the development process and unreachable by the people. The previous literature found disparities and inequality in terms of NSDP and GSDP in the Indian states, however, very few studies found the convergence in the Indian states and seven sister states. There were contradictory results about the concept of disparities and inequalities and mountainous states have not been subjected to analyse these issues. There is a need for an independent study to find the conclusion regarding the disparities and performance of the mountainous states.

The growth process in the mountainous states may be sluggish as compared to the major states because mountainous states have reserved the natural resources and green economy, which is known as the term of "Resource Curse". Despite having been abounded the natural resources and green economy, there may be sluggish growth rates. The performance is the basic idea for to measure the disparities and variations and also to find out the causes that increase the growth rate in the mountainous states. The study has been divided into two sub-periods as 1980-81 to 1996-97 and 1997-98 to 2014-15. The performance of mountainous states is measured along in their NSDP growth and output stages. The study has been calculated the growth rate of NSDP on the basis of compound annual growth rate.

Table 1 presents the growth rate of NSDP and performance both at all India level and in mountainous states during 1980-81 and 1996-97 and 1997-98 and 2014-15. A perusal of the table shows that the growth rate of NSDP accelerated both at the all India level and average growth rate of mountainous states from 5.31 percent to 7.22 percent and 5.52 percent to 7.39 percent during 1980-81 and 1996-97 to 1997-98 and 2014-15. Taking the entire period (1980-81 and 2014-15), the growth rate of NSDP recorded both at all India level and an average of mountainous states at 6.62 percent and 6.55 percent. The growth rate of different mountainous states are concerned the table shows that

Sikkim registered the highest growth rate of 8.57 percent and followed by Arunachal Pradesh (8.45 percent) and Nagaland (7.44 percent) during 1980-81 and 1996-97.

Table 1: Compound Annual Growth rates of NSDP in the Mountainous States During the Period of 1980-81 to 2014-15 (Constant Prices 2011-12)

Mountainous States	1980-81 to 1996-97	1997-98 to 2014-15	Entire Period (1980-81 to 2014-15)	Acceleration/ Deceleration Growth Rates of NSDP during 1980-81 and 1996-97 to 1997-98 and 2014-15
Arunachal Pradesh	8.45	6.85	6.76	-1.60
Assam	3.26	4.60	3.46	1.34
Himachal Pradesh	5.12	7.00	6.32	1.88
Jammu & Kashmir	3.03	4.93	4.19	1.90
Manipur	4.46	4.92	4.72	0.46
Meghalaya	5.08	6.79	6.17	1.71
Mizoram	NA	8.06	8.06	NA
Nagaland	7.44	7.60	7.13	0.16
Sikkim	8.57	11.84	8.66	3.27
Tripura	5.93	8.33	7.53	2.40
Uttarakhand	3.84	10.35	9.09	6.51
Average Growth Rates of Mountainous states	5.52	7.39	6.55	1.87
Average Growth Rate of All India Level	5.31	7.22	6.62	1.91

Sources: *Website of RBI,* **Note:** *growth rate observed in Mizoram during 2001-02 to 2014-15 and Uttarakhand during 1994-95 to 2014-15 as the availability of data on the RBI site.*

The states recording higher growth rate than the all India level were Arunachal Pradesh (8.45), Nagaland (7.44), Sikkim (8.57) and Tripura (5.93) during 1980-81 to 1996-97. The six mountainous states that registered lower growth rate in comparison to all India level were Assam, Himachal Pradesh, Jammu & Kashmir, Manipur, Meghalaya and Uttarakhand during 1980-81 and 1996-97.

The three states recorded lower growth rates of NSDP were Assam (3.26), Jammu & Kashmir (3.03) and Uttarakhand (3.84) during the same period. The four mountainous states also registered higher growth rate of NSDP in comparison to an average of mountainous states were Arunachal Pradesh, Nagaland, Sikkim and Tripura. The average growth rate of mountainous states recorded higher in comparison to all India level.

During 1997-98 and 2014-15, the five out of eleven states registered higher growth rates of NSDP in comparison to all India level were Mizoram (8.06), Nagaland (7.6), Sikkim (11.84), Tripura (8.33) and Uttarakhand (10.35). The states that recorded lower growth rates in comparison to the all India level were Arunachal Pradesh, Assam, Himachal Pradesh, Jammu & Kashmir, Manipur and Meghalaya during this period. The five mountainous states also recorded higher growth rates than the averages of mountainous states were Mizoram, Nagaland, Sikkim, Tripura and Uttarakhand during 1997-98 to 2014-15. The lower growth rates than the averages of mountainous states were recorded by Arunachal Pradesh, Assam, Himachal Pradesh, Jammu & Kashmir, Manipur and Meghalaya. The state of Sikkim was recorded higher growth rate of 11.84 percent and lower in Assam at 4.60 percent during1997-98 to 2014-15. During the entire period (1980-81 and 2014-15), the three mountainous states recorded less than five percent growth rate of NSDP were Assam, Jammu & Kashmir and Manipur.

2.4. Acceleration/Deceleration Growth Rates of NSDP

The growth rates of NSDP both at all India level and an average of mountainous states accelerated from 5.31 percent to 7.22 percent and 5.52 percent to 7.39 percent during 1980-81 and 1996-97 to 1997-98 and 2014-15. A perusal of the table shows that two mountainous states increased higher the growth rate of NSDP during 1980-81 and 1996-97 to 1997-98 and 2014-15 were Sikkim and Tripura. The state of Arunachal Pradesh recorded deceleration in the growth rate of NSDP from 8.45 percent to 6.85 percent during 1980-81 and 1996-97 to 1997-98 and 2014-15. The nine out of eleven mountainous states recorded acceleration in the growth rate of NSDP were Assam, Himachal Pradesh, Jammu & Kashmir, Manipur, Meghalaya, Nagaland, Sikkim, Tripura and Uttarakhand during 1980-81 and 1996-97 to 1997-98 and 2014-15.

The table 2 shows that increased the mean and standard deviation during 1980-81 and 1996-97 to 1997-98 and 2014-15. However, the coefficient of variation registered that decreased from 0.369 to 0.305 during 1980-81 and 1996-97 to 1997-98 and 2014-15. It indicates that inequalities have declined in term of NSDP growth rates among the mountainous states during 1980-81 and 1996-97 to 1997-98 and 2014-15.

Table 2: The Results of Coefficients of Variation in the Mountainous States; 1980-81 and 1996-97 to 1997-98 and 2014-15

Periods/Mean/SD/CV	1980-81 to 1996-97	1997-98 to 2014-15
Mean Value	5.520	7.390
Standard Deviation	2.037	2.251
Coefficients of Variations	0.369	0.305

Sources: *RBI Site*

The results also indicated that there was convergence in the mountainous states, for the reason that values of coefficient of variation declined during 1980-81 and 1996-97 to 1997-98 and 2014-15.

2.5. Interstate Growth Linkages in the Mountainous States

This section presents the spillover effects of the growth rate of NSDP among the mountainous states and tested Granger Causality test (GCT). It is the econometric tool that finds out the Granger causes of one variable in the past value would be affected by the future value; however, the past value is the Granger cause of the future value or prediction of future value. This section covers three steps; one is that to the test of the unit root test (Phillips-Perron) in the NSDP growth rate of mountainous states; the second is the Dickey-Fuller GLS (ERS) Unit Root Test in the NSDP growth rate in mountainous states and last is the pair-wise Granger causality test. These tests have been needed for our study; because these tests have been observed the relationship and to find out the pair-wise relationship in the NSDP of mountainous states. The results of statistical methods of unit root test have been presented in Table 3 and 4.

The results have been indicated that stationary series for each state has a unit root in NSDP level, whereas states of Mizoram and Uttarakhand were not in stationary at 1 percent level. These states are significant at the 5 and 10 percent level and however, Uttarakhand has been significant on the basis of trend and intercepts level.

Table 3: Results of Phillips - Perron Unit Root Test in the Mountainous States

Mountainous States	Coefficient (Level & Intercept)	Adj. T-Stat	T-Statistic
Arunachal Pradesh	-1.31	-7.09***	-7.13***
Assam	-0.93	-4.89***	-4.78***
Himachal Pradesh	-1.11	-6.23***	-5.81***
Jammu & Kashmir	-1.26	-6.79***	-6.81***
Manipur	-1.33	-15.96***	-7.40***
Meghalaya	-1.13	-6.39***	-5.92***
Mizoram	-1.02	-3.30**	-3.30**
Nagaland	-1.02	-8.86***	-5.32***
Sikkim	-0.94	-4.90***	-4.90***
Tripura	-0.82	-5.28***	-5.01***
Uttarakhand	-0.58 (-1.02)	-2.57 (-3.79**)	-2.52 (-3.62**)

Sources: RBI site **Note:** *(1) *** indicates Statistically Significant at the 1 % level (2) ** indicates Statistically Significant at 5% & the 10 % level, not in 1% level.*

The unit root test constantly measured in the negative value of coefficient and t-statistic. The results have been indicated that Uttarakhand and Mizoram states are not significant at the 1 percent level; these states are significant at the 5 and 10 percent level. Most of the mountainous states have recorded at 1 percent significant level; these states showed stationary series for all mountainous states except Uttarakhand and Mizoram. The states of Mizoram and Uttarakhand have been significant at the 5 and 10 percent level.

Table 4: Results of Dickey-Fuller GLS (ERS) Unit Root Test in the Mountainous States

States	Coefficient	T-Statistic
Arunachal Pradesh (Level & Intercept)	-1.308	-7.25***
Assam (Level & Intercept)	-0.907	-4.78***
Himachal Pradesh (Level & Intercept)	-1.092	-5.81***
Jammu & Kashmir (Level & Intercept)	-1.109	-2.29**
Manipur (Level & Intercept)	-1.255	-6.87***
Meghalaya (Level & Intercept)	-0.98	-5.171***
Mizoram (Level & Intercept)	-1.008	-3.39***
Nagaland (Level & Intercept)	-0.92	-4.92***
Sikkim (Level & Intercept)	-0.91	-4.82***
Tripura (Level, Trend & Intercept)	-0.274 (-0.789)	-1.37 (-4.45***)
Uttarakhand (Level, Trend & Intercept)	-0.281 (-0.939)	-1.34 (-3.67**)

Sources: *RBI site* **Note:** *(1) *** indicates Statistically Significant at the 1 % level (2) ** indicates Statistically Significant at 5% & the 10 % level, not in 1% level.*

Further, the tests (Phillips-Perron and Dickey-fuller test) have been needed for our study because it is the technique to find out the stationary series in the mountainous states. Dickey-fuller test (Table 4) results have shown that only two states namely Uttarakhand and Jammu Kashmir states have not been significant at the 1 percent level; however, they significant at the 5 and 10 percent level. Therefore, results have shown that the series were stationary at the 5 and 10 percent level, not at the 1 percent level. Most of the mountainous states have been stationary series in NSDP at the 1 percent level; however, Tripura and Uttarakhand states have been significant on the basis of the level, trend and intercept.

Thus, all mountainous states have stationary series integrated with the trend and intercept; however, three states were integrated with level, trend and intercept. Tables 3 and 4 presented that all states were significant at the 1, 5 and 10 percent level as mentioned in the tables. The most important question in this study is that there is any relationship in the long run equilibrium of NSDP among the mountainous states and pair-wise relationship in these states. If we want to find the answer to this question, we apply and test the Granger of Co-integration method. The results are presented in the table of 5. We analysed the test in the all mountainous states series values and found that very less interdependency in the growth rate of NSDP among the mountainous states.

The results clearly indicated that very less interdependency among the mountainous states in the growth rate of NSDP. The F-statistics results showed that the growth rate of NSDP in Sikkim Granger cause of the growth rate of NSDP in Mizoram.

Table 5: Pair-wise Granger Causality Tests (F- Statistic) in the Mountainous States

Mountainous States	Arunachal Pradesh	Assam	Himachal Pradesh	Jammu & Kashmir	Manipur	Meghalaya	Mizoram	Nagaland	Sikkim	Tripura	Uttarakhand	Total no. of states affecting
Arunachal Pradesh	----	0.21	3.52**	0.63	0.1	3.06***	1.03	3.76**	1.08	2.15	0.46	3
Assam	0.48	----	0.82	6.49**	1.02	0.9	0.89	1.65	0.71	0.64	2.70***	2
Himachal Pradesh	0.31	1.05	----	0.97	1.13	5.59*	1.2	0.7	0.02	1.95	1.16	1
Jammu & Kashmir	0.35	1.13	0.57	----	0.1	3.08***	0.93	1.52	0.31	1.08	0.05	1
Manipur	1.22	0.15	0.89	0.35	----	1.38	0.79	1.07	0.07	0.18	0.62	0
Meghalaya	0.03	0.16	1.94	0.55***	0.44	----	0.79	0.58	0.51	0.27	0.009	1
Mizoram	0.84	8.60*	0.44	0.76	0.05	3.84***	----	0.15	9.20*	2.41	0.81	3
Nagaland	2.89***	0.88	2.04	2.54**	0.23	0.69	0.6	----	0.05	5.54*	1.41	3
Sikkim	0.34	0.76	0.31	0.24	0.77	0.77	6.80**	0.11	----	0.01	0.62	1
Tripura	5.39*	2.19	2.41***	2.79**	0.05	3.94**	0.62	0.001	0.09	----	0.47	4
Uttarakhand	5.34**	2.70***	0.44	3.16***	0.1	0.42	1.2	0.21	1.93	0.86	----	3
Total No. of states affecting	3	2	2	5	0	5	1	1	1	1	1	22

Sources: *RBI site*;

Note: (1) * indicates Statistically Significant at the 1 % level (2) ** indicates Statistically Significant at 5% and (3) *** indicates Statistically Significant at the 10 % level

Mountainous states have not Granger cause in terms of NSDP growth rates among the mountainous states. However, some mountainous states are interdependent in the significant level of 1, 5 and 10 percent level. These states are Sikkim and Mizoram, they are interrelated and Granger caused between each other. In the polarisation effect, the state of Manipur is indicated to no polarisation effect in any other mountainous states. However, Tripura found to polarisation effect in many of them namely Arunachal Pradesh, Himachal Pradesh, Jammu Kashmir and Meghalaya.

Arunachal Pradesh, Mizoram, Nagaland and Uttarakhand states recorded that to polarisation effect in only three states as mentioned in the table above. Arunachal Pradesh, Jammu & Kashmir and Meghalaya states found that to trickle down effect only in three, five and five mountainous states. In the polarisation and trickle-down effect, twenty-four times states have been affected or caused in terms of growth rate of NSDP among each other. The study results have found that most of the states have not been Granger caused among each other. However, some states have been significant at the 1, 5 and 10 percent level that means some states affected the growth rate of NSDP by the Granger cause. Thus, the study observed bidirectional growth causality among the mountainous states at the significant level in terms of polarisation and trickle-down effect. The growth rate of Sikkim, Himachal Pradesh, Jammu & Kashmir and Meghalaya is found to polarisation effect only in one state; and Sikkim, Mizoram, Tripura and Uttarakhand indicated to trickle down effect in one state as mentioned in the above table. The states of Jammu & Kashmir and Meghalaya growth rates found to trickling down effect in five mountainous states. The state of Arunachal Pradesh indicated to trickle down effect only in three states; which were Nagaland, Tripura and Uttarakhand.

Conclusion and Summary

The study has observed that there was variation in term of NSDP growth performance among the mountainous states. The study results showed that the growth rate of NSDP accelerated both at the all India level and average growth rate of mountainous states during 1980-81 and 1996-97 to 1997-98 and 2014-15. Regarding mountainous states, Sikkim recorded highest growth rate and followed by Arunachal Pradesh and Nagaland during 1980-81 and 1996-97. The four mountainous states also registered higher growth rate of NSDP in comparison to an average of mountainous states were Arunachal Pradesh, Nagaland, Sikkim and Tripura. The average growth rate of all mountainous states recorded higher growth rate in comparison to all India level. In comparison during 1997-98 and 2014-15, the five mountainous states also recorded higher growth rates than the averages of mountainous states were Mizoram, Nagaland, Sikkim, Tripura and Uttarakhand. The state of Sikkim was recorded higher growth rate of NSDP and lower in Assam. During the entire period, three mountainous states recorded less than five percent growth rate of NSDP were Assam, Jammu & Kashmir and Manipur.

The growth rates of NSDP both at all India level and an average of mountainous states accelerated during 1980-81 and 1996-97 to 1997-98 and 2014-15. Three mountainous states increased higher the growth rate of NSDP during 1980-81 and 1996-97 to 1997-98 and 2014-15 were Sikkim, Tripura and Uttarakhand. The state of Arunachal Pradesh recorded deceleration in the growth rate of NSDP during 1980-81 and 1996-97 to 1997-98 and 2014-15. The nine out of eleven mountainous states recorded acceleration in the growth rate of NSDP were Assam, Himachal Pradesh, Jammu & Kashmir, Manipur, Meghalaya, Nagaland, Sikkim, Tripura and Uttarakhand during 1980-81 and 1996-97 to 1997-98 and 2014-15. The coefficients of variation indicate that inequalities declined in term of NSDP growth rates among the mountainous states during 1980-81 and 1996-97 to 1997-98 and 2014-15. The results also indicated that there was convergence in the mountainous states, for the reason that values of coefficient of variation declined.

In the spillover effects, the results clearly indicated that very less interdependency among the mountainous states in term of the growth rate of NSDP. The F- statistics results showed that the growth rate of NSDP in Sikkim, Granger cause of the growth rate of NSDP in Mizoram. However, Tripura as a most influential state in term of NSDP growth causation many of them namely Arunachal Pradesh, Himachal Pradesh, Jammu Kashmir and Meghalaya. The study observed bidirectional growth causality among the mountainous states at the significant level in terms of trickle-down effect and polarisation effect. In consequence, our study exposes a mixture of polarisation and trickling down effects of the growth rate of NSDP within mountainous states. The study only examines to exploring the growth of NSDP linkages among mountainous states of India.

There is an urgent requirement to reinforce the investment of infrastructure and increase public investment in basic core sectors, namely, agriculture and micro small scales industries. There is an urgent necessity to improve the human capital and technology by investing in health, education, skill and training and also to expand economic activities to boost economic growth opportunities in mountainous states. Unneeded to say that, while above issues are critical to attaining the goal of high growth of NSDP; efficient implementation and scrutinising of growth policy changes will be of extreme importance. In the future research, the research should analyse the different socioeconomic factors to identify some factors that influence the growth and development linkages among Indian states and different countries.

References

Ahluwalia, M. S. (2002). State level performance under economic reforms in India; Economic policy reforms and the Indian economy, pp. 91-125.

Bhide, S., Kalirajan, K. & Chadha, R. (2006). Growth Interdependence Among Indian states: an Exploration. *Asia-Pacific Development Journal*. Vol. 12, No. 2, pp. 59-80.

Cherodian, R., & Thirlwall, A. P. (2013). Regional disparities in per capita income in India: convergence or divergence. *Journal of Post Keynesian Economics*, Vol. 37, No. 3, pp. 384-407.

Debnath, A., & Roy, N. (2012). Testing spillover effects of economic growth: The case of India's northeastern region. *IUP Journal of Applied Economics*, Vol. 11, No. 3, pp. 84.

Dholakia, R. H. (2009). Regional Sources of Growth Acceleration in India. *Economic and Political Weekly*. Vol. 44, No. 47, pp. 68-72.

Gaile, G. L. (1980). The spread-backwash concept. *Regional Studies*, Vol. 14, No. 1, pp. 15-25.

Higgins, B. (1983). From Growth Poles to Systems of Interactions in Space. *Growth and Change*, Vol. 14, No.4, pp. 3-13.

Kokko, A., Zejan, M., and Tansini, R. (2001). Trade regimes and spill-over effects of FDI: Evidence from

Uruguay. Weltwirtschaftliches Archiv, Vol. 137, No.1, pp. 124-149.

Reserve Bank of India (2017) Data Base on Indian Economy (National Income). Retrieved from: http://dbie.rbi.org.in/DBIE/dbie.rbi?site=statistics

Shetty, S. L. (2003). Growth of SDP and structural changes in state economies: Interstate comparisons. *Economic and Political Weekly*, pp. 5189-5200.

Zhang, Q. and B. Felmingham (2002). The Role of FDI, Exports and Spill-Over Effects in the Regional Development of China. *The Journal of Development Studies*, Vol. 38, No. 4, pp. 157-178.

CHAPTER: 3
A COMPARATIVE ANALYSIS OF SMALL SCALE INDUSTRIES: PRE AND POST ERA OF GLOBALIZATION

Bishwajeet Prakash and Rakesh Kumar Gautam

Abstract

Globalization is the process by which regional economies, societies, cultures have opened the national border and interconnection with global countries through free movement of goods, services, resources and capital. In connection with India its means to integrating the country with world economy through trade, foreign direct investment, capital flow, migration and spread of technology.(Bishnoi,2015). In 1991 India after suffering from huge financial and economic crisis Dr. Manmohan Singh brought new economic policy known as Liberalization, Privatisation and Globalization Policy (LPG Policy), through the policy the Indian market was open their border for a global world. Globalization can bring enormous opportunities for developing countries like India in terms of economic growth, the flow of capital, technology and other resources but on the other hand its effect to the dearth of various sectors. The Small Scale sectors form a dominant part of Indian industry and contribute a significant role in the production, employment, and export of the country. The launching of LPG policy the Small Scale Industries adopt new technology, new market management system and other effective resources. On the other hand, this sector faces huge competition with large industries in terms of production, technology, and capital. The completion with large industries creates unequal competition among these sectors. Therefore, there is a need to study and analyse the impact of globalization on Indian Small Scale Industries . The paper would evaluate the performance of Small Scale Industries in both `period pre-globalization and post-globalization. The study is based on the descriptive study of the secondary data. The result of the study shown that globalization leads a negative effect on the Small Scale Industries in all segments.

3.1. Introduction

Globalization refers to an increase in economic integration among the nations. It signifies as a process of internationalization plus liberalization and become a world as a small village in the globalization (Khatri & Manglani, 2013). It's gradually referred as closer economic integration among the various nations. The whole world becomes the economic interdependence to each other through free movement of goods, services and capital. The official meaning of globalization for the WTO is "Movement of the economics of the world towards the unrestricted cross-border movement of goods and services, capital and the labour forces." The world becoming a flat surface level –field emerging in the due process of time (Singh,2012). This process has brought a magnificent change in the micro level of the economy. Due to the crisis of BOP during the eighties, the Congress-led government has introduced the Liberalization, Privatization and Globalization (LPG) policies in 1991.That policy was brought to open the Indian markets for the world market.

In order to bring to redevelop and strength the Small Scale Industries a separate policy statement has been announced for the small, tiny and village enterprise on 6th August 1991.This was the first time when a separate policy was introduced for the small scale and village enterprise (Asra & Prasad, 2011). Main features of small Industrial Policy 1991 were
1. Emphasis on cheap credit to adequate credit.
2. Introducing factoring services by the bank.
3. Setting up of an Export Development Centre in the Small Industries Development Organization (SIDO).

4. Setting up technology development cell and quality counselling information centre.
5. Market promotion of Small Scale Industries products through cooperative societies or public sector lending.

3.2. Role of Small Scale Industries in Indian Economy

The development of developing countries based on the growth of industries. The mass expansion of industrial sectors leads to greater utilization of natural resources, higher production of goods and services, mass export of products, the creation of employment opportunities, improvement of standard of living, higher technological and entrepreneurial innovation. Since second planning commission focused on the highest industrial growth, special emphasis on small-scale industries was leads to higher employment opportunities with low capital investment. The contributions of Small Scale Industries are remarkable in Indian industrial system(Singh,2014). This sector contributes 40% share in industrial production and 35% share in export of the country. In terms of employment generation, this sector contributes 16 million directly or indirectly employment opportunities (Kansal et al., 2009) The definition of Small Scale Industries is broader and changes their applicability according to the structure of the economy. In India, the Small Scale Industries were reconstituted and became the Micro, Small and Medium Enterprises in India, the definition of this sector become change according to new MSMEs act 2006.

The development of Small Scale Industries is being given due to importance due to order to achieve following objectives:
1. To removal of regional disparities and economic backwardness of states.
2. To attain the self-reliance of the country.
3. Reduction in disparities in income, wealth, consumption & standards of living and to facilitate mobilization of resources, the creation of new capital and development of entrepreneurial skill.
4. Create large employment opportunities and raise levels of output, income and standard of living.

5. Meet substantial part of the economy's requirement of consumer goods and
6. To facilitate industries as a helping hand.

Table 1: Classification of MSMEs on the basis of Investment

Manufacturing Sector (Investment in Plant and Machinery)	Enterprise	Service Enterprise (Investment in Equipment)
Up to 25 lakhs	Micro	Up to 10 lakhs
More than 25 lakhs up to Rs.10 crores	Small	More than 25 lakhs up to Rs.10 crores
More than 25 lakhs up to Rs.10 crores	Medium	More than 25 lakhs up to Rs.10 crores

Source: Micro, Small & Medium Enterprise Development Act 2006

3.3. Literature Review

Various studies have been conducted from time to time in different states of India. Few of the literature based on the globalization impact on Small Scale Industries are presented below:

Mathew M.C (2004) highlighted in his study that the vibrancy and dynamical of the sector anticipated under the era of deregulation and de-reservation. The study revealed that small-scale industries are worked as a backbone of the country, its need a strong small and medium enterprise policy which closely linked with international commitment. The study suggested that at the strategic level there is the need of mechanism which changes the demography of small scale enterprise.

Bishnoi M (2015) discusses a comparative study of growth and performance of the small scale and Medium industries during the pre and post reform period. The study describes that globalization can bring enormous opportunities for economic growth as well as well as some important challenges for the developing countries like India. The small scale enterprises are facing unequal completion with large scale MNCs. The result of the study shows that globalization is almost a complete failure on the growth front. On conclusion, the recent trend of the growth of SSIs sector showed the trust of Indian economy on globalization and liberalization which failed to rendered positive impact on the Small Scale Industries .

Kansal et al. (2009) in their study, an attempt has been made to analyze the impact of globalization on the growth and performance of Small Scale Industries in India. The study was a comparative analysis of growth pattern of key parameters between Pre- and Post – Globalization periods reveals that the "globalization" had a negative impact on the growth of small scale sector measured in terms of a number of units, production, employment and exports. It shows that globalization had a negative impact on the growth of SSI.

Rathod, C. B. (2007) discussed the importance of the Small Scale Industrial sector and also the contribution of Indian small scale entrepreneurs in the world economy. The major objective of the study was to study the growth and pattern of the Small sector and recognize the reasons for success/ failures,of these industries.The study was also evaluate the impact of globalization on SSIs and export opportunity, to identify the barriers and constraints that SSIs were facing to cope with globalization.

Kasal and Sonia (2009) described the impact of globalization on the Small Scale Industries in India. The paper evaluates the performance of SSI before and after the liberalization period. The data was based on secondary data sources and study period is 1973-2007.The paper analyzed that there was the negative impact of globalization on the growth, in terms units, employment, production and exports.

Hashim,(2004) has provided an insight into the strengths and weaknesses of small and medium-sized enterprises. It can also be concluded that there are certain weaknesses that prevail in SMEs and need to be removed.

Hussain, V, Syed. (2004) analyzed that to survive in the world market SSIs should have to lay greater emphasis on international standards with regard to quality, health and hygiene to be offered by them. Sahoo, K, Sukanta. (2004) examined the contribution of SSI in the industrial sector and concluded that with the decline in agricultural employment and virtual stagnation in the organized manufacturing sector, employment in SSI sector has emerged as the only ray of hope.

Rajyalakshmi, N. (2004) reviewed the productivity awareness among SSI units in Visakhapatnam district of Andhra Pradesh at the micro level and explored small- scale entrepreneurs, how they measured productivity in their units. The study based on primary data collected by using structured schedule through personal interviews. A sample of 200 SSI units has been selected for the study. The study found that Chemical units were more capital intensive and it was low in food and agro units. Productivity awareness was not noticed in the SSI units. The study concluded that Success in the small industry will be best achieved if the productivity culture will be clearly understood by all the employees.

Subrahmanyabala, M.H. (2004) highlighted the impact of globalization and domestic reforms on small-scale industries sector. The study stated that small industry had suffered in terms of growth of units, employment, output and exports. Researcher highlighted that the policy changes had also thrown open new opportunities and markets for the small-scale industries sector. The author suggested that the focus must be turned to technology development and strengthening of financial infrastructure in order to make Indian small industry internationally competitive and contribute to national income and employment.

3.4. Data Source And Methodology

In the current study, an attempt has been made to analyze the impact of globalization on the growth of Small Scale Industries in India. For this, the growth of SSI over the period has been considered and the major factors affecting SSIs have been analyzed. The study has been conducted with reference to the data available related to employment, no. of units and productivity of SSIs in India. The SSI sector has been studied with the proven fact that they hold the largest share of Industrial Sector in India. For this, the period of globalization has been taken into consideration. The relevant data have been collected from different sources viz. Ministry of Commerce and Industry, Ministry of Micro, Small and Medium Enterprises, Office of the Development Commissioner (SSI), Government of India, New Delhi, Annual Survey of Industries (Central Statistical Organization), Ministry of Planning (GOI), Census of Small Scale Industries (GOI), Yojna, Monthly Commentary on Indian economic conditions, The Journal of

Entrepreneurship, various bulletin of Reserve Bank of India, etc.

3.5. Objectives

1. The comparative study of small scale sectors during pre and post-globalization.
2. Opportunities and Challenges for the Small Scale Industries in India

3.6. Analysis of Data

The data collected tabulated, processed and analyzed on the basis of various statistical tools such as Percentage, Annual Growth Rate Annual Average Growth Rate (AAGR) and Compound Annual Growth Rate (CAGR).

Annual Growth Rate is based on the formula mentioned below

Annual Growth Rate = $\frac{\text{Current year value-Previous year value}}{\text{Previous year value}}$

Compound Annual Growth Rate is calculated by using below formula

CAGR = (Ending value / Beginning value) ^ (1/n) − 1

3.7. Result and Discussion

3.6.1. Number of Units of SSIs.

The number of units in Small Scale Industries over the year shows the growth of small industries in the country. The working number of units in small scale sectors in pre and post-globalization period in India shown in below table.

Analysis: The table 2 clearly show that the Annual Average Growth Rate of a number of units in the pre-globalization period from 1973-74 to 1991-92 was 23.96% but in the post-liberalization period between 1992-93 to 2010-11 in terms of units the Annual Average Growth Rate was 11.25%.The Compound Annual Growth rate before globalization was 16.01% but on the same period in post-globalization was 9.21%.The table indicates that in the period of 1990-91 was high growth rate but its reduced next year to 3.98%.In terms of units in numbers was increased but in terms of average and yearly growth rate shows in the post-globalization period was lower than pre-globalization.

Table 2: Units in Millions

Pre- Globalization			Post Globalization		
Year	Units	% growth	Year	Units	% growth
1973-74	0.42		1992-93	7.35	4.11
1974-75	0.5	19.05	1993-94	7.65	4.08
1975-76	0.55	10.00	1994-95	7.96	4.05
1976-77	0.59	7.27	1995-96	8.28	4.02
1977-78	0.67	13.56	1996-97	8.62	4.11
1978-79	0.73	8.96	1997-98	8.97	4.06
1979-80	0.81	10.96	1998-99	9.34	4.12
1980-81	0.87	7.41	1999-00	9.72	4.07
1981-82	0.96	10.34	2000-01	10.11	4.01
1982-83	1.06	10.42	2001-02	10.52	4.06
1984-85	1.24	6.90	2003-04	11.4	4.11
1985-86	1.35	8.87	2004-05	11.86	4.04
1986-87	1.46	8.15	2005-06	12.34	4.05
1987-88	1.58	8.22	2006-07	12.84	4.05
1988-89	1.71	8.23	2007-08	27.27	112.38
1989-90	1.82	6.43	2008-09	28.15	3.23
1990-91	6.79	273.08	2009-10	30.25	7.46
1991-92	7.06	3.98	2010-11	39.23	29.69
AAGR		23.96 %	AGAP		11.25 %
CAGR		16.01%	CAGR		9.21%

Source : Annual Report of Micro, Small and Medium Enterprises (GOI)

3.6.2. Employment Growth by SSIs

The most important argument to promoting the Small Scale Industries is that this sector contributes higher employment opportunities. The following table provides the information of Small Scale Industries.

Analysis: The above table 3 shows that Annual Average Growth Rate(AAGR) of employment by the small industries in the pre-globalization period, from 1973-74 to 1991-92 was 8.46% percent and in the post- liberalization between 1992-93 to 2010-11 it was 7.27%. During pre- globalization 1974-75 to 1978-79 periods, the yearly growth rate was more than average growth rate and after the rate of growth was decreased. In the period of 1990-91, the rate of annual average growth rate much increased to 32.36%.

Table 3: Employment in Millions

Pre-Globalization			Post-Globalization		
Year	Employment	% growth	Year	Employment	% growth
1973-74	3.97		1992-93	17.48	5.30
1974-75	4.04	1.76	1993-94	18.26	4.46
1975-76	4.59	13.61	1994-95	19.14	4.82
1976-77	4.98	8.50	1995-96	19.79	3.40
1977-78	5.4	8.43	1996-97	20.59	4.04
1978-79	6.38	18.15	1997-98	21.32	3.55
1975-80	6.7	5.02	1998-99	22.06	3.47
1980-81	7.1	5.97	1999-00	22.91	3.85
1981-82	7.5	5.63	2000-01	24.09	5.15
1982-83	7.9	5.33	2001-02	25.23	4.73
1983-84	8.42	6.58	2002-03	26.37	4.52
1984-85	9	6.89	2003-04	27.53	4.40
1985-86	9.6	6.67	2004-05	28.25	2.62
1986-87	10.14	5.63	2005-06	29.99	6.16
1987-88	10.7	5.52	2006-07	31.25	4.20
1988-89	11.3	5.61	2007-08	47.34	51.49
1989-90	11.96	5.84	2008-09	49.35	4.25
1990-91	15.83	32.36	2009-10	50.25	1.82
1991-92	16.6	4.86	2010-11	58.27	15.96
AAGR		8.46	AAGR		7.27
CAGR		7.82	CAGR		6.54

Source: Annual Report of Micro, Small and Medium Enterprises (GOI)

In the post- globalization period, in 1992-93 to 2010-11 was 7.27 % and Compound average growth rate was 6.54%.Only in 2007-08 and 2010-11 the average growth rate much higher than the annual average growth rate.

3.6.3. Production Contribution by SSIs

The Small Scale Industries produced more than 8000 varieties of product ranging customer goods to machinery and cover almost all varieties of products. This sector contributes 40% to the value added in the industrial manufacturing sector. The below table provides the information about the growth of Small Scale Industries on production during the period of 1973-74 to 2010-11.

Table 4: Production in Millions

Pre-Globalization			Pre-Globalization		
Year	Production	% growth	Year	Production	% growth
1973-74	7200		1992-93	84,413	4.71
1974-75	9200	27.78	1993-94	98,796	17.04
1975-76	11,000	19.57	1994-95	122,154	23.64
1976-77	12,400	12.73	1995-96	147,712	20.92
1977-78	14,300	15.32	1996-97	167,805	13.60
1978-79	15,800	10.49	1997-98	187,217	11.57
1975-80	21,600	36.71	1998-99	210,454	12.41
1980-81	28,100	30.09	1999-00	233,760	11.07
1981-82	32,600	16.01	2000-01	261,297	11.78
1982-83	35,000	7.36	2001-02	282,270	8.03
1983-84	41,600	18.86	2002-03	314,850	11.54
1984-85	50,500	21.39	2003-04	364,547	15.78
1985-86	61,200	21.19	2004-05	429,796	17.90
1986-87	72,300	18.14	2005-06	497,842	15.83
1987-88	87,300	20.75	2006-07	585,112	17.53
1988-89	106,400	21.88	2007-08	790,759	35.15
1989-90	132,300	24.34	2008-09	880,805	11.39
1990-91	78,802	(40.44)	2009-10	904,637	2.71
1991-92	80,615	2.30	2010-11	990,365	9.48
AAGR		15.80	AAGR		14.32
CAGR		13.56	CAGR		13.84

Source: Annual Report of Micro, Small and Medium Enterprises (GOI)

Analysis: The above table indicates that the Annual Average Growth Rate of production in the pre-globalization period from 1973-74 to 1991-92 was 15.80% and post-globalization period during 1992-93 to 2010-11 it was 14.32%.The Compound annual average growth on the same period was 13.56 and 13.84%

respectively.

3.6.4. Contribution in Export Sector by SSIs

Small Scale Industries are playing a major role in the promotion of the export sector in India. According to SIDBI total contribution of this sector in the export of India is around 30%.Besides direct export, this sector provides raw materials to industries this take an indirect support to promote the export sector in India. The below table indicates the performance of SSIs during pre-globalization and post-globalization period in the export of the country.

Table 5: Exports in Millions

Year	Exports	% growth	Year	Exports	% growth
1973-74	400		1992-93	17,784	28.10
1974-75	500	25.00	1993-94	25,307	42.30
1975-76	500	-	1994-95	29,068	14.86
1976-77	800	60.00	1995-96	36,470	25.46
1977-78	800	-	1996-97	39,248	7.62
1978-79	1,100	37.50	1997-98	44,442	13.23
1975-80	1,200	9.09	1998-99	48,979	10.21
1980-81	1,600	33.33	1999-00	54,200	10.66
1981-82	2,100	31.25	2000-01	69,797	28.78
1982-83	2,000	(4.76)	2001-02	71,244	2.07
1983-84	2,200	10.00	2002-03	86,013	20.73
1984-85	2,500	13.64	2003-04	97,644	13.52
1985-86	2,800	12.00	2004-05	124,417	27.42
1986-87	3,600	28.57	2005-06	150,242	20.76
1987-88	4,400	22.22	2006-07	182,538	21.50
1988-89	5,500	25.00	2007-08	202,017	10.67
1989-90	7,600	38.18	2008-09	213,040	5.46
1990-91	9,664	27.16	2009-10	224,332	5.30
1991-92	13,883	43.66	2010-11	238,432	6.29
AAGR		22.88%	AAGR		16.58%
CAGR		20.52%	CAGR		14.64%

Source: Annual Report of Micro, Small and Medium Enterprises (GOI)

Analysis: The above table indicates that in the pre-reform period the exports increased 400 crores in 1973-74 to Rs.13,883 crores in 1991-92.The average annual growth in the same period was 22.88% and Compound Annual Growth Rate was 20.52%.The data observed that 1982-83 the export growth was in negative. During post-globalization period SSI exports Rs.17,785 crores in 1992-93 to 238,432 crores in 2010-11.The Annual Average growth in the same period was 16.58% and Compound average growth rate was 14.64%.The table indicates that the export rate was high during the period of 1994-95 immediately after the reform but gradually the percentage decreased to 2.07 % in 2001-2002.However, the export rate increased later during the same period.

3.8. Opportunities and Challenges

The LPG process leads to open the domestic market to world market. The exposure of openness of market creates an unequal competition among large industries and Small Scale Industries. The challenges are in the form of due to reduction of tariff barriers, finance such as inadequate source of finance, scarcity of cheap credit ,lack of raw materials, wear bargaining power, lack of policy, low recognition from the society, lack of infrastructure facilities, in experience marketing skill, low innovation technique, lack of well innovative technology and ideas ,underutilization of capacity. The Small Scale Industries have been huge opportunities such as capped various service sector, hardware and software industries, a variety of raw materials, including hosiery, leather products and others.

Conclusion

In this study, an attempt has been made to analyses a comparison between pre and post-globalization on the growth of Small Scale Industries in India. The comparisons between both the period reveals that globalization has a negative effect on the growth of Small Scale Industries in terms of units, employment, production and exports. A negative growth rate of Small Scale Industries in all sectors indicates a major set for the indigenous economy of India. The reform of 1991 has not ideally suitable for the growth of small scale sectors and a serious cause of concern for the policy makers. No indicators have been shown a positive impact hence the average annual growth rate was much higher in the pre-globalization period as compare to post-globalization period. In concluding the study shows the LPG policy is negatively affected the Small Scale Industries in India.

References

Asra, S & Prasad. K (2011). Impact of Economic Reform on Small Scale Industries in India, *International Journal of Business Management, Economics and Information Technology*, 2, 317-321.

Bishnoi, M (20115). Indian Small Scale Industries: An Analysis of Pre and Post Globalization Period, *EPRA International Journal of Economic and Business*, 4, 269-273.

Government of India- Annual Report (2012-13) Ministry of Micro, Small and Medium Enterprises, New Delhi.

Hashim. (2004), Relative strengths and weaknesses of SMEs in Malaysia: A Review of Literature", *Asian Economic Review*. 1, 43-54.

Hussain, V, Syed (2004). Performance of SSI in India and the challenges ahead, The Indian Journal of Industrial Relations, Vol. 39 No. 3, Jan 2004, pp: 391-401.

Kansal, R., & Sonia, (2009). Globalization and Its Impact on Small Scale Industries in India", *PCMA Journal of Business*, 1, 135-146.

Mathew, M. C (2004). Small Industry and Globalization, *Economic and Political Weekly*, 20, 1999-2000.

Ministry of Micro, Small and Medium Enterprises (2010): Annual Report 2009-10, Government of India, New Delhi.

Nag, B (2000). WTO Regime and Its Implications for Indian Small and Medium Enterprise Sector, *SEDME*, 3, 1-7.

Rathod, C.B (2007). Contribution of Indian Small Scale Entrepreneurs to Economic Growth in India: Opportunities and Challenges in Global Economy, *Prabadh-Journal of Management & Research*,.23,1-12.

Sahoo, K, Sukanta (2004). Small Scale manufacturing Industries in India, *The Indian Economic Journal*,1, 2003-2004.

CHAPTER: 4
MAHATMA GANDHI NATIONAL RURAL EMPLOYMENT GUARANTEE SCHEME (MGNREGS): A LITERATURE REVIEW

Monika Devi and Aman Sharma

Abstract

Unemployment remained a major issue in India in the past few decades. The Government of India has launched a flagship programme, i.e. "National Rural Employment Guarantee Act (NREGA)" to overcome this intensifying issue. This act was launched in 2005 with an aim to provide employment in rural areas for better upbringing of the lives of the poor and further renamed as "Mahatma Gandhi National Rural Employment Guarantee Act (MGNREGA)" in 2009. "Mahatma Gandhi National Rural Employment Guarantee Scheme (MGNREGS)" is known as "Silver Bullet" due to its sturdy effectiveness. The mainstay of this scheme relies on funding from the centre which ensures at least 100 days of guaranteed wage employment per year to every rural household whose adult member volunteer to do unskilled manual work. One-third of beneficiaries should be women and it provides equal opportunities for SCs, STs & other weaker sections. The present research work aims to provide a general review of MGNREGS studies from 2005 to 2017, which majorly comprises of qualitative work. It is hoped that it will be further useful for concerned individuals, scholars and researchers in this field of study. Apart from this, the paper also investigates the prevalence of political involvement in allocation of benefits under this scheme.

4.1. Introduction

Although the Mahatma Gandhi Rural Employment Guarantee Act (MGNREGA) was notified on September 7, 2005, came into effect on 2 February 2006 and it was implemented in a phased manner. In phase 1 it was started in the 200 most backward districts of the country. It was implemented in an additional 130 districts in Phase 2 (2007-2008). This Act was notified in the remaining rural district of India in phase 3 from 1st April 2008. This is the biggest employment program launched in the country for the development of its rural areas. Its goal is to provide 100 days of guaranteed wage employment for every rural family in a financial year, whose adult members are unskilled manual volunteers. This scheme is different from the first employment programs started by the Indian government. This plan is demand-driven on one hand and on the other hand, considers employment as the right of rural households. Thus, this scheme provides direct income to unskilled workers in rural areas.

4.2. Literature Review

This paper examines the detailed literature review of the MGNREGS and covers the research conducted in this area over a decade. The first ever research in this filed was conducted by Dreze **(2005)**. In his article, he discussed the pros and cons of the proposed Act and expressed three common fears. One is that the money will be wasted due to widespread corruption. The second fear is that Employment Guarantee Act will lead to financial bankruptcy. The third fear is that the government will get entangled in endless litigation, as holders of aggrieved laborers take the local authorities to court. To dispense these fears, however, he said that the proposed Act aimed at empowering the disadvantaged, and included extensive safeguards against and dereliction of duty from the concerned authorities.

Vasta (2006) evaluates the effectiveness of the Employment Guarantee Scheme (EGS) in the paper, which has the potential to reduce risk and vulnerabilities. They argue that if the NGA has intervened due to erosion of poverty and drought rather than short-term intervention in the form of EGS as EGS, interim intervention and short-term intervention are necessary. He concluded that EGS gave positive results in many ways: effective dry relief, increase in rural employment, supplementary sources of income, women workers of a significant category and income-courage and social cohesion, if interventions to reduce NGE Instead of working in emergence as EGS, poverty and lack, a good definition strategy should be followed.

Kumar (2007) performed a detailed analysis of the effects of various anti-poverty programs, including wage and self-employment programs. He said that most of the targeted programs for poverty alleviation show good politics, but show some bad economics. Micro-level studies on poverty alleviation programs in self-employment programs have evaluated the effectiveness of wage employment programs and national social assistance programs and concluded that poverty alleviation programs are above the poverty line in the group of people, poverty eradication Through the abolition of the program area, in this book, many limited careers Apart from recognizing the political economy of poverty, enough light can be highlighted.

Dreze (2007) In the newspaper article in Orissa, the Rural Employment Program looks at corruption and how it continues in NREGS also. However, he believes that NREGA has tremendous potential in the survey areas. Where the work was available, it was generally found that workers were earned from legal minimum wage (and sometimes more) of Rs. 70 per day and the wages were paid within 15 days. This is an unprecedented opportunity for the rural poor and it was clearly admirable between the other workers of the population and the other disadvantaged sections. There is hope among the workers that NREGA will enable them to avoid long distance seasonal migration. Apart from this, there is considerable scope for producing NREGA in this area, whether it is in the area of water conservation, rural connectivity, elevation of forest and improvement of private agricultural land.

Pankaj (2008) He said the house due to the income of the total annual income plan (Bihar and the total annual number of income jobs in Jharkhand, the beneficiary of about 2 houses and Jharkhand, at home to many low-income families in Bihar families' beneficiary in Bihar is a new level of consciousness about the owner families, the minimum wage. work participation rate increased (Dabbler), but availability and other Due to low employment levels under the Jana had no affect the prevailing local labor.

Narayanan (2008) An article is based on the findings of the Social Audit Survey on Crutch Facilities and Child Care under NREGS in Villupuram district of Tamilnadu. It expands the difficult practices of young mothers who worked under MGNREGS and provides adequate proof of the necessity for childcare facility on all activities. He suggested the government to develop the cost related rules with the instructions for preparing the template for childcare facilities and incorporating these expenses in financial estimates. He has determined that at least five laborers (men and women) have demanded this because many employees are not ready to bring their children to the workshop till child care is available.

Ghosh (2008) He said that direct and indirect employment through MNREGA in India, an important value of reviving rural economy, providing sustainability of basic consumption for poor families and improving the ability of the hiring of rural workers to be easier Will be done. He said that, the level of livelihood of rural people can be elevated by MGNREGA programme.

Dreze & Khera (2009) They found that most of the workers of MNREGA were from the most deprived sections of society and the level of awareness level among the workers of MNREGA was very low. There was insufficient shelf of work, delay in payment of wages, lack of basic work facilities, behind these failures, the existence of deep structural problems, including poor flow of money, lack of staff, faulty records and lack of grievance redress mechanism. This survey found that 27 percent sample work involves participation of contractors. In the end, the authors concluded that the best weapon against corruption is strict adherence to transparency measures.

Swaminathan (2009) He emphasized that priority is important under MGNRGS to strengthen the ecological base of agriculture. It has also commented that a major weakness was the lack of effective technical guidance and support from agriculture and rural universities and institutions. They suggested the need to bring convergence of child care, nutritional health and education programs in MGNREGS activities for sustainable rural development with human development. He believed that MNREGA workers should be engaged in checking the environmental destruction. For sustainable ecological development with environmental saving personnel, MGNREGS workers can get recognition for their outstanding work.

Singh & Nauriyal (2009) He evaluated the effect of MGNREGS in three districts of Uttarakhand and said that the activities of NREGS were found to be 10-20% due to the expansion of the household income and hence there was no significant improvement in their income and employment level. In addition, marginal improvements have been found in migration and debtor's deduction. The increase in consumption level and savings in sample households was also marginally improved. It has been stated in the report that in the sample districts poor performance of MGNREGS, lack of procedures, low levels of awareness and weak Panchayat Raj institutions.

Nair, Sreedharan & Anoopkumar (2009) He studied the effect of NREGS in three Gram Panchayats of Kadgarh district, i.e. used Madki, Ajanoor and Tripurpur with secondary data. Various institutional aspects have also been examined in the form of guidelines, rules and regulations brought by the Government of Kerala. Worker registration is very good in all three Gram Panchayats. Registration of Scheduled Castes and Scheduled Tribes is also effective. This scheme has been successful in increasing the level of employment and income of the rural level, thereby increasing their purchasing power. Working in groups has given women social rights. In some cases, NREGA works and agricultural work has progressed with an increase in the problem of labor shortage in agriculture sector. They concluded that some changes in the existing operating system were recommended to make the program more effective.

IAMR (2009) This study is based on the evaluation of NREGS, in which 20 districts and 300 beneficiaries of India, North, Western, Southern and Northeast areas will be covered. Studies show that in many districts, photographs are not checked on job cards and in some places the beneficiary has given money to get it. Job cards were not ready for all entries; In many homes, work was not received during scheduled period of 15 days, nor did they receive a graduate allowance. Due to the extra income generated through this scheme, the number of beneficiaries at the low earning level decreases in almost half the size, which is being spent more on the rise of families and on food and non-food items.

Sainath (2009) In his newspaper article, he asked for expansion of MGNREGS, spending more than 101 PDS on universal access, health and education. He remarked that the Rural Development Ministry has taken a positive step. It allows small but important assets such as farm ponds on each farm, which should be the purpose of every government. A major expansion of MGNREGS will provide cushion to lakhs of workers struggling to find work and will be devastated by the increase in food costs. But under the scheme, the number of days of work will be asked to throw the limit. He explained that the Prime Minister should call the measures of drought being called "level of war" and it must be time to do it.

Bassi & Kumar (2010) Impact in Kalyan NREGS promises to provide a lot of water management on the promise of the largest social security initiative in the world, but the types of intervention and the limited area's evidence show that due to absence of WM schemes, planning and execution are critically flawed Are there. Hypnosis and economic analysis are different in different areas. Today, agriculture climate is not based on the ideas of hydrology and geographical structures, which are important in determining the effect of land and water-based intervention. To determine the nature of water management interference in any area of India, we have identified three broad and different types of features, including agricultural climate, hydrology and geological settings. He said that in each typography, technical knowledge of water management functions in any area will require many scientific information, some of which will be examined with detailed investigation of submarine hydrology, geophysics, topography and slope characteristics.

Dhakal (2010) said that MNREGA is playing an important role in generating income for informal sector stakeholders and it has been helpful in employment generation in Chit Van district of Nepal. Poverty has contributed to the income of the informal sector in removing houses and nearly half of the households have been taken to the middle income level and higher income category, the role of informal sector has been played in reducing poverty. Apart from this, it also shows the possibility of having a better source of income in the informal sector for many people, however, what does the above analysis show that if the state is not completely absent then the support of the state has been greatly reduced.

Sudarshan, Bhattacharya & Fernandez (2010) Women's Participation in the NREGA: Some Observations from Fieldwork in Himachal Pradesh, Kerala and Rajasthan. The ability of the program has been seen everywhere to allow women to save some. The nature of the work shows that there is a need to give some serious consideration to develop comprehensive activities under NREGA. For example, while young women coming with elderly women and infants have confirmed their need to earn wages, hard labor labour is not desirable from their own health or the viewpoint of their infants. The design of the program needs to be adjusted to accommodate these variations in the life cycle and the physical ability to do hard physical work.

Pankaj & Tanka (2010) examined the impact of MNREGA on the empowerment of rural women in Bihar, Jharkhand, Rajasthan and Himachal Pradesh. They found that women workers have received this scheme primarily because of the opportunities for salaries and the benefits have been obtained through the effects of income-consumption, the impact of the house and the increase of choice and capacity.

Jha, Gaiha & Shankar (2010) investigated that "information, access and targeting: National Rural Employment Guarantee Scheme in India", is kept in place, keeping track of this relationship, its accessibility and efficacy in India. (NREGS) in three states Results show that the link between information, access and delivery of the plan is not easy. Information can increase the trend for the program used by those who are not their primary target population, and can increase the efficacy of distribution for such beneficiaries. On the other hand, lack of information, the ability of citizens to benefit from this scheme, especially the poorest of the poor, decreases.

Vij (2011) The right wing framework and detailed social audit mechanism in MNREGA design is the first step in the right direction; To give social justice, its ideology should be fully accepted by the implementing agencies. The Social Audit Mechanism is a forum where the government, NGO and the public can come together and can be comprehensive to ensure effective policy implementation, monitoring and evaluation. Through the civil society, its technical expertise and outreach can help in the monitoring and implementation of the government, while empowering the poor so that they can gain access to the schemes' benefits. Last but not least, to deliver these organizations, they should be supported by the administration. This is the only way for MNREGA and sustainable development.

Murthya & Indumati (2011) In the logic of using macro level and the lack of economic labor, this study proves that income in MNREGA is not rural wage. In rural areas, any price in agriculture and rural areas Farming and compared to non-agricultural workers the difference between rain and irrigated agriculture is relatively small. Therefore, the AP does not cause the state of irrigation state, NREGA labor wages, but non-due to an increase in agricultural wage employment due to an increase in agricultural wages to attract rural youth, almost a 'home village These policies are out of date houses made of parts and labor shortage that subsidies for agricultural machinery, drought-affected farmers, protect the livelihood of agriculture and irrigation oriented states Sector is not even.

Sudarshan (2011) Scheme to the diversity seen in women's local economy is very closely related to the characteristics - what options are available, the market gets to pay how it compares with the salaries of NREGA, the best men's market wages for women and the highest gender gap and men in Kerala and enough work to a higher level of participation in Rajasthan wages Plbd to rationalize the domestic response to wage the highest in the market. The second major factor is women's responsibility to take care of, which limits the available mobility and time to speed up payments. Entire whole, the study value of women's program empowerment perspective in went confirmed and suggests that enhancing the discrimination results by the region and needs analysis and policy will further be embedding the feedback process.

Ahuja, Tyagi, Chauhan & Chaudhary (2011) He concluded that this scheme is not interested in covering farmers and animals at large, because they are busy in their activities. Small land for farmers and animal resources, they are more interested in working on this project and their participation is also high. Thus, this scheme protects the livelihood of poor rural people. It was found that all the variables (important loans) selected for analysis were important, which resulted in the log-in coefficient in MNREGA, the value of these variable value, negative signals had a negative effect, "It is not interested" animal husbandry employment and borrowing In order to take a large number of other "MNREGA".

Hirway (2011) He studied and explained that a well-designed wage-employment program with a guaranteed component not only addresses the immediate problem of ensuring employment and wages to the poor, but contributed to the promotion of poor economic development. In his study, he used the village-level social audit matrix (SAM) to estimate the employment, income and production multiplier effects of NREGA in the village of Gujarat and said that multiples increase over time. He further said that NREGA has contributed a lot to women by relieving the local infrastructures such as water, fuel, timber, fodder, shelter etc. for women, relieving local infrastructures and giving relief from unpleasant work.

Harisha, Nagarajb, Chandrakantha, Murthy, Chengappa, Basavaraj, Chengappac & Basavarajb (2011) They say that the implementation of MNREGA programs has been very helpful in the homes required to provide Karnataka jobs. Analysis has shown that workers' jobs affect the employment of workers under the gender, education and family size programs. MNREGA has contributed to the increase in consumption expenditure which reduces the debt burden of the beneficiaries.

Imbert & Papp (2011) He used the stable roll-out of the program and guessed the changes in the districts which used to get the MNREGA program, which would later get the program. They estimate that after starting the program, in the initial districts, in the initial districts of the rest of India, the increase in the public employment of the head-age group has increased to three days per month (1.3 percent of the private sector employment). Their results suggest that private sector wages increase in public sector recruitment in the functioning of the private sector.

Poonia (2012) This paper reviews India's approach to social conservation since independence and places NREGA within the broad social protection discourse. In India, public policy and public works have generally tried to include women as a percentage of the beneficiaries, but have not given enough attention to gender sensitive design. NREGA has tried some gender sensitivity in its design. Although one of the provisions of the Act is that one third of those jobs should be of women, very differently, finally, they concluded that the major majority of workers in the informal economy were excluded from social security provisions. Overall, initial conclusions confirm that NREGS has the potential to promote local development, if management and distribution are good; and in the labor market, women's weak position has helped very much.

Nayak (2013) To participate in this program, it has been found to be very marginal in comparison to men in tribal women where more women were abused than NREGA. their male counterparts. Studies have shown that in the NREGA scheme, lack of aboriginal women, lack of crush feature worksheets, ownership of accounts and women's women bank, and lack of gender discrimination among women. It has been concluded that the operational guidelines clearly state that the seal roll is basically a register of daily wages and should include an explanatory role that should be free of wages in the right amount for each day, on labor days, the need to reduce the effect and their testimony of their initial or thumb, adjust an essential attribute. Should be modified for the purpose.

Kumar & Joshibt (2013) In the implementation of MNREGA, there is a direct way of increasing the income of the rural poor. It has provided almost equal employment benefits for all categories of agricultural-size, domestic type and income groups. State-wise studies have shown that all states have benefited from MNREGA, but with a wide variety. This has made the country more economically vulnerable. In rural areas, food consumption of both cereals and grains has increased in all categories. Diversification of different families is also celebrated in a diversification, which again is a strong signal of better consumption of food. Calorie intake has increased significantly and the amount of protein increased by families of different categories, which has reduced the number of families with malnourishment and nutritional deficits by 8 to 9 percent. In essence, the effect of MGNERAAG has been positive and effective for increasing the consumption of food items, changing the pattern of diet and providing nutritional food security to the poor rural households of India.

Panda & Majumder (2013) About 70 percent of Indian population lives in rural areas. Rural Employment Guarantee Act (MNREGA) is considered as a "silver bullet" to eliminate rural poverty and unemployment through the demand of productive labor force in rural Indian villages. It provides an alternative source of livelihood that can be used for reducing labor, child labor, reducing poverty, making productive property through self-dependent villages, construction of roads, water tanks, soil and water conservation etc. is. It can be concluded that the success of this act depends on its proper implementation and in this scenario, community participation is very important in making this program more effective.

Tripathi (2013) MNREGA is absolutely right for women's participation, we understand regional differences related to culture and conferences, infrastructure, awareness level, etc. There is no similarity in our country for participation of women in this scheme, but we have made a major initiative of rural initiatives. Rural positive aspects allow women to employ and make them financially stable and they cannot ignore empowerment by oath by working in their own moves. Panchayat and women's participation and other stories of their success in reference to examples. Constant growth in partnership throughout India.

Girarad (2014) Physical and Rural India, 33% of women in formal political processes, women's education, social status of women, employment, economic status, employment, labor force development (development), labor force (MNREGA) study opportunities are related to profit. Formal procedures for women involvement for women's duties and formal global institutional correlation is fine, which means that the area will increase their political awareness. Second, the underlying dependence on formal political processes - where women were not only public decisions, but in order to get information publicly, instead of their demands, they need to express policies, government institutions, hold and gender quota creation in India Formally, formal genders are changing with mobility.

Roy & Gowda (2015) Prior to the implementation of the MNREGA program, the life expectancy of the respondents was less than 31.3%, whereas only 16.0% of the respondents were falling below the lower level, before implementation of the MNREGA program, 28.0% Were living in While the implementation .of the MNREGA program, 39.3% of the respondents were living at a high level. Before and after the implementation of MNREGA, there was a positive and significant difference between the level of life of the beneficiaries. Prior to the MNREGA program, after implementation of MNREGA, the total value was 36.55, it was 36.55 against 60.16. Before and after the implementation of the MNREGA program, 65 percent of the intermediate, the increase in the average values of the level of life before and after the MNREGA program was found very important at one percent level.

Ranaware, Das, Kulkarni, Narayanan (2015) This study says that MNREGA is considered anti-farmer because it employs a large number of workers. This work is encouraged for agriculture and it is mainly beneficial for small and marginal farmers. This plan cannot still be productive or many working papers, it seems that the property is somewhat or very useful, there is another asset for the notion that this plan is non-sustainable, it is not entirely correct; Many work on local land is done regularly, if there is no local government, users have the argument that the ability to pay more attention to design and maintenance was a good way to ensure that the work was Assessment is a good format, now encourage local partnerships. Attempts to improve will be a better, more careful selection of tasks, and now HRR designs Will ensure that the livelihood of the effective support scheme.

Shalla & Fazili (2015) He said that MNREGA has offered rights based agreements for the rural poor, especially for the disadvantaged sections like Scheduled Castes and Scheduled Tribes. This Act envisages significant reforms in the socio-economic conditions of the rural poor, which acts as a vibrant force in fulfilling the said objectives of the State Governments. This study appears and according to other research, which is still a major difference, JNRA is present in the state in implementation of MNREGA, which needs to be addressed for the state so that major socio-economic indicators. In the context of Jammu and Kashmir, the involvement of local people in the capacity building and skill building, awareness campaign of Panchayat workers and government officials, supervision of vigilance at the state level, identification and execution of work under NREGA in the state should be done. To be done at the very end of the important publicity, property properties should be increased, if the state's goal is to make permanent livelihood for the rural poor.

Das (2015) In developing economies, decentralization at the local level gives more power to people so that they can get more in terms of public decision-making and implementation of policies. However, for their needs, the problem of political consumerism can be imminent, where public resources are allocated for individuals or specific groups, which are related to the local political party in power. In this context, the paper examines the role of local officials in the role of working under MNREGA, which is implemented locally. It was found that the supporters of the ruling party, who are politically active, are more likely to get these benefits. Studies have shown that primary behavior is available in access to public resources.

Khan & Saxena (2016) believed that MNREGA has had a positive impact on both rural and rural areas. MNREGA is a boon for rural households because they have been kept with guaranteed employment for their free time because they have got jobs from one side and secondly, their income has increased. Secondly, their income has increased. Due to MNREGA, the level of life of the rural people has also increased. It was found in this study that rural women feel like men and men. There was no difference between the men and women in the wages of MNREGA. This fact for women was the most important confidence booster. Prior to MNREGA, they did not enjoy equal opportunities as men and remained similar to the walled housewives. MNREGA is the first task, which has made rural women feel better under these important provisions. It shows that money is being spent on MNREGA after improving the quality of life and human development issues.

Bhat & Mariyappan (2016) Implementation of MNREGA has made an important initiative for the poor people of rural areas by their better efforts. One-third of MNREGA workers were women. MNREGA provides remuneration in the hands of beneficiaries, especially women help in changing their life without intermediaries and changing their behavior towards their life and work. Therefore, especially on the beneficiaries, women have an impact on MNREGA, which allows them to take their own steps. It is interesting to note that beneficiaries have good knowledge about MNREGA and its related activities in the area and they believe that MNREGA has done similar work and has given wages since gender discrimination. However, beneficiaries have to face some challenges in the management process of MNREGA, which seeks appropriate initiatives and solutions by the implementing agency.

Devi, Balasubramanian & Kumar (2016) evaluated the effect of NREGS and PDS on domestic food consumption using the cross-partial survey data of Tamil Nadu state. Describes the result of domestic spending that NREGA participates in removing the extra income to improve the lifestyle of your family members, such as purchasing durable assets such as furniture and health education. In addition, participants of NREGA change in the cost of food grains, milk, meat and eggs, such as grain, and these foods NREGA non-employment went seen a considerable increase in overall expenditure in relation to the participants the program over the provision of basic food commodities in order to ensure and improve the nutritional security of rural households, increase the purchasing power of rural areas to be a strong emphasis on MGNREGA.

Singh (2016) In this study, a comprehensive evaluation and ranking of 31 states has been presented on the world's largest social welfare scheme to eliminate poverty through employment generation in rural areas. This scheme consists of socially and economically weaker sections (Scheduled Castes and Scheduled Tribes) and women's priority groups. In the performance rankings, Tamilnadu is in top position, followed by Pondicherry, Punjab, and Rajasthan. This research, policy makers and governments recognize sources of deficiency in the MNREGA scheme. To prove and improve their performance proves to be useful guidelines for determining maximum goals for infiltration of states' future, it can be used as a policy document to encourage best policies so that in future children The situation could be motivated to perform well.

Jha, Mishra, Sinha, Alatalo & Pandey (2017) He studied MNREGA in India (Madhya Pradesh), an incentive-based program which includes MNREGA, water harvesting and conservation under poverty, climate change and sensitive nature of the NSS (water, land, soil) and human system (employment opportunity). Many great assets have been made and re-evaluated in all sample villages. Property: Surface water, ground water take a good look, stop storing tank, dams and ponds. Remove the effects of climate change.

4.3. Methodology

4.3.1. Objectives

An assessment of the impact of MNREGA on employment, income and savings, women's participation, agriculture, economic empowerment and various rural development programs. Whether MNREGA work is getting support from the convergence system with the concerned department. Is there the availability of work in the growing villages of MNREGA?

4.3.2. Content Analysis

Most areas have been studied where there has been a great deal of impact on MNREGA's employment, income, savings, economic empowerment, women's empowerment and other effects like travel etc. In rural areas, many development programs have been made to improve through this medium, which have a positive effect. With the participation of women, they can be expected to live at a higher level. Many results show that MGNREGA increases employment, enhances the income, savings and investment of rural people. The small landlord has a lot of land this is an alternate income tool. MNREGA is possible to improve the lives of rural people.

4.3.3. Qualitative Research

In this paper, MGNREA's qualitative study has been done. This study is between the period 2005 to 2017. Studies by researchers show that MNREGA has had an impact on unemployment, income, savings and rural life. It has a positive effect on all of these. The situation of women has improved; they are paid equal pay for men. Food improvement has improved in the rural areas, which is controlling the problem of fever. MNREGA has benefited small farmers.

4.3.4. Data Source

Secondary – Research Papers, Books, Journals, Websites.

4.4. Analysis

Summary Table of literature review

Sr.	Year	Author(s)	Title	Place
1	2005	Dreze	Employment Guarantee Act: promise and demise.	India
	Results/ Findings		• Money will be wasted due to corruption. • Employment Guarantee Act will lead to financial bankruptcy.	India

#	Year	Author	Title	Location
2	2006	Vasta	Employment Guarantee Scheme in Maharashtra: It's Impact on Drought, poverty and Vulnerability	Maharashtra
	Results/Findings		• EGS has given positive results.	
3	2007	Kumar	Political Economy of Poverty : A Micro Level Study	India
	Results/Findings		• The programs targeted for poverty alleviation show good politics, but some bad economics displays.	
4	2007	Dreze	NREGA: Dismantling the Contractor Raj	Orissa
	Results/Findings		• NREGA is able to avoid seasonal migration. • There are plenty of possibilities for production	
5	2008	Pankaj	Processes, Institutions and Mechanisms of Implementation of NREGA: Impact Assessment of Bihar and Jharkhand	Bihar and Jharkhand
	Results/Findings		• Increased work participation, but there was no impact on the existing local labor due to the availability and low employment level among the others.	
6	2008	Narayan	Employment guarantee, women's work and childcare	m district of Tamilnad

	Results/ Findings	• The students suggested to develop plans for the students. • The evidence required for childcare facility is provided.		
7	2008	Ghosh	"Far from Failure", Journal of Transparency Studies	India
	Results /Findings	• The level of livelihood of rural people can be raised by the MNREGA program.		
8	2009	Dreze & Khera	Battle for work: NREGA is making a difference to the lives of the rural poor	North India
	Results/ Findings	• The level of awareness was very low. • The measures of transparency against corruption are correct.		
9	2009	Swaminathan	The Synergy between NREGA and Food Security Act	India
	Results/ Findings	• There is a need to bring convergence of child care, nutritional health and education programs.		
10	2009	Singh & Nauriyal	System and Process Review and Impact Assessment of NREGA in the State of Uttarkhand	Uttarkhand
	Results/ Findings	• There was no significant improvement in income. • Low level awareness and poor performance of Panchayat Raj institutions.		

11	2009	Nair, Shreedharan & Anoopkumar	A study of National Rural Employment Guarantee Programme in three grama panchayats of Kasaragod district	Kasaragod district
	Results/ Findings	• Employment and income levels have been successful in increasing their purchasing power.		
12	2009	IAMR	All India Report on Evaluation of NREGA: A Survey of Twenty Districts	India
	Results/ Findings	• Work is not available during the scheduled period of 15 days, nor does he receive an unemployment allowance.		
13	2009	Sainath	Drought of justice, flood of funds	India
	Results/ Findings	• Millions of workers have been provided employment.		
14	2010	Bassi & Kumar	NREGA and rural water management in India: Improving the welfare effects	India
	Results/ Findings	• WM Department Agriculture are recognizing the characteristics of climate, hydrology and geological settings.		
15	2010	Dhakal	Impact of Informal Sector on Poverty and Employment in Nepal: A Micro Level Study of Chitwan District	Chitwan District
	Results/ Findings	• MNREGA plays an important role in generating income		

16	2010	Sudarshna, Bhattacharya & Frenandez	Women's Participation in the NREGA: Some Observations from Fieldwork in Himachal Pradesh, Kerala and Rajasthan	Himachal Pradesh, Kerala and Rajasthan
	Results/ Findings	• Positive results were met in relation to women's involvement.		
17	2010	Pankaj & Tanka	Empowerment effects of the NREGS on women workers: a study in four states.	Bihar, Jharkhand, Rajasthan and Himachal Pradesh
	Results/ Findings	• Impact of MNREGA on the empowerment of rural women Women have received the benefit of the salary from this plan.		
18	2010	Jha, Gaiha & Shankar	National rural employment guarantee programme in Andhra Pradesh and Rajasthan	Andhra Pradesh and Rajasthan
	Results/ Findings	• Information, access and distribution of plans is not easy. • Lack of information reduces the ability of profit		
19	2011	Vij	Collaborative governance: Analysing social audits in MGNREGA in India	India
	Results/ Findings	• Social audit system can be comprehensive to ensure effective policy implementation, monitoring and evaluation.		

20	2011	Murthy & Indumati	Economic analysis of MGNREGA in the drought–prone States of Karnataka, Rajasthan and irrigation–dominated State of Andhra Pradesh	Karnataka, Rajasthan & Andhra Pradesh
	Results/ Findings		• Under the MNREGA, there has been an increase in the agricultural sector and rural living standards	
21	2011	Sudarshna	India's National Rural Employment Guarantee Act: Women's Participation and Impacts in Himachal Pradesh, Kerala and Rajasthan	Himachal Pradesh, Kerala and Rajasthan
	Results/ Findings		• Women empowerment, women have the opportunity to get salaries..	
22	2011	Ahuja, Tyagi, Chuhan & Chudhary	Impact of MGNREGA on rural employment and migration: a study in agriculturally-backward and agriculturally-advanced districts of Haryana	Haryana
	Results/ Findings		• This scheme protects the livelihood of poor rural people who have less land.	
23	2011	Hirway	Providing employment guarantee in India: Some critical issues	Gujraat

	Results/ Findings	• MGNREGA contributes to the promotion of poor economic development		
24	2011	Harisha, Nagaraj, Chandrakantha, Murthy, Chengappa, Basavaraj, Chengappa & Basavaraj	Impacts and implications of MGNREGA on labour supply and income generation for agriculture in central dry zone of Karnataka	Karnataka
	Results/ Findings	• NREGA has been very helpful in providing employment.		
25	2011	Imbert & Papp	Government hiring and labor market equilibrium: Evidence from india's employment guarantee	India
	Results/ Findings	• Private sector wages have increased in the private sector wages in public sector recruitment.		
26	2012	Poonia	Critical Study of MGNREGA: Impact and 7 women's part 8 cipation	India
	Results/ Findings	• NREGS has the potential to promote local development, if management and distribution are good.		
27	2013	Nayak	Impact of Mgnrega on Status of Tribal Women in Odisha: A Case Study of Rajgangpur Block of Sundergarh District	Rajgangpur Block of Sundergarh District
	Results/ Findings	• More women were misused than NREGA. • The objective should be modified to get it.		

28	2013	Kumar & Joshibt	Household Consumption Pattern and Nutritional Security among Poor Rural Households: Impact of MGNREGA	India
	Results/ Findings		• There is a direct way of increasing the income of the rural poor • This is the way to provide food security.	
29	2013	Panda & Majumdar	A Review of Rural Development Programmes in India	India
	Results/ Findings		• Provides an alternative source of livelihood.	
30	2013	Tripathi	MGNREGA-A Ray Of Hope For Women Or A Myth	India
	Results/ Findings		• For women's empowerment, 1/3 participation has also been kept in the program.	
31	2014	Girard	Stepping into formal politics: Women's engagement in formal political processes in irrigation in rural India	India
	Results/ Findings		• Formal procedures for women participation are fine, their political awareness will increase.	

32	2015	Roy & Gowda	Impact Analysis of Mahatma Gandhi National Rural Employment Guarantee Programme in Dhalai District of Tripura	Dhalai District of Tripura
	Results/ Findings	• There is a positive and significant effect on the level of life of the beneficiaries.		
33	2015	Ranaware, Das, Kulkarni & Narayanan	MGNREGA Works and their impacts	India
	Results/ Findings	• MNREGA is considered anti-farmer. • It is mainly beneficial for small and marginal farmers.		
34	2015	Shalla & Fazili	Impact Of Employment Guarantee On Livelihood Security: Evidence From The Mgnrega In J&K	Jammu & Kashmir
	Results/ Findings	• Property properties should be increased, if the state's goal is to make permanent livelihood for the rural poor.		
35	2015	Das	Does political connections and affiliation affect allocation of benefits in the Rural Employment Guarantee Scheme: Evidence from West Bengal, India	India
	Results/ Findings	• Primary behavior is available in access to public resources. • The problem of political consumerism can be imminent,		

36	2016	Khan & Saxena	Economic Impact of MGNREGA: A Micro-Case Study of Bisalpur Sub-division of District Pilibhit in Uttar Pradesh	Uttar Pradesh, District Pilibhit
	Results/ Findings	• The level of income and the level of life of rural people has increased.		
37	2016	Devi, Balasubramanian & Kumar	The Impact of MGNREGA on Household Nutritional Security–An Economic Analysis in Tamil Nadu	Tamil Nadu
	Results/ Findings	• There has been significant increase in overall expenditure in respect of food items.		
38	2016	Singh	Evaluation of world's largest social welfare scheme: An assessment using non-parametric approach	India
	Results/ Findings	• The first goal of eliminating poverty through employment generation is the first goal. • The priority group of weaker sections and women covers the group.		
39	2017	Jha, Mishra, Sinha, Alatalo & Pandey	Rural development program in tribal region: A protocol for adaptation and addressing climate change vulnerability	Dhar, district of Madhya Pradesh state. India
	Results/ Findings	• MNREGA, an incentive program that improves rural life.		

4.5. Discussion

Top topics were identified:
- Women's economic empowerment, take wages directly through their accounts.
- Increasing expenditure of income from NREGA on food, consumer goods, education of children and loan repayment.
- Availability of work in villages increased NREGA.
- Increase in decision to create NREGA for women with additional income
- Incentives to work hours, work easily available.
- Breaking issues of caste and community, socio-economic benefits
- Easy access to credit efforts for convergence with health-HIV awareness through self-help groups, literacy, hope, ICDS.

One important initiative of the Government of India, the priority is given to the rural poor to create better life support programs in their unskilled workers, which will be one-third of the beneficiaries. In order to make the work more effective, the government should promote convergence in order to get financial assistance from the respective departments.

Conclusion

About 70 percent of Indian population lives in rural areas. Mahatma Gandhi National Rural Employment Guarantee Act (MNREGA) is considered as a "silver bullet" to eliminate rural poverty and unemployment through the demand of productive labor force in Indian villages. It provides an alternative source of livelihood which can be used to reduce migration, to limit child labor, to eliminate poverty, to make productive properties like roads, soil and water conservation etc. For which it has been considered as the world's largest poverty program. This plan is taking place from time to time for the undetermined period and the area is being expanded in terms of specific disparities and results etc. Rural development programs should be thoroughly reviewed with two different strategies, i.e. (i) keeping in mind the signs from all corners of the country, keeping in mind all areas and (ii) Mango The broad coverage of all the people covered by the objectives and the currents. Thus, the implementation process of this program should be critically examined and the people of rural people It should have a bearing on living. It can be concluded that the success of this act depends on its proper implementation and in this scenario, community participation is very important in making this program more effective.

References

Dreze, J. (2005). Employment Guarantee Act - Promise and Demise. *Kurukshetra*, 53(7), 9-13.

Vatsa, K. S. (2006). Employment Guarantee Scheme in Maharashtra: Its Impact on Drought, Poverty and Vulnerability. *Indian Journal of Labour Economics*, 49(3).

Kumar, M. (2007). *Political Economy of Poverty : A Micro Level Study.* New Delhi: Deep & Deep Publications.

Dreze, J. (2007). NREGA: Dismantling the Contractor Raj. *The Hindu*, November 20.

Pankaj, A. (2008). *Processes, Institutions and Mechanisms of implementation of NREGA: Impact assessment of Bihar and Jharkhand.* Delhi: Institute for Human Development.

Narayanan, S. (2008). Employment guarantee, women's work and childcare. *Economic and Political Weekly*, 10-13.

Ghosh, J. (2008), "Far from Failure", Journal *of Transparency Studies*, Vol. 1, No. 4, April 2008, 5-7.

Dreze, J., & Khera, R. (2009). Battle for work: NREGA is making a difference to the lives of the rural poor. *Frontline, 26*(1), 3-16.

Swaminathan, M. S. (2009). The Synergy between NREGA and Food Security Act. *The Hindu*, June 1.

Singh, S. P., & Nauriyal, D. K. (2009). *System and Process Review and Impact Assessment of NREGA in the State of Uttarkhand.* Indian Institute of Technology, Roorkee.

Nair, K. N., Sreedharan, T. P., & Anoopkumar, M. (2009). A study of National Rural Employment Guarantee Programme in three grama panchayats of Kasaragod district.

IAMR. (2009). *All India Report on Evaluation of NREGA: A Survey of Twenty Districts.* Delhi: Institute of Applied Manpower Research.

Sainath, P. (2009). Drought of justice, flood of funds. *The Hindu*, August 15.

Bassi, N., & Kumar, M. D. (2010). NREGA and rural water management in India: Improving the welfare effects. *Occasional paper, 3*.

Dhakal, R. C. (2010). Impact of Informal Sector on Poverty and Employment in Nepal: A Micro Level Study of Chitwan District. *The Economic Journal of Nepal, 33*(2), 106-125.

Sudarshan, R. M., Bhattacharya, R., & Fernandez, G. (2010). Women's Participation in the NREGA: Some Observations from Fieldwork in Himachal Pradesh, Kerala and Rajasthan. *IDS Bulletin, 41*(4), 77-83.

Pankaj, A., & Tankha, R. (2010). Empowerment effects of the NREGS on women workers: a study in four states. *Economic and Political Weekly*, 45-55.

Jha, R., Gaiha, R., & Shankar, S. (2010). National rural employment guarantee programme in Andhra Pradesh and Rajasthan: Some recent evidence. *Contemporary South Asia, 18*(2), 205-213.

Vij, N. (2011). Collaborative governance: Analysing social audits in MGNREGA in India. *IDS Bulletin, 42*(6), 28-34.

Murthya, P. S., & Indumatib, S. (2011). Economic analysis of MGNREGA in the drought–prone States of Karnataka, Rajasthan and irrigation–dominated State of Andhra Pradesh. *Agricultural Economics Research Review, 24*, 531-536.

Sudarshan, R. M. (2011). *India's National Rural Employment Guarantee Act: Women's Participation and Impacts in Himachal Pradesh, Kerala and Rajasthan.*

Ahuja, U. R., Tyagi, D., Chauhan, S., & Chaudhary, K. R. (2011). Impact of MGNREGA on rural employment and migration: a study in agriculturally-backward and agriculturally-advanced districts of Haryana. *Agricultural Economics Research Review, 24*, 495-502.

Hirway, I. (2004). Providing employment guarantee in India: Some critical issues. *Economic and Political Weekly*, 5117-5124.

Harish, B. G., Nagaraj, N., Chandrakanth, M. G., Murthy, P. S., Chengappa, P. G., & Basavaraj, G. (2011). Impacts and implications of MGNREGA on labour supply and income generation for agriculture in central dry zone of Karnataka. *Agricultural Economics Research Review, 24*(3), 485-494.

Imbert, C., & Papp, J. (2011). Government hiring and labor

market equilibrium: Evidence from india's employment guarantee. In *ISI conference, New Delhi, December.* Retrieved from: http://www.isid.ac.in/~pu/conference/dec_11_conf/Papers/ClementImbert.pdf [Accessed on: 18 June, 2017].

Poonia, J. (2012). Critical Study of MGNREGA: Impact and women's participation. *International Journal of Human Development and Management Sciences*, 1(1), 35-55.

Dr. Smita Nayak (2013), *"Impact of Mgnrega on Status of Tribal Women in Odisha: A Case Study of Rajgangpur Block of Sundergarh District",* Journal of Agriculture and Environmental Sciences, Vol. 2 No. 2, December 2013.

Kumar, P., & Joshi, P. K. (2013). Household Consumption Pattern and Nutritional Security among Poor Rural Households: Impact of MGNREGA. *Agricultural Economics Research Review*, 26(1).

Panda, S., & Majumder, A. (2013). A Review of Rural Development Programmes in India. *International Journal of Research in Sociology and Social Anthropology1, 2,* 37-40.

Tripathi, R. (2013). MGNREGA-A RAY OF HOPE FOR WOMEN OR A MYTH. *International Journal of Advanced Research in Management and Social Science*, 2(6), 146-150. Retrieved from: http://garph.co.uk/IJARMSS/June2013/12.pdf [Accessed on: 19 June, 2017].

Girard, A. M. (2014). Stepping into formal politics: Women's engagement in formal political processes in irrigation in rural India. *World Development, 57,* 1-18.

Roy, J., & Gowda, K. N. (2011). *Impact Analysis of Mahatma Gandhi National Rural Employment Guarantee Programme in Dhalai District of Tripura.* Doctoral dissertation, University of Agricultural Sciences, GKVK. Retrieved from: http://www.krishisanskriti.org/vol_image/11Sep2015090957 16.pdf [Accessed on: 12 June, 2017].

Ranaware, K., Das, U., Kulkarni, A., & Narayanan, S. (2015). MGNREGA Works and their impacts. *Economic & Political Weekly, 50*(13), 53-61.

Shalla, S. A., & Fazili, A. I. (2015). Impact of Employment Guarantee on Livelihood Security: Evidence from the MGNREGA in J&K. *Asia Pacific Journal of Research,* 1(30).

Das, U. (2015). Does political activism and affiliation affect allocation of benefits in the rural employment guarantee program: Evidence from West Bengal, India. *World Development*, 67, 202-217.

Khan, M. I., & Saxena, S. (2016). Economic Impact of MGNREGA: A Micro-Case Study of Bisalpur Sub-division of District Pilibhit in Uttar Pradesh. *International Journal of Pure and Applied Management Sciences*, 1(1).

Devi, T. S., Balasubramanian, R., & Kumar, B. G. (2016). The Impact of MGNREGA on Household Nutritional Security– An Economic Analysis in Tamil Nadu. *International Journal of Scientific Research in Science and Technology (IJSRST)*, 2(3).

Singh, S. (2016). Evaluation of world's largest social welfare scheme: An assessment using non-parametric approach. *Evaluation and Program Planning*, 57, 16-29.

Jha, S. K., Mishra, S., Sinha, B., Alatalo, J. M., & Pandey, R. (2017). Rural development program in tribal region: A protocol for adaptation and addressing climate change vulnerability. *Journal of Rural Studies*, 51, 151-157.

CHAPTER: 5
GROWTH AND STRUCTURE OF ORGANIZED MANUFACTURING SECTOR OF HIMACHAL PRADESH

Sanjeev Kumar and Falguni Pattanaik

Abstract

The role of manufacturing sector in generating employment and accelerating the economic growth is quite discussed in the literature at national level as well as sub-national level for few states of India. Few studies have investigated the growth of manufacturing sector in the context of emerging state economies. Observing the recent economic growth and increasing the importance of the state in the national economy, it is significant to estimate the growth and structure of manufacturing sector of individual state. With this motivation present study has examined the growth and structure of organized manufacturing sector of Himachal Pradesh by using the Annual Survey of Industries (ASI) data from 1981 to 2014. The study has shown that over the period organized manufacturing sector of Himachal Pradesh in term of GVA and employment grow with higher rate against the selected states and national figures especially during the recent period. The resultant employment elasticity in the state is also noted quite high in relation to the national economy and selected states. Most of the industries in the states grew in the range of 8 to 20 percent in term of GVA, while in term of employment 5 industries have achieved more than 10 percent of growth rate during the study period. This extremely high performance of Himachal

Pradesh in organized manufacturing in both GVA and employment has possibly a lot to do with the tax exemptions providing to industrial units set up in the state.

5.1. Introduction

A number of studies have studied the issue of employment, productivity and wage of organized manufacturing sector in India using the Annual Survey of Industries data (Goldar, 1989a 2000b; Nagaraj, 1994a, 2000b, 2004c; Mazumdar, 2003;Rani and Unni, 2004; Majumder, 2006; Sen and Dasgupta, 2006). These studies clearly showed that employment and gross value added in Indian manufacturing sector has experienced an uneven pattern. From 1950 to mid-1960s, industrial sector of India had experienced a high rate of growth. In the next fifteen years, industrial growth was not prosperous particularly in the heavy industries and up to the end of 1970s the signs of revival were seen in this sector (Thomas, 2013). Lack of investment in infrastructure by the public sector, slow growth in agriculture income, restrictive trade and industrial policies were some of notable reasons for this sluggish growth. During the 1980s the jobless growth pattern was noticed in the manufacturing sector by the several researchers. The increase in the wage rate, job-security regulation, contracting out work, more use of capital intensive technique of production, limited structural transformation, changes in industrial composition, increased in actual hours worked per workers are well established facts for this jobless growth (Papola 1994; Bhalotra, 1998; Goldar, 2000; Nagaraj, 2000, Bhattacharya and Sakthivel 2004; Ghose, 2005; Kannan and Raveendran, 2009; Sen and Das 2015).

Several other researchers have found inconsistency in the pattern of manufacturing growth during the 1990s and in the recent years. Thomas (2013) explained that during the initial years of economic reform around 1.5 million job were created in the manufacturing sector. In the next six years around more than one million job were lost in the manufacturing sector. Goldar (2011) invalidate the phenomena of jobless industrial growth. He claimed that during the period from 2003-04 to 2008-09 employment increased with a growth rate of around 7.5 percent per annum in the manufacturing sector.

The studies on the manufacturing sector are also available at the state level, some of them have mainly dealt with the growth and structure of manufacturing sector at the individual state level or in comparative perspective (Albin, 1990; Upendranath, Vijayabaskar and Vyasulu, 1994; Burange, 1999; Trivdedi, 2004; Kumar, 2006; Mitra, 2007; Das, 2007; Ghose and Roy, 2007; Prakash and Balu, 2013; Jana and Adhikary, 2016; Kukreja, 2016).

From the above citations, it is clear that the role of industrial sector in generating employment and accelerating the economic growth is quite discussed in the literature at national level as well as sub-national level for few states of India, few or none have investigated the growth of industrial sector in the context of emerging state economies. Observing the recent economic growth and increasing the importance of the state economy in the national economy, it is significant to estimate the growth and structure of manufacturing sector of individual state. With this motivation present study examined the growth and structure of organized manufacturing sector of Himachal Pradesh in comparative perspective since 1981 to 2014. The remaining part of this paper is structure in the following manner. Section 2 deals with the data source, methodology and time period covered. Section 3 provides the detail of result and discussion. Summary and conclusions are presented in the last section.

5.2. Data Source and Methodology

The study is mainly based on secondary data and data has been collected from Annual Survey of Industry (ASI) published by Central Statistical Organization. The study uses data on aggregate as well as industry levels on the various variables such as gross value added, total person engaged, fixed capital, number of factories, total Emoluments. At the aggregate level time series data have been collected since 1981 to 2014. At the industry level, data have been used since 1999-2000 onwards because previous year's data is not available for the state variables. ASI data are available in various National Industrial Classification (NIC) such as NIC- 1998, NIC-2004, and NIC-2008. The concordance has been done between NIC- 1998, NIC-2004, and NIC-2008 to make uniformity and consistency in the data at the 3-digit NIC 2004 classification. The growth is estimated using following semi-log model:

$$\ln Y_0 = \beta_1 + \beta_2 t + u_t$$

This model is like any other regression model in which

β_1 and β_2 are linear. The only difference is that controlled variable is the logarithm of Y and the control variable is time and take values of 1, 2, 3, 4, 5 etc. β_2 represent the slope coefficient which measure the relative change in Y for a given change in the value of t. Further, employment elasticity is calculated using following log linear regression model:

$$\ln L = \alpha + \beta \ln Y$$

Where, L represents employment, Y stands for output, and ln indicates the natural logarithm of the variable β coefficient stands for the employment elasticity.

5.3. Results and Discussion

5.3.1. Growth of Organized Manufacturing Sector of Himachal Pradesh

The present section analyzes the growth of employment and GVA and employment elasticity of organized manufacturing sector of Himachal Pradesh in comparison with national figures over a period of 34 years to find out the growth and structure of organized manufacturing sector of the state. Apart from the aggregate growth, industries wise growth is also analyzed in this section.

5.3.2. Growth of Employment and GVA and Employment Elasticity

The results indicate that over a period of 34 years Himachal Pradesh economy in term of GVA and employment grow with higher rate against the national figures. The resultant employment elasticity in the state is also noted quite high in relation to the national economy. The high value of employment elasticity indicates that with a 1 percent increase in GVA, employment increases with 0.28 percent in the Himachal Pradesh (Table 1).

A breakup of the study period into different periods reflect differences in the pattern of growth. It may be noted that in Himachal Pradesh, the GVA growth rate have increased with high rate during the recent period (2000-2014), as compared to the starting period of 1981 -1990. On the other hand, employment growth in the state marginally improved to 6.74 percent in 2000-14 from 4.47 percent in 1981-1990. But what is important to note is that in spite of high growth of GVA, employment elasticity in the state declined to 0.58 percent from 0.62 percent during the said period (Table 1). With the declined growth rate of GVA during 1991-2000 in Himachal Pradesh, it can be said that there was hardly any impact of economic reforms on employment generation in the state.

Turning to the national figures, a slightly comparable trend can be observed during the sub-periods wherein GVA and employment growth have marginally improved over the period. GVA growth increases to 6.6 percent in 2001-14 from 5.79 percent in 1980-81, while employment growth increased to 2.18 percent from less than one percent growth rate during the same period. As a result, employment elasticity increased to 0.33 percent in the current period (Table 1).

Table 1: Growth of Employment and GVA and Employment Elasticity of Organized Manufacturing Sector in Himachal Pradesh and India, 1981 to 2014 (in percent)

Years	Himachal Pradesh			India		
	Growth of Employment	Growth of Gross Value Added	Elasticity	Growth of Employment	Growth of Gross Value Added	Elasticity
1981-1990	4.47	5.94	0.62	0.008*	5.79	0.007*
1991-2000	-1.22*	5.87	-0.01*	0.28*	6.04	0.09*
2001-2014	6.74	11.38	0.58	2.18	6.6	0.33
1981-2014	1.96	7.56	0.28	0.59	5.64	0.11

Source: Author estimation based on Annual Survey of Industries data.
Note: *Estimates are insignificant.

Industries wise growth pattern shows some interesting results in the state. Most of the industries in the states grew in the range of 8 to 20 percent in term of GVA during the 1981-2014. Only one industry, i.e. tobacco products (160) in the state grew with negative rate. The industries which have experienced growth in the range of 2 to 6 percent are beverages (155), spinning, weaving and finishing of textiles (171), non-metallic mineral products (269), and medical appliances and instruments (331+333) (Table 2).

Table 2: Growth of Employment and GVA and Employment Elasticity across the Industries in Himachal Pradesh, 2000-2014 (in percent)

Sr. No.	NIC-Code	Growth of Employment	Growth of Gross Value Added	Elasticity
1	151	2.98	9.41	0.35
2	153	2.63	9.19	0.36
3	154	8.65	10.27	0.65
4	155	0.41*	3.98	0.11*
5	160	-4.15	-3.95	-0.04
6	171	0.64	2.94	0.21
7	172	3.26	8.08	0.59
8	210	17.49	16.16	0.99
9	251	8.3	17.91	0.44
10	252	6.59	14.45	0.42
11	261	3.04	12.99	0.23
12	269	2.24	4.52	0.33
13	271	8.09	14.54	0.50
14	272	8.98	13.30	0.62
15	273	4.09	11.72	0.29
16	281	4.02	10.67	0.32
17	289	3.62	10.02	0.37
18	291	2.73	9.55	0.23
19	292	4.69	8.39	0.29
20	293	13.83	18.38	0.72
21	311+312	8.93	11.73	0.74
22	315	12.73	19.62	0.65
23	319	13.07	19.01	0.57
24	321	4.12	10.20	0.41
25	331+333	-0.13*	5.22	0.11
26	343	10.08	11.18	0.74

Source: Author estimation based on Annual Survey of Industries data.
Note: *Estimates are insignificant.

As far as the growth rate of employment is concerned, out of 26 industries in the state 5 industries have grown more than 10 percent growth rate during the study period. Within these five industries, paper and paper product (210) has grown with the highest rate in the state. Tobacco products (160)), and medical appliances and instruments (331+333) have experienced negative growth rate over the period (Table 2).To know, which industries in the state performed well in term of employment generation with respect to GVA during 1981 to 2014. Industries wise employment elasticity is calculated for this purpose. On the basis of the high value of employment elasticity, paper and paper product (210) observed highest employment generating industry in the state. The industries which have experienced the value of employment elasticity in the range of 0.50 to 0.75 percent are other food products (154), other textiles (172), basic iron and steel (271), basic precious and non-ferrous metals (272), domestic appliances (293), electric motors, and electricity distribution (311+312), electric lamps and lighting equipment (315), other electrical equipment (319), and parts and accessories for motor vehicles and their engines (343). Only one industry (tobacco products, 160) has witnessed negative value of employment elasticity in the state (Table 2).

5.3.3. Wage and Labour Productivity

We now look at the wage and the labour productivity performance of an organized manufacturing sector of Himachal Pradesh. It may be noted that over the period wage share in the GVA has declined in the state and this is reflected in its negative growth rate. With this negative growth rate it can be argued that the rise in the productivity growth is not progressed into more wage share. Similarly, trends of negative growth rate of the wage share in GVA are also observed in the case of national economy over the period. The average share has also experienced a marginal declined in the state as well as national level. The state average wage growth declined to 4.23 percent in 2001-14 from 5.11 percent in 1981-90. Whereas in the national economy, it declined to 4.01 percent from 5.13 during the same period.

Table 3: Growth of Wage and Labour Productivity in Himachal Pradesh and India, 1981 to 2014, (in percent)

Years	Himachal Pradesh			India		
	Wage share in GVA	Average wage	labour Productivity	Wage Share	Average Wage	labour Productivity
1981-90	3.65	5.11	1.46	-0.65	5.13	5.78
1991-00	-2.86	4.23	7.09	-1.37	4.39	5.75
2001-14	0.09*	4.73	4.64*	-0.39	4.01	4.41
1981-14	-1.37	4.23	5.6	-1.04	4.01	5.05

Source: Author estimation based on Annual Survey of Industries data.
Note: *Estimates are insignificant.

Table 4: Industries wise Growth of Wage and Labour Productivity in Himachal Pradesh, 2000 to 2014, (in percent)

Sr. No.	NIC-Code	Wage Share in GVA	Average Wage	labour Productivity
1	151	-2.74	3.68	6.43
2	153	-2.36	4.21	6.56
3	154	3.04*	4.66	1.62*
4	155	-0.33*	3.9	3.56
5	160	2.88	3.08	0.20*
6	171	1.58	3.89	2.3
7	172	-1.29*	3.53	4.82
8	210	5.82*	4.5	-1.33*
9	251	-2.21	7.4	9.6
10	252	-3.63	4.22	7.85
11	261	-6.6	3.36	9.95
12	269	3.08	5.37	2.28
13	271	-2.70*	3.74	6.44
14	272	0.49	4.81	4.32
15	273	-4.16	3.46	7.62
16	281	-1.79*	4.86	6.64
17	289	-1.96	4.44	-6.4
18	291	-3.6	3.22	6.82
19	292	0.97*	4.68	3.71
20	293	-0.43*	4.13	4.55
21	311,312	0.59*	3.39	0.28
22	315	0.79*	7.79	6.99
23	319	-0.23	5.72	3.26
24	321	-5.09	1.82*	6.91
25	331,333	-1.95	3.41	5.63
26	341	1.12*	2.22	1.09

Source: Author estimation based on Annual Survey of Industries data.
Note: *Estimates are insignificant.

As far as the labour productivity growth is concerned, in Himachal Pradesh it has grown almost at par with the national figure with small variation over the period. But within sub-periods, growth in labour productivity shows the differences. It may be noted that during 1981-90, growth in labor productivity in the state was very low in comparison to the period of 1991-00 and 2001-14. In case of national economy, labour productivity has experienced opposite trends, where labour productivity growth declined over the period (Table 3).

Industries wise growth of wage and labour productivity in the state mirror divergences. In terms of the wage share in GVA, most of the industries in the state experienced negative and statistically insignificant growth rate over the period. About the average wage share, the two industries have experienced more than 7 percent of growth rate in the state. These industries are rubber products (251) and electric lamps and lighting equipment (315). The rest of the industry has experienced growth rate in the range of 2 to 5 percent. Similarly, in terms of labour productivity there is also a difference in the growth pattern across the industries. Glass and glass products (261) are noted highest labour productivity industry in the state, while electrical distribution, control apparatus insulated wire and cable (311+312) industry is noted lowest labour productivity industry in the state (Table 4).

5.3.4. Growth of Structural Ratios

To study the growth of industrial production in Himachal Pradesh, it is meaningful to analyze the growth of key structural ratios. The growth of key structural ratios at the aggregate level for the Himachal Pradesh and India has been presented in the table 5. The results show that over the period GVA per unit in the state grew with a growth rate of 4.18 percent, fixed capital per unit grew by 3.10 percent, employment per unit grew with a negative growth rate of -1.42 percent and capital intensity increased by 4.15 percent. The national figures for all these variables is observed relatively high during the same period.

Sub-period wise growth of GVA per unit, fixed capital per unit, employment per unit and capital intensity shows discrepancies. During the decade of the 1980s the growth of all these variables in the state was noted quite high in comparison to the decade of 1990s except capital intensity. The growth of capital intensity in the state was noted very low and statistically insignificant during 1980s. But in the decade of 1990s, its growth accelerated with a growth rate of around 8.65 percent. What is important to note is that during the current decade growth in two variables, i.e. GVA per unit and fixed capital per unit accelerated in the state and grown with a growth rate of around 4.62 and 3.34 percent respectively. But the growth in other two structural ratios, i.e. employment per unit and capital intensity declined with rapid rate in the state.

At national level sub-period wise growth of these structural ratios also shows the differences. The growth in all the structural ratios observed highest during 1980s except employment per unit in relation to the decade of 1990s. In the decade of 2000s growth in three structural ratios declined. These structural variables are GVA per unit, fixed capital per unit and employment per unit. But capital intensity increased to 5.59 percent 2000-14 from 4.66 percent.

Table 4: Per Unit Growth of GVA, Fixed Capital and Employment, and growth of Capital Intensity in Himachal Pradesh and India, 1981-2014

Years	Himachal Pradesh				India			
	GVA per Unit	Fixed Capital Per Unit	Employment per Unit	Capital Intensity	GVA per Unit	Fixed Capital Per Unit	Employment Per Unit	Capital Intensity
1981-90	86.5 (3.86)	280.4 (5.45)	160.8 (2.39)	0.2 (1.17)*	27.9 (5.40)	60.2 (5.50)	78.8 (0.38)*	0.23 (5.47)
1991-00	208.5 (3.19)	541.6 (2.93)	137.5 (-3.89)	0.8 (8.65)	32.0 (5.06)	69.3 (4.89)	72.0 (0.69)	0.25 (4.66)
2001-14	759.5 (4.62)	1277.7 (3.34)	73.6 (-0.02)*	2.2 (2.43)	36.3 (4.47)	79.5 (4.50)	64.4 (-0.05)*	0.28 (5.59)
1981-14	399.5 (4.18)	767.8 (3.10)	118 (-1.42)	1.2 (4.15)	41.5 (4.67)	91.2 (4.46)	71.2 (0.37)	0.22 (4.67)

Source: Author estimation based on Annual Survey of Industries data.
Note: *Estimates are insignificant.
Figure in parenthesis shows growth rate (in percent).

5.3.5. Relative Performance of Organized Manufacturing of Himachal Pradesh

In this section, relative performance of Himachal Pradesh organized manufacturing is analyzed with the selected major state of India. GVA and employment share to all India total and the employment elasticity of respective state is used for this purpose. It is observed that Himachal Pradesh contributes a smaller share in both GVA and employment in comparison to selected states. What is interesting to note is that over the period its contribution in both GVA and employment increased significantly. To be specific, in term of GVA, its share incessantly increased to 0.7 percent in 1990-91 from 0.5 percent in 1980-81 and further to 2.5 in 2013-14 from 0.9 percent in 2000-01. But the speed of acceleration is noted after the decades of 1990s.

Table 5: State Wise Share of GVA in all India total, 1981 to 2014, (in percent)

States	1980-81	1990-91	2000-01	2013-14	Average share of GVA (1981-14)	AAGR of GVA (1981-14)
Andhra Pradesh	5.0	6.2	6.2	2.5	6.14	5.64
Assam	1.0	1.4	0.9	0.9	1.11	5.00
Bihar	5.2	5.1	0.5	0.5	3.3	0.36*
Gujarat	9.8	8.8	12.9	14.6	11.9	6.27
Haryana	3.0	3.1	4	4.2	3.55	6.26
Himachal Pradesh	0.5	0.7	0.9	2.5	1.14	7.57
Karnataka	5.1	5.3	5.7	6.4	6.02	6.31
Kerala	3.2	2.2	2.3	1.4	2.14	4.32
Madhya Pradesh	5.1	6.1	4.2	2.4	4.35	4.26
Maharashtra	24.0	22.7	21.1	21.5	21.54	5.49
Orissa	1.9	2.4	1.7	2.8	2.12	6.18
Punjab	3.4	3.7	2.9	2.2	3.14	5.22
Rajasthan	2.9	3.1	3.6	3.1	3.05	5.18
Tamil Nadu	10.1	11	11.4	10	9.98	5.54
Uttar Pradesh	6.1	9.3	7	4	7.39	4.84
West Bengal	10.9	5.9	4	2.6	5.32	3.93

Source: Author estimation based on Annual Survey of Industries data.
Note: *Estimates are insignificant.

Table 6: State Wise Share of Employment in all India total, 1981 to 2014, (in percent)

State	1980-81	1990-91	2000-01	2013-14	Average Share of Emp (1981-14)	AAGR of Emp (1981-2014)
Andhra Pradesh	8.79	10.22	11.36	3.86	9.90	0.36
Assam	1.59	1.33	1.41	1.38	1.41	0.43
Bihar	4.89	4.39	0.79	0.84	2.62	-2.79
Gujarat	9.10	8.32	9.41	10.14	9.29	0.79
Haryana	2.39	3.10	3.77	4.52	3.63	1.42
Himachal Pradesh	0.29	0.65	0.49	1.44	0.67	1.97
Karnataka	5.12	5.13	5.94	6.85	5.84	1.15
Kerala	3.59	3.31	3.92	2.60	3.37	0.55
Madhya Pradesh	4.17	5.08	3.17	2.38	3.76	-0.61
Maharashtra	17.27	15.17	14.68	13.93	14.86	0.30
Orissa	1.71	1.87	1.61	1.93	1.85	0.57
Punjab	3.13	4.97	4.49	4.45	4.49	0.87
Rajasthan	2.47	2.96	2.91	3.47	3.04	0.87
Tamil Nadu	10.31	11.80	14.23	15.12	13.19	1.19
Uttar Pradesh	9.92	9.69	6.76	2.86	7.95	-0.27
West Bengal	12.20	9.01	7.13	4.77	7.92	-0.72

Source: Author estimation based on Annual Survey of Industries data.

Another important feature of industrial development of Himachal Pradesh is that up to 2000s its contributions in term of GVA was lowest among the selected states. But in 2013-14, its contribution marginally improved and it became tenth highest contributing state in term of GVA to all India total. At present the states like Bihar, Assam, Kerala, Punjab and Madhya Pradesh are contributing lower share than the Himachal Pradesh.

In analyzing the pattern of employment growth it is noticed that up to 2000-01 the contribution of Himachal Pradesh was lowest among the selected states. In 2013-14, its employment contribution slightly improved and it became fourteenth largest contributing state in the country. At present Himachal Pradesh contributing a highest share in employment than the Bihar and Assam, and from the rest of the states its contribution is lower. The resulting employment elasticity value of Himachal Pradesh is also comparable in size with the selected state. Himachal Pradesh is one of the second largest state in the country in term of employment generation with respect to GVA growth rate after the state of Bihar. The rest of the state has lowest elasticity value in comparison to these two states (Figure 1). As far as the growth rate is concerned, the Himachal Pradesh economy grew both in GVA and employment with the highest rate among the selected states in the country during the 1981-2014.

Figure 1: State Wise Employment Elasticity, 1981 to 2014 (in percent)

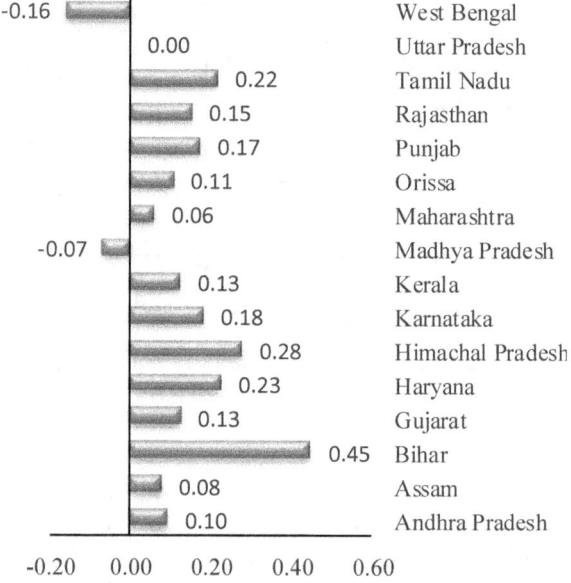

Source: Author estimation based on Annual Survey of Industries data.

This extremely high performance of Himachal Pradesh in organized manufacturing in both GVA and employment has possibly a lot to do with the tax exemptions providing to industrial units set up in the state (Goldar, 2011). Similarly, growth differences across the states in the organized manufacturing is a lot to do with poor physical infrastructure, i.e. the poor quality of power supply, ports and airports and railway and road networks are some of the responsible factors (Kappor, 2014). There is a set of literature who argued that labour market rigidities is an important cause for the poor performance of growth of organized manufacturing in India. But another set of studies explained that during the recent period some of the states have relaxed the labour laws at ground level. As a result growth of organized manufacturing increases in those states who have relaxed the labour laws (Papola, 2008).

Summary and Conclusion

The paper concludes that the organized manufacturing sector of Himachal Pradesh has witnessed very high rate of growth during the recent period 2000-2014, as compared to the starting period of 1981-1990. Industries wise growth pattern shows some interesting results in the state. Most of the industries in the states grew in the range of 8 to 20 percent in term of GVA during the 1981-2014. Only one industry, i.e. tobacco products (160) in the state grew with negative rate. As far as the growth rate of employment is concerned, out of 26 industries in the state 5 industries have achieved more than 10 percent growth rate during the study period. On the basis of the high value of employment elasticity, paper and paper product (210) observed highest employment generating industry in the state. It may be noted that over the period wage share in the GVA has declined in the state and this is reflected in its negative growth rate. With this negative growth rate it can be argued that the rise in the productivity growth is not progressed into more wage share. Another important feature of industrial development of Himachal Pradesh is that up to 2000s its contributions in term of GVA and employment was lowest among the selected states. But in 2013-14, its contribution marginally improved. In term of employment generation with respect to GVA growth rate Himachal Pradesh is one of the second largest state in the country after the state of Bihar. As far as the growth rate is concerned, the Himachal Pradesh economy grew both in GVA and employment with the highest rate among the selected states in the country during the 1981-2014 and this is lot to do with the tax exemptions providing to industrial units set up in the state.

References

Albin, A. (1990). Manufacturing Sector in Kerala: Comparative Study of Its Growth and Structure. *Economic and Political*

Weekly, 25(37), 2059-2070.
Bhalotra, S. R. (1998). The Puzzle of Jobless Growth in Indian Manufacturing. *Oxford Bulletin of Economics and Statistics*, 60(1), 0305-9049
Bhattacharya, B. B., & Sakthivel, S. (2004). *Economic Reforms and Jobless Growth in India in the 1990s*. Working Paper, No. 245/2004. New Delhi, India: Institute of Economic Growth.
Burange, L. G. (1999). Industrial Growth and Structure: Manufacturing Sector in Maharashtra', *Economic and Political Weekly*. 34(9), M39-M48.
Das, P. (2007). Economic Reform, Output and Employment Growth in Manufacturing: Testing Kaldor's Hypotheses. *Economic and Political Weekly*, 42(39), 3978-3985.
Ghose, A. K. (1994). Employment in Organized Manufacturing in India. *Indian Journal of Labour Economics*, 37(2), 141-162.
Ghose, A., and Roy, S (2007) Inter-State Disparity in the Growth and Determinants of Wage Rate for Industrial Labour in India. *Indian Journal of Labour Economics*, 50(4), 975-990.
Goldar, B. (2000). Employment Growth in Organized Manufacturing in India. *Economic and Political Weekly*, 35(14), 1191-1195.
Goldar, B. (2004). Indian Manufacturing: Productivity Trends in Pre- and Post-Reform Periods. *Economic and Political Weekly*, 39 (46/47), 5033-5043.
Goldar, B. (2011). Growth in Organised Manufacturing Employment in Recent Years. *Economic and Political Weekly*, 47(7), 20-23.
Goldar, B., & Seth, V. (1989). Spatial Variations in the Rate of Industrial Growth in India'. *Economic and Political Weekly*, 24(22), 1237-1240.
Kannan, K., & Raveendran, G. (2009). Growth Sans Employment: A Quarter Century of Jobless Growth in India Organised Manufacturing. *Economic and Political Weekly*, 44 (10), 80-91.
Kapoor, R. (2014). *Creating Jobs in India's Organized Manufacturing Sector*. Working paper No. 286/2014. New Delhi, India: Indian Council for Research on International Economic Relations.
Kukreja, P. (2016) The Relationship between Trade Openness and Regional Inequality: Case of Indian manufacturing industries. *Journal of Regional Development and Planning*, 5(2), 33-44.
Majumder, R. (2006). Employment and Wages in the Liberalised

Regime: A Study of Indian Manufacturing Sector. *The Indian Journal of Labour Economics*, 49(4), .611-624.

Mazumdar, D. (2003). Trends in employment and the employment elasticity in manufacturing, 1971—92: An international comparison. *Cambridge Journal of Economics*, 11(1), 152-194.

Mazumdar, D., & Sarkar, S. (2004). Reforms and Employment Elasticity in Organised Manufacturing. *Economic and Political Weekly*, 39 (27), 3017-3029.

Mitra, A. (2007). Industrialization and Poverty Evidence: From Indian States. *Indian Journal of Labour Economics*, 50(2),

Nagaraj, R. (1994). Employment and Wages in Manufacturing Industries: Trends, Hypotheses and Evidence. *Economic and Political Weekly*, 29(4), 177-186.

Nagaraj, R. (2000). Organised Manufacturing Employment. *Economic and Political Weekly*, 35 (38), 3445-3448.

Nagaraj, R. (2004). Fall in Organised Manufacturing Employment: A Brief Note. *Economic and Political Weekly*, 30(30), 3387-3390.

Papola, T. S. (1994). Structural Adjustment, Labour Market Flexibility and Employment. Indian *Journal of Labour Economics*, 37(1), 3-16.

Papola, T., S, ed. (2008): *Labour Regulation in Indian Industry*, 1-10 (New Delhi: Bookwell Publishers).

Rani, U., & Unni, J. (2004). Unorganised and Organised Manufacturing in India: Potential for Employment Generating Growth. *Economic and Political Weekly*, 39(41), 4568-4580

Sen, K., & Das, D. K. (2015). Puzzle of Declining Labour Intensity in Organized Indian Manufacturing. *Economic and Political Weekly*, 50(23), 108-115.

Thomas, J.J. (2013). Explaining the 'Jobless' growth in Indian manufacturing. *Journal of the Asia Pacific Economy*, 18(4), 673-692.

Trivedi, P. (2004). An Inter-State Perspective on Manufacturing Productivity in India: 1980-81 to 2000-01. *Indian Economic Review*, 39 (1), 203-237.

CHAPTER: 6
HEALTHCARE SERVICE QUALITY IN PUBLIC HOSPITALS FROM THE PERSPECTIVE OF OUTPATIENTS-AN EMPIRICAL ASSESSMENT FROM JAMMU CITY OF INDIA

Shahid Hamid Raina, Khursheed Hussain Dar and Waseem Hassan Khan

Abstract

Purpose: (a)To evaluate the service quality of public hospitals of Jammu City from the perspective of outpatients (b) to determine impact of service quality dimensions on patient satisfaction.(c) to find the differences (if any) in service quality perceptions among various socio-demographic groups.

Results: Healthcare is one of the key services under the ambit of services sector of Indian economy. The study evaluated the service quality of Public Hospitals of Jammu City from the perspective of outpatients, by the help of a standardized healthcare service quality scale. The study found that the perceptions of quality at Public Hospitals in the study area not very rosy, with the overall service quality (OSQ) or mean service quality being below average. The multivariate regression analysis revealed that among the five dimensions of service quality, doctor behavior was found to be having the largest impact on outpatient satisfaction, followed by infrastructure and staff behavior. The results also revealed statistically significant differences in quality perceptions among various socio- demographic groups. The quality perceptions of highly educated people were low as compared to less educated or illiterate patients. Similarly patients from poor economic background had high quality perceptions as compared to patients from good economic background.

Implications: The study concluded that the public hospitals in the study area ought to improve their service quality and patient satisfaction with immediate attention being given to interpersonal skills and infrastructure. However, this doesn't mean that other areas of service quality can be neglected; they too need to be improved.

6.1. Introduction

Healthcare is one of the key services under the ambit of services sector of any economy. Healthcare is a host of services provided by government, non-government and private organizations for promoting and restoring health of individuals and communities. In India bulk of the healthcare service are of private origin. At the dawn of independence private healthcare sector in India accounted for only 5-10% of patient care (Rao, 2012). However, over the years private sector has become the main source of treatment for majority of the households in India. According to National Family Health Survey (NFHS) III (2005-06), 70% of urban households and 63% of rural households in India seek treatment from private sector. Several factors have led to the massive growth of private healthcare sector in India. Some of the major factors are perception of better quality of care, inadequate public health facilities, low government spending on health sector, huge disease burden, growing population, growing middle class, and concessions by government for establishing private hospitals in the form of subsidized land, reduced import duties on medical equipment etc. Having said that, public hospitals at each level of care are still very much relevant and rendering services to large segments of population, especially the underprivileged ones.

The public hospitals in India have been facing two major challenges- improving access and delivering quality services. As far as the first challenge is concerned significant progress has been made, especially in the last decade after the launch of National Rural Health Mission (NRHM) in 2005 by Government of India. In the post 2005 era the network of primary health centers, district and sub-district hospitals has been strengthened throughout the length and breadth of the country. It has brought a huge share of underprivileged and marginal groups within the ambit of public healthcare delivery system, which were earlier neglected. As far as the second challenge is concerned, the public hospitals have a long way to go. The perception of quality in public hospitals among the masses is very poor. Research has shown the perceived quality of health care services has a relatively greater influence on patient behaviors (satisfaction, referrals, choice, usage, etc.) compared to access and cost. In Nepal, for example, the government made substantial investments in health care to increase access. Yet, utilization of the facilities remained low because of clients 'negative perceptions of quality (Andaleeb, 2000). The perception of poor quality of care in public hospitals is one of the main reasons of burgeoning private healthcare sector in India. Hence, providing access to healthcare services should not be the sole motive of government but access coupled with quality services. Poor quality not only extends the recovery period of patients but also elevates psychological barriers of using the system. Therefore, it is imperative for healthcare providers to focus on delivering quality services for gaining patient confidence.

The study has two main objectives (a) To evaluate the service quality of public hospitals of Jammu City from the perspective of outpatients (b) to determine impact of service quality dimensions on patient satisfaction. The study was carried out on outpatients of selected public hospitals of Jammu city of Indian State of Jammu and Kashmir.

6.2. Service quality and patient satisfaction

Service quality is an abstract and elusive construct. Bitner *et.al.* (1994) defined service quality in terms of the consumer's overall impression of the relative inferiority or superiority of the organization and its services. Cronin and Taylor (1992) view service quality as a form of attitude representing a long-run overall evaluation. Parasuraman *et.al.* (1985) define service quality as the discrepancy between consumer's perceptions of services offered by a particular service provider and the expectations about the service provider. Service quality has been increasingly identified as a key factor in differentiating services and building competitive advantage. Therefore, understanding, measuring and improving quality is a formidable challenge for all organizations, since they compete to some degree on the basis of service (Taner & Antony, 2006).

Service quality is more difficult for customers to evaluate than goods quality because services possess four distinct characteristics - intangibility, heterogeneity; perishability and inseparability. Customers evaluate service quality both on the outcome of the service and the process of service delivery. As far as healthcare services are concerned, it becomes even more difficult to evaluate because of high credence element involved. Historically, the establishment of quality standards in healthcare has been delegated to the medical professionals and has been defined in terms of technical delivery of care or outcome of care (Andaleeb, 2000). The healthcare service comprises of two quality dimensions- technical quality and functional quality (Donabedian, 1980). Technical or medicare quality is considered as the accuracy of diagnoses and procedures according to the professionals' specifications and functional quality as the way in which the service is delivered to the patient. However, in the last two decades patients' assessment of quality known as functional quality has begun to play an important role and has become the primary determinant of patient's quality perceptions.

Intertwined with the quality of health care services is patient satisfaction. In the Western world, there is evidence that the public is inclined to pay more for care from quality institutions that are better disposed to satisfy customer needs (Andaleeb,2000).Patient satisfaction should be as indispensable to assessments of quality as to the design and management of health care systems (Donabedian, 1988). Service quality and customer satisfaction are two closely related but distinct constructs (Dhabolkar, 1996). Satisfaction is an evaluative, affective or emotional response (Oliver, 1989). According to Kotler (1991), satisfaction is the post purchase evaluation of products or services given the expectations prior to purchase. While service quality judgments are quite specific to the service delivered, satisfaction can be determined by a broader set of factors including those which are outside the immediate service delivery experience (Padma *et.al*, 2010). Researchers have found it useful to differentiate between general patient satisfaction and patient perceptions of quality. Patient satisfaction reflects the extent to which expectations of service standards have been met and is typically operationalized by asking patients about general satisfaction with care received (Rao et .al, 2006).

Research has established that service quality is an antecedent of customer satisfaction in various service settings. In healthcare setting, service quality has also been found to be an important determinant of patient satisfaction. Andaleeb (2001) in a study in Dhaka found that service quality dimensions (Responsiveness, Communication, Discipline and Assurance) had a statistically significant impact on patient satisfaction. Rao et.al (2006) in their study in UP, India also found that medicine availability, medical information, doctor behavior and staff behavior had significant impact on patient satisfaction. Duggirala.et.al. (2008) in a study on Indian hospitals concluded that all the service quality dimensions were significant predictors of patient satisfaction Padma et.al (2010) in their study in Tamil Nadu found that four service quality dimensions (Personnel Quality, Process of clinical care, Trustworthiness and Hospital image) had significant impact on patient satisfaction.

In the light of above discussion and evidence, the study examines the relationship between service quality dimensions and patient satisfaction in the context of public hospitals of Jammu city of India.

6.3. Sampling and Data Collection

The study was carried out in Jammu city of Jammu and Kashmir State of India. Sample was drawn from the outpatient Departments of four selected public hospitals of Jammu city using purposive sampling technique. The population consisted of outpatients visiting these four public hospitals. Only those outpatients were considered for the study who were at least on their second visit to the hospital. A sample of 280 outpatients was drawn from the selected hospitals through purposive sampling technique. The sample was equally distributed among the four sample hospitals. Data on various service quality items and satisfaction was collected by making use of a standardized questionnaire developed by Rao. *et al* in 2006. The respondents were asked to reveal their perceptions regarding service quality on a 5- point Likert scale ranging from 1 -5, with 1 standing for strongly disagree and 5 for strongly agree. Similarly data on overall or general satisfaction level with the care received was collected on a 5 point scale ranging from with higher value indicating higher satisfaction level. The 3 items used for measuring general satisfaction and the 16 items constituting the five service quality dimensions are given in Appendix. The characteristics of sample are given in Table 1. .However, the distribution of sample across various socio- demographic characteristics is just co-incidental.

Table 1: Socio- Demographic Profile of the Respondents

Demographic variable		Number	Percent
Gender	Male	120	42.60
	Female	160	57.40
	Total	280	100
Residence	Rural	95	33.93
	Urban	185	66.07
	Total	280	100
	APL*	215	76.78
	BPL**	65	23.22
	Total	280	100
Education	Illiterate	45	16
	Primary	38	13.57
	Middle	51	18.21
	high school	70	25
	Graduate	46	16.42
	Postgraduate	30	10.71
	Total	280	100

Source: Field Survey
*Above Poverty Line ** Below Poverty Line

6.4. Results

6.4.1. Descriptive statistics

The data on five service quality dimensions and satisfaction construct was collected from outpatients of selected public hospitals of Jammu city by making use of a standardized scale developed by Rao.*et.al.* in 2006 for Indian context. The data was analyzed by making use of *Spss* software. The reliability of the scale dimensions was tested by Cronbach alpha. It was found that all the five service quality dimensions are reliable with a reasonable alpha score. Further descriptive statistics were also calculated for all sub-scales and satisfaction construct. From Table 2 it could be seen that the 16 item scale measuring perceived service quality is a reliable one with an alpha score of 0.79. Also the sub-scales or dimensions are very much reliable with an alpha score in the range of 0.75-0.82. Similarly the three item satisfaction scale is also very much reliable with an alpha score of 0.73.

Table 2: Descriptive Statistics

Dimension	Cronbach Alpha	Mean perception	Standard deviation
Doctor Behavior(DB) (5 items)	0.78	2.60	0.85
Staff Behavior(SB) (2 items)	0.75	2.40	0.79
Medical Information(MI) (3 items)	0.80	2.20	1.20
Medicine Availability(MA) (2 items)	0.79	2.00	0.95
Hospital Infrastructure (HI) (4 items)	0.82	2.70	0.73
Overall perceived Quality(16 items)	0.79	2.38	0.90
Overall satisfaction (3 items)	0.73	2.65	0.65

Source: Authors own Calculations

Table 2 reveals that the overall perceived service quality in public hospitals of Jammu city is below average with a mean value of 2.38. The individual mean value of perceived quality dimensions or subscales is also on the lower side, with a mean value of 2 for medicine availability being the lowest. It could be inferred from Table 2 that the administrators of public hospitals of Jammu need to have a better understanding of patient expectations and align their services in line with those in order to have a better perceived service quality. Similarly the overall satisfaction score of outpatients with the hospitals services is found to be slightly above average. It could be understood from the fact that the overall perceived service quality is a precursor to the overall satisfaction. Hence, lower overall service quality value translates into a lower satisfaction value. Therefore, the public hospitals of Jammu city ought to improve their service delivery mechanism for enhancing the satisfaction levels of their outpatients.

6.4.2. Influence of service quality on patient satisfaction

It is well document in the service quality literature that service quality and satisfaction are two closely related but distinct constructs, with the later being influenced by the former. In order to determine the impact of perceived hospital service quality dimensions on outpatient satisfaction, a multiple regression analysis was done. The regression equation thus formulated is given below.

Satisfaction = $\alpha + \beta_1(DB) + \beta_2(SB) + \beta_3(MI) + \beta_4(MA) + \beta_5(HI) + error$

The results of multiple regression are provided in Table3 and it could be seen that the model is a significant with F=12.53, P<0.001, explaining a variation of 68% in the dependant variable as indicated by the value of adjusted R square. All the service quality dimensions were statistically significant (at 0.01 and 0.05 levels) in predicting the patient satisfaction.

Table 3: Regression results: Overall satisfaction as dependent variable

Independent Variables	Standardized Beta	Significance
Doctor Behavior(DB)	0.35*	0.000
Staff Behavior(SB)	0.25*	0.000
Medical Information(MI)	0.15*	0.0001
Medicine Availability(MA)	0.13**	0.001
Hospital Infrastructure (HI)	0.30**	0.004

R Square=0.69, Adjusted R Square=0.68, F=12.53, P<0.001
*Significant at 0.001 and ** 0.05 levels

The regression results show that all the service quality dimensions have a significant and positive impact on patient satisfaction. Among the five dimensions doctor behavior has the largest impact with a beta value of 0.35, meaning that overall satisfaction of outpatients followed by hospital infrastructure and staff behavior. The results of regression analysis clearly indicate that greater gains in overall satisfaction can be realized by focusing on interpersonal skills (doctor and staff behavior) and infrastructure. However, it does not mean that other dimensions can be overlooked.

In order to test for the differences in service quality perceptions among patients having different education levels and economic background, a one way ANOVA was performed. The results of one way ANOVA revealed that there existed statistically significant differences in overall service quality perceptions among patients with different education levels and economic background with $F(5, 274)= .8.80$, $P=0.000$ for various education levels and $F (1, 278)=10.40$, $P=0.000$ for patients with APL and BPL background.

Discussion

The overall mean perception score of 2.38 for service quality in sample public hospitals of Jammu from the perspective of outpatients on a 16 item scale clearly indicates that their expectations are in no way met or even closer to being met. The poor service quality in public hospitals in the study area is forcing even the poorer strata of the society to look for private hospitals and clinics as revealed by the ever expanding private health sector in Jammu city. The hospital administrators in the study area ought to align their services with the expectations of patients, so that the lost faith in public hospitals is regained. Among the five dimensions of service quality the lowest mean score of 2.00 for medicine availability dimension reflects that the public hospitals in Jammu city do not have adequate prescribed medicines. Similarly the mean perception score of 2.60 and 2.40 for doctor behavior and staff behavior respectively indicates that the interpersonal communication between doctors and outpatients and hospital staff and outpatients needs to be addressed. However, the low mean scores for these two dimensions could be partly attributed to the huge rush of outpatients in the sample hospitals and shortage of manpower. Therefore, if overall service quality and patient satisfaction has to be enhanced, the State government should equip the public hospitals with adequate number of doctors and other support staff. As far as the overall satisfaction of outpatients with the hospital services is concerned, the situation is grim with the mean satisfaction level being just2.65.

The results of multiple regression depict that service quality dimensions have a statistically significant effect on outpatient satisfaction in the sample public hospitals. However, the most significant dimensions are related to communication of doctors and other hospital staff with the outpatients and hospital infrastructure. The hospital administrators can use the results to identify the grey areas of service delivery and improve them for enhancing their service quality and thereby patient satisfaction. Given the resource constraints in public hospitals, it may not be possible for the hospital administrators to focus on all the service quality dimensions Therefore; immediate focus should be given to those aspects of service delivery which have the most significant impact on satisfaction. In the context of this study, utmost attention should be given to doctor behavior, staff behavior and infrastructure. in order to improve the interpersonal skills of medical and other hospital staff orientation programmes should be held by the Health Department of the State. The hospital administrators of the sample hospitals can look at the individual service quality items constituting these three dimensions of service delivery and take initiatives to improve them.

References

Andaleeb, S.S. (1998).Determinants of customer satisfaction with hospitals: a managerial model. *International Journal of Healthcare Quality Assurance*, (11) (6), 181-187.

Andaleeb, S.S. (2000).Public and Private Hospitals in Bangladesh; Service Quality and Predictors of Hospital Choice. *Health Policy and Planning*, (15) (1), 95-102.

Andaleeb SS. (2001).Service quality perceptions and patient satisfaction: a study of hospitals in a developing country. *Social Science & Medicine*, (52), 1359–1370.

Bitner, M.J., Booms, B.H. & Mohr, L.A. (1994). Critical Service Encounters: The Employee. Viewpoint. *Journal of Marketing*, (58) (4), 95-106

Cronin, J.J., Taylor, S.A (1992). Measuring Service Quality: A Re-

Examination and Extension. *Journal of marketing*, 56(3), 55-68.

Dabholkar, P.A. (1996). Consumer evaluations of new technology-based self-service operations: an investigation of alternative models. *International Journal of Research in Marketing*, (13), 29-51.

Donabedian, A. (1980). Exploration of Quality Assessment and Monitoring, Volume 1. The Definition of Quality and Approaches to its Assessment. *Health Administration Press*, Ann Arbor, MI.

Duggirala, M., Rajendran, C., and Anantharaman, R.N. (2008).Patient-perceived dimensions of total quality service in healthcare. *Benchmarking: An International Journal* (15), 560-83.

)Kotler, P. (1991), Marketing Management: Analysis, Planning, Implementation and Control, *Prentice-Hall*, Englewood Cliffs, NJ.

National Family Health Survey (NFHS-111) (2005-2006). *Indian Institute of Population Sciences. India. Mumbai*

Oliver, R.L.(1989). Processing of the Satisfaction Responses in Consumption: A Suggested Framework and Research Propositions. *Journal of Consumer Satisfaction, Dissatisfaction and Complaining Behavior*, (2) (1), 1-16.

Padma, P.,et.al.(2010).Service Quality and its Impact on Customer Satisfaction in Indian Hospitals. *Benchmarking: An International Journal*, (17)(6), 807-841.

Parasuraman A., Zeithmal V.A., and Berry L.L (1985). A Conceptual Model of Service Quality and its Implications for Future Research. *Journal of Marketing*, (49), 41-50.

Rao, K.D.,et.al (2006). Towards patient – centered health services in India-a scale to measure patient perceptions of quality. *International Journal for Quality in Health Care*, (18)(6), 414-421.

Rao, P.H (2012). The Private Health Sector in India: A Framework for Improving the Quality of Care. *ASCI journal of Management*, (41) (2), 14-39

Taner T, Antony J: Comparing public and private hospital care service quality in Turkey. *Leadership in Health Services*, (19), 1-10.

Appendix

Dimension	Items
Doctor Behavior	You are given enough time to tell the doctor everything
	Doctors listen carefully to what you have to say.
	The doctor checks patients properly.
	The doctor is always ready to answer your questions.
	The doctor gave you adequate time.
Staff Behavior	Hospital workers talk politely.
	Hospital workers are helpful to you.
Medical Information	The doctors gave you advice about ways to avoid illness and stay healthy.
	The doctor gave you complete information about your illness.
	The doctor gave you complete information about your treatment
Medicine Availability	This hospital has all the medicines needed by you.
	You are able to get all the necessary medicines easily.
Hospital Infrastructure	The cleanliness of the hospital is adequate.
	The condition of the toilets is good.
	Drinking water is easily available in the hospital.
	This hospital has all the requisite amenities.
Overall satisfaction with hospital services	Overall how satisfied are you with the services at this hospital?
	How satisfied are you with the services you received at this hospital compared with what you paid?
	Are you completely satisfied with your treatment?

Source: Rao, K.D., et.al.(2006)

CHAPTER: 7
RURAL TOURISM AS A SOURCE OF RURAL DEVELOPMENT IN MAWLYNNONG VILLAGE IN MEGHALAYA: A CASE STUDY OF THE CLEANEST VILLAGE OF ASIA

Elwin Kro Nihang

Abstract

North Eastern state of India is regarded to be one of the best naturally gifted states of India whether it may be Sikkim, Meghalaya or Mizoram. The hills, mountains, valleys, water falls and specially the suitable climate are the best things available to attract the national and international tourist. Moreover the uniqueness in culture and food habit of the people of north eastern states of India is also a talking point among various tourists. Mawlynnong a small village hosts a variety of tourist by showing off the rural attracting things since the last few years these paper deals to find out the amount of growth of rural tourism in the area of Mawlynnong village and find out its impact on the development process of the village through social and economic means. This paper specially adapts the following objectives; of the economic and social impacts on the people. The methodology used in this paper is comparative analysis, and secondary as well as primary data is used in the process of this research paper. Through the analysis of the data it has been known that the rural tourism in Mawlynnong has been growing and putting positive impacts on the social and economic condition of the people in Mawlynnong, although there have been some loopholes in the tourism infrastructure and many things. And this positive impact of rural tourism on the economic and social condition of the people has brought a considerable development in the rural areas of Mawlynnong.

7.1. Introduction

Mawlynnong village need no introduction because this interior village in Meghalaya has created its own fame in the world by achieving the cleanest village not only of india but also of asia in the year 2013. Mawlynnong village is located 90 km away from the rush rush urban scenario of shillong, not only the village has created a sense of honour for the north eastern state of india but also it created new buzz of hungerness for the people outside the state to know more and more about the village. The sudden feet of achievement as the cleanest village of asia has brought the village to limelight in the media and became a centre of attraction for the tourist, since it was like a new world of discovering by the tourist. And this sense and curiosity by the travelers as well as tourist made the so called rural tourism grow in this place, which became a help in disguise for the people to upgrade their economic condition and to fight against poverty and bring established economic condition in the economy, the village has a great help from the tourist visit to them which has driven the economy to prosperity and brought self employed activities to the people of the villages. The growth of rural tourism in the village has also contributed to the increase in education among the villagers and also bring financial steadiness among them. Its has been a great achievement by the village because being an interior village it was always very tough for a village ligto create such a outstanding scenario of tourism and creating lot of attraction among the tourist, and presently the village is not only bringing tourist but also to the whole Meghalaya by the declaration of the village as the cleanest village the number of tourist visiting Meghalaya has increased. So since then it has been a clear interesting topic for the researcher to move into it and carry on their research. Mawlynnong has been to the peak of its economy through tourism development in the village. This paper deals with the impact on education economy of the villagers through the development of rural tourism in the village mawlynnong

7.2. Literature Review

Rathor Nisha (2013) "Rural tourism impacts, challenges and opportunities" rural tourism or tourism in rural areas is a new form of activity that can bring economic and social benefits to the society. In Asia, especially in India, rural tourism in its true form is relatively new. Rural tourism can help in shaping our society. It can have both positive and negative impacts on both rural and urban communities. There is a scope of rural tourism in India. The govt should encourage private enterprises to promote tourism in rural areas, for developing rural areas we have to understand the rural environment, demography, socio- culture economic and political background of that place. How we can involve the rural people to enhance their socio economic condition.

Milli Nitashree (2006) Rural tourism Development: An overview of tourism in tipam pakey village of Naharkatia, Dibrugarh district Assam, Rural tourism is a recent offshoot of tourism sector that has grown up to be a potential business in its own space. Rural tourism is a form of natured based tourism that uncovers the rural life, culture, art and heritage at local communities socially and economically .Such form of tourism has created tremendous impact on the local economy and socio-cultural scenario of the concerned area on one hand and carries a potential scope for the rural resident on the other hand. Rural tourism is an opportunity for rural development.

The Tipam phakey village of naharkatia has a great diversity of culture, tradition and natural resources which makes it every attractive tourist destination. It has a great of a unique budhist culture that has formed the basis of attraction for the outsiders, here rural tourism promotes socio economic changes, local economy and culture and lifestyle of the local residing people. This paper aims at exploring the rural tourism at tipam pakey village, which act as an incentive to promote local, socio-economic, cultural and lifestyle of the people residing in around this tourist location and also to find out various constraint and possibilities of tourism development in the study area.

Tiwari Munish (2012) Making of Indian tourism in 21st century challenges and prospect, This article made an attempt to show the rise and fall of tourist visitors to India due to the miscalculation of future demand and supply of tourist visitors, and it mentions the critical role of government in the process of development of tourism in India

Michotthiboult (2010) Pro poor tourism in Kumarakom district of Kerala, policy implementation and impacts, This article has suggested that tourism is harmful to the society and the environment as well, without proper government regulation and policies, and has mentioned the importance of proper policy implemented bt Kerala government named as "responsible tourism "which had a great impact on the sustainable development of tourism in the said district of Kerala

Sharma Neha and Tiwari Amar (2014), rural tourism: a prominent niche for Indian tourism. This article has made attempt to show the role of rural tourism in reviving rural economy through traditional way of living, art and craft etc, and in this context the govt of India through the union ministry of tourism in collaboration with UNDP has committed 2.5 million US dollar in the 10th five year plan for the development of rural tourism in the country. So this article study of the impact of the above project on rural tourism on the country

Literature Gap

It is very important to know the impact of rural tourism on the people of mawlynnong relating to social and economic impacts, since no particular study on economic impacts has been carried on.

7.3. Objectives of the Study

1. To Find out the economic impacts of rural tourism on the people of Mawlynnong.
2. To Find out the social impacts of rural tourism on the people of Mawlynnong village

7.4. Methodology

The study is mainly based on primary data. To collect primary data a census was conducted with the help of semi structured questionnaire in the village of Mawlynnong. Required information was collected from the head of the household. Besides interview, focus group discussion was also conducted in the village. Descriptive statistics analysis was used in the study to find the factors which affect household income. Depending on needs, the study has also utilized bar diagram. And most importantly it is comparative study with people engaged in rural tourism and other occupation.

7.5. Result of the Study Through the Census Conducted in the Village

Through the census conducted by by the researcher the following data on occupation and income of the people of mawlynnong was attained

Type of Occupation	Percent
Agricultural Labour (with own land)	23.2
Agricultural Labour (landless	22.2
Tourism	6.3
Other Labour	2.5
Tourism with other occupations	46.0
total	100

Total agricultural labour- 45.20, Total Tourism related- 52.30, Others- 2.5 Graphical representation of the above data

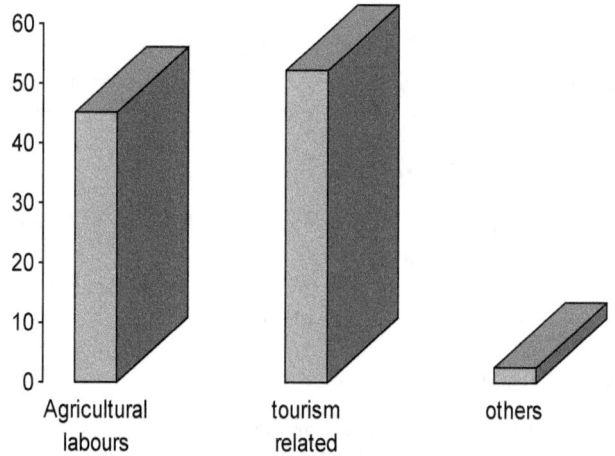

Income of the people of Mawlynnong village

sectors	Per capita income(annually)
Agricultural Labors	Rs.35048
Tourism related people	Rs. 56760
others	Rs. 43080

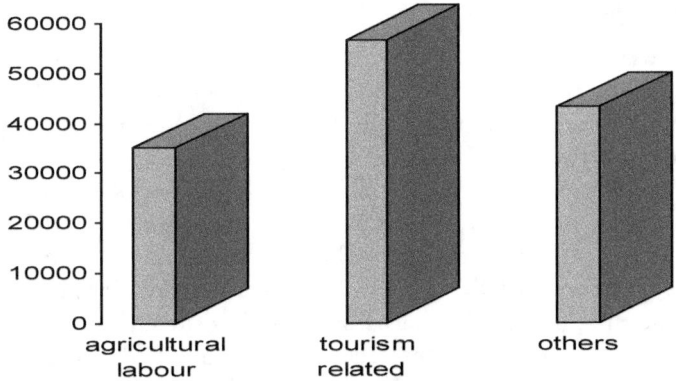

From the above collected data it is clear that the income of the people related to rural tourism has a higher level of income compared to other occupation.

Literacy Rate-

The literacy rate of all the people related to different occupation has been collected by the researcher through a designed questionnaire,

Sectors	Literacy rate
Agricultural labors	53.80%
Tourism related people	89.60%
Others	67.50%

The above data also shows that the literacy rate is also been higher for the people engaged in the rural tourism than some other occupation in the village among the people who resides there. The diagrammatic representation of the above table Is shown below-

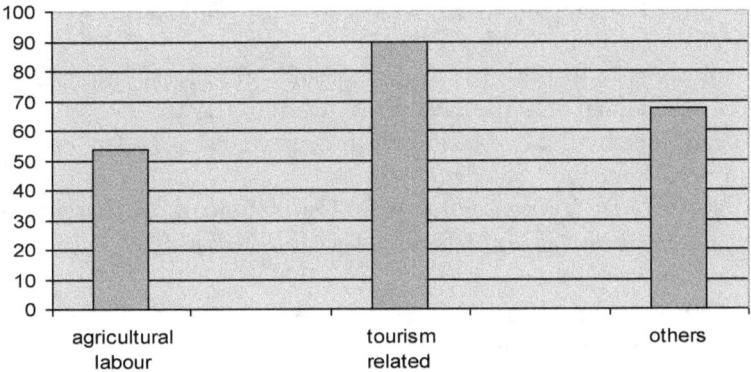

Conclusion

The above study has a certain results based on the data collected by the researcher. The data represents or shows that the people related to rural tourism in mawlynnong Village has a higher rate of income as well as higher literacy rate, than the other people engaged in other occupation. So from this range of income and literacy rate of the people of mawlynnong working in different sectors has a huge difference when its comes to economic and social conditions of the people. Moreover it is important to note that the rural tourism has successfully and positively impacting the economic as well as the social condition of the people of mawlynnong village. So rural tourism can be hugely regarded as a serious source of rural development in some parts of the North eastern states of India where there is a potential of rural tourism. This growth of rural tourism can really upgrade the economic condition of the people of the region in the economic social and cultural ways.

References

RathorNisha (2013) "Rural tourism impacts, challenges and opportunities"

Campbell, L.M (1999), "Ecotourism in Rural Developing Communities, Annals of tourism research 26(3), pp.534-553.

Sharma Neha and Tiwari Amar (2014), rural tourism: a prominent niche for Indian Research Annals of Tourism research, 14, pp.71-87.

Hampton,M.P (2003), "Entry points for local tourism in developing countries; Evidence from Yogyakarta *Annals of Tourism Research*, 14, pp.71-87.

Hampton, M.P. (2003), "Entry points for local tourism in developing countries: Evidence from Yogyakarta

TiwariMunish (2012) Making of Indian tourism in 21st century challenges and prospect,

Milli Nitashree (2006) Rural tourism Development: An overview of tourism in tipam pakey village of Naharkatia, Dibrugarh district Assam

Michotthiboult (2010) Pro poor tourism in Kumarakom district of Kerala, policy implementation and impacts.

CHAPTER: 8
DEVELOPMENT OF RURAL AREA AND HUMAN RESOURCE: REAL OVERVIEW
Praveen Prakash

Abstract

Poor rural masses and backward rural areas are not at fault for their plight but something else and that is, exclusion due to inaccessibility to institutions and (Infra) structures. Rural development is directly related to the efforts on the part of the system/dispensation, because poverty is lack of ownership to sources/resources to meet the bare dignified living standards in a country, which also has the bearing on the future of that household and the area; thus onus squarely lies on the systems and institutions, when the State/Nation comes into being.

In the present millennia it (poverty/backwardness/non-development) is an indicator of the failure of the systems in a country, and is not at all related to the phony indicators like calorie consumption standards and dollar per day. Of course poverty is the main cause of inequality/sub-standard living conditions. Efforts should have been made to make the masses 'developed' (the saturation point of development where people are having basic traits and skills to live with dignity and, ever ready to evolve without much efforts (because of the basic skills and traits) in a changing (technologically/economically) world). Indian masses are in a stage of melting-pot, as things are synthesizing, though slowly and chaotically due to systems and institutions in place, and also due to aheadness of general masses when compared to the exploitative institutions/systems. They are ahead due to information technology and aspirations thereon to lead dignified life as other nationals are leading since decades ago, which now abundantly evident on LED/Touch screens. Medieval social and political mindset are being cornered in debates and discussions at national and international forums and, on the other hand, skills and capabilities as well as concepts of non-exploitative management of every economic and political activities are gaining ground. Dealing based on Upper- hand or Up-manship is defunct now, but neither arrogance or exploitation by domination and organization in its place is going to be accepted; so inclusiveness is the answer, not thrusted poverty and inequalities due to intentional under-development and pseudo-spiritualism by the systems (misuse of 'Karmaa' concept of cause and effect).

8.1. Development of Rural Area and Human Resource: Real Overview

Rural India remained neglected due to over-emphasis on industry based urban areas development activities. Whereas it has been said innumerable times that India's real development would be possible only when villages of it would be deservedly developed (and not developed into urban areas). This paper is also based on the first hand experiences, observations and analysis of the rural areas on the basis of residing in it continuously for the last 23 years by the author. This study is basically exploratory, done on the basis of general observations by the author (Economic (Man) Observer).

Agriculture development and its allied activities remained obscure to the planners that is why the very vital component in Indian context, the irrigation facilities, are not developed and provided (accessible), therefore the responsibility of the failure is being digressed/forwarded to 'monsoon dependency' and 'poor monsoons'.

Modern corporate world in India is now divesting to rural areas for Fast Moving Consumer Goods (FMCG) sector; then why not Human Resource Development (HRD) and skills be created in the rural masses, or the planners just want to create consumers in these areas for the FMCG MNCs, as this sector is volume driven and have low margins.

FMCG's standard Indian version i.e., Patanjali Limited, is based on new business concepts and, it is based on revenue increase (in place of higher margins) and customer base; thus, can be the case study material for all and more so to the components of the 'system'.

Rural development (RD) basically suffered from lack of precise definition and policies. But to put it in perspective the appropriate concept related to rural development would be to increase the Quality of Life of rural masses and decreased / low cost of living standards.

In India it is basically the general stage of development, nationally, and the culture (and quality of the democracy) that would decide the development of the rural areas. Emphasis should be on raising the Quality of life among rural masses and Quality of the region.

Earlier there used to be somewhat self-reliant rural areas as conceived by Mahaatamaa Gandhi, but now due to diverse complexities of general modern life it has become retrogressively 'backward rural areas'.

Rural areas are places less densely populated, and are farther to the reach of cities and towns. These areas predominantly are farm-based allied activities based economy. Another main distinction can be drawn on the basis of public services like, street-lighting, water, garbage disposal and management, transportation etc., in rural and urban areas. From another point of view, there used to be distinction (between rural and urban) on the basis of quality of air, water, milk and milk products, vegetables etc., and values based general human behaviour / daily dealings in rural areas and just the opposite in urban areas.

After observing the rural-urban divide I can state that due to ill managed and 'planned policies' (to create and reinforce the vote bank politics by the system), it has generated the rat race/chaos among hitherto simple village gentry, as "... government cannot invest effectively in this sector; if it does, it will carry with it lots of bureaucracy, red tape, and resultant corruptions." (Kalam & Rajan, 2014).

System cheated them on the lines of social backwardness, politics, local caste based manipulations and lack of IT enabled telephony/technology as well as pseudo-spirituality. But things have gone out of the hands of the system (very due to IT and Digital Revolution) and villagers have now become very much aware and ahead of the systems (one can easily infer that same situation was present more than couple of decades ago, initially, among all types of separatists, as they were ahead when compared to the rest of the nation and, there was the factor of 'developing the regions on their own' as they were exposed to the development in foreign countries and ideologies and, also on the other hand, because of snail paced development in India and especially of rural areas along with all pervasive culture of corruption ; later on this former factor (to develop their regions on their own) in these movements was successfully diluted and polluted by some 'sections') . At national level also, many observers have felt that rural areas are changing, "... development aspirations have changed in rural areas..." (Dev, 2015).

More villagers (except those politically motivated / instruments of politics) now know the causes of backwardness (and more so the young village dwellers/villagers), again due to digital telephony/media; and thus, assert main stress to the causes like principle-less politics, ethic-less society and livelihood/occupation base. On the other hand, to earn living; systems (of vote bank creation) have cornered them to become street-smart, corrupt, superficial and made them to adopt the ways of the world having no values and therefore no norms (negative values and negative norms; i.e., Deviants/ potential revolutionist).

It makes no sense that to imitate the good works of NGOs, SOs and VOs blindly (to cite a general reference), systems have distributed the sewing machines to the rural women whose main occupation remained to be the agricultural and allied activities, therefore in-spite of getting sewing machines and there by developing the skill related to it and savings thereof, women still preferred working in the fields because of its being permanent income generation source.

Another main point observed is that the systems have remained very formal and goal achievement oriented (based on other analytical tools like SWOT, goal formation, strategy formulation, programme formulation, implementation) but totally detached from the realities including, being incomplete on the basis of feedbacks, control/regulations as well as mid-course corrections.

On the other hand, markets of all types in rural areas are / were absent or highly backward and under-developed/un-organized. Rural areas all in general require uniformly adequate rural infrastructure to serve the entire regional rural population, whereas things were inadequately and biasedly implemented/executed as per vote banks.

It is apt to mention that UAE is also having 60% of the population below the age of 30yrs but things are totally different of late and they have changed (and still changing) the face of gulf ecology sustainably. Systems being having privy to various conditional points, have used it to manipulate political system as well as to dominate and gain bargaining power and, for competitive advantage when dealing with local rural masses along with political masters.

Intentional negative and dull presentations and usage of colors and imagery in schemes and programmes were somewhere being perceived by the system as factors like, gaining the confidence of rural people and thus indirectly an effort to look as the harbinger of points of purity, honesty and hardwork, whereas the reality is just the opposite.

Planners and systems remained focused on to serve the 30% of the total population i.e., urbanites and, in the process neglected 70% of the population residing in rural areas, and thus further pushed them to be exploited by the urban areas and by the systems in the rural areas. Systems in these areas never provided any world-class (standardised) products and services (especially HRD&M) and if ever provided, generally, it remained marred in corruption thereby making these worst cost-effective deals having weak and inefficient distribution network of public utilities and thus, harmed the (image of) systems and masses (State Transport and Railways etc., can be observed and analysed).

Emphasis was on glossing annual reports and papers; for example in general it has been deducted that in 1st plan community development and national extensive services were basis of RD; in the 2nd plan co-operative farming and local participation got the focus; in the 3rd plan stress was on decentralized democratic mechanism through panchayati raj; in the 4th plan special area programme was launched for backward areas; in 5th plan system resorted to minimum needs programme to eradicate rural poverty; in the 6th plan focus was on developing social-economic infrastructure and IRDP for equality; in 7th plan strategy was to create skill-based employment through different schemes. By now (by 7th plan) we would have developed rural areas but nothing sort of that have happened.

The importance of RD can be adjudged/assessed by the fact that ¾ of the population resides in rural areas and add quite a chunk to the national income by the agriculture and it provides (and have great potential) major occupation avenues to the rural India (around 70% of employment, of whatever types to disguise the hopelessness), bulk of raw materials to the industries come from agriculture and rural areas, demand for industrial goods and services and development of industries is generally dependent on the demand by the rural masses' motivation and preference and increased spending/purchasing power of rural population.

8.2. The backdrop

Planners made schemes for backward and rural areas for the rural welfare especially for the education development, economic development, health and housing etc., they thought it to be supplemental, and benefits of these would give the impetus to the other general national level developmental programmes, and, are shown being achieving something on the papers/ files/ in annual departmental reports. Instead efforts should have been made to provide Quality of life at less cost. No permanent measures have been taken earlier which were to be considered as local area friendly based so as to reduce and eliminate inhuman living conditions and there of assist in acquiring modern day minimum living needs like education, health facilities, food security, transportation, telephony, skill training, financial securities etc., i.e., a radical and paradigm shift to develop and extend just and productive economy because "… just society needs to guarantee to each individual (permanent)… income and basic dignity of life." (Parikshit, 2017).

Due to reinforced political manipulations (i.e., assisted by the bureaucratic organizational setup) the things were made to trickle down intentionally slowly (after applying divisive policies) so that masses could be used as vote bank for future as well, continuously. It (aim of having vote banks) was also achieved by cashing in on the ignorance of people by systems.

Whereas, development could have been achieved simply by making available the provisions and facilities in rural areas 24x7 and 365 days, along with changes at demographic and psychographic levels.

8.3. The Ways to Go Ahead

The rural areas cannot develop on their own due to lack of any developmental structures and HR development and management concepts, and green technologies. Following are few factors that can be pondered upon for RD:

- Compatibility between rural occupations / vocations and technologies.
- Immediate efforts should be made to release the agriculture sector from the exploitative clutches of intermediaries/agents' tight knit network of mafia and cartel like mechanism (papaya producers sell their produce to the big commission agents at the price of rupees 40/- per Quintal during harvest season (because papaya plants get over-laden with fruits and therefore could break the plant and thus incur the loss to the farmers (a distressed situation of farmers being mercilessly exploited thus by the brokers & agents) , whereas in the retail market, to the end user its being sold at the price of more than rupees100/- per Kg)
- Demographic changes be generated, like at education level, income generation vocations level, health, life-expectancy etc.
- Psychographic changes like values awareness and its application, creating positive attitude and aptitude, health consciousness, feeling of nationalism etc., thus be achieved
- Public relations and participation regarding rural programmes and projects including highlighting the strong points of these through opinion creators and communicators, among masses.
- Values (and ethics) creation among people and standardised delivery procedures and systems.
- There should be selective specialization and holistic basic traits development efforts i.e., in HR of the systems and HR of rural areas.
- Ideation and concept development and its short time bound efficient launch.
- Provision of providing good quality products and services at less cost in less time to the rural masses.
- Developing the strong feeling of village community development and nationalism among masses.
- There should be Problem-solving govt. programmes / policies, and, not otherwise in the name of democracy or awareness generation.

8.4. Development Basics

Rural areas are regions having ecology, environment and natural resources including culture, traditions, ethos, ethics etc., vital to the nation and therefore all types of environment and their analysis be done to make a data base on the basis of which transformational efforts be made viz Political (politics which needed to be mature, stable, promoting/encouraging, cooperative, consistent and expansionary in operations), economic (economic factors should include less or no inflationary effects on rural masses or activities, low cost of standard livelihood, permanent/durable income generation resources, development of local raw-material then its processing/value-addition, marketing (developed traditional and modern markets), packaging and storage (including consumption), social (health awareness and programmes, life-style changes, shedding ill-traditional values, non-exploitative and exhaustive peaceful progressive positive values and norms base including positive ethos and ethics etc.), technological (favourable and cheap technologies w.c.t., economic activities, health, education, transportation, storage, marketing, civil amenities (can adopt good practices from China and Japan),communication and IT etc.), environmental (anti-polluting, non-polluting, non-hazardous, conservationist, propagating, eco-friendly, waste-disposal and management etc.), industrial (agro-based, eco-friendly, self-reliant as well as small, modern-cottage and handloom and handicraft based); and' suitable well managed outcome thereon be implemented.

System used spin masters and experts to oppress (India Against Corruption (IAC) can be recalled) whereas these would have been used to infuse positive points of programmes and social innovations. Also, existing schemes be made to penetrate / reach the deserved and targeted beneficiaries and, schemes be diversified so that all the rural youths be covered and benefitted (as schemes and programmes have a time-line, starting from the introduction of the programmes to progress and growth, saturation and obsolescence and decline if these are not diversified).

It is not appropriate to cut corners (cutting amount of allowance/fund) while serving the deserved beneficiaries especially when the person / household is poor and discouraged by the ideologies of the systems; stress is also needed to be given on developing a human into a balanced / good citizen, "... we need development of rural infrastructure by focusing on developing Human dimensions. We need to give quality of life to people on personal and occupational fronts to create better rural economy." (Narula, 2010)

Also, increasing sustainable and adequate distribution agencies and institutions including other support systems and infrastructure in all of the rural areas is the issue to be remain focused on. It is unbelievable that if the private sector can penetrate the rural areas and create its markets and consumers then how come public sector fails (that means there is intentional non-serious and inconsistent work-culture so as to indirectly encourage private sector to earn profits and exploit rural markets (state transport, state schools, national airlines, telecommunication and state based media/news channel are few examples)).

All that rural areas require is the knowledge about the management concepts; then be it organic or inorganic, agricultural or related to allied activities. These concepts are needed to be freely disseminated to all (if the aim of the system is to unite and develop and, not divide to gain say in the bargaining) irrespective of their need or not, so that all shall come to know the ways of doing things from idea level to planning to implementation and then to follow-ups etc., as, suppose if only few be made to learn these concepts and apply this knowhow then others (individuals/groups/organisations) develop complexes and start creating hurdles / disruptions and, this thus fails, for the time period, the propagation of positive changes in the society.

Patanjali limited is espousing significantly the professionalism in the management, processes and work culture: same can be replicated within the rural areas (with natural resources (with zero-waste and waste disposal management) and HR). The aim of HRD&M should be providing at least world class curriculum and tools in training or information modules for imbibing the values and norms, ethics and ethos into the HR, which will advance and increase the national developmental efforts manifolds.

It is overwhelming to know that Patanjali limited is pro-change and thus has employee friendly organizational culture. It is mainly due to lots of training and developmental programmes (though these do have Indian positive ethics and ethos, values and norms also) for its employees as well as, it also extends career counseling and mentoring activities to the rural youth and local masses, in other words it is engaged in HRD&M also.

It is apt here to mention the positive outcome that Indian media has been able to bring about successfully and that is, giving the impetus to the 'proper' growth of governments and governance, which in response has given rise to 'government development' (because govt is averse to reforms of any type).

Each one now in new millennia aspire to become organized and want to live in organized and dignified way (that is why most of us prefer to live in foreign countries over our own). Chaotic / ill-organised environment indicates the political manipulations, wastage, prejudice, corruption ridden, delay tactics based, and raise the cost, delivery of sub-standardised products and services etc,.

Thus the aims of the development should be to raise skills and capacities creationas well as increase general managerial and social standards so as to get values imbued masses as, "... responsible citizenhood behavior of individuals and community, which bring out an attitude and self-motivation to utilize the opportunities and resources for self and community. Citizenhood behavior among the bureaucrates and politicians who have power..." (Gupta and Maiti,2008), bring about positive changes (private sector gives training and skill development courses once again to even the MBAs at the entry level).

In rural areas, initially, effective HRD&M activities should be to develop skills, positive attitude and employability for frictionless functioning. Unorganized and planless economic activities and (thereon unjust competition) (due to) political hyper-activism made these areas the fertile grounds for manipulations and exploitations and thus these remained backward and underdeveloped (in a state of an unorganized entity).

In India divisive politics and pseudo-spirituality strive on the chaos and unorganized environment (and vested players use incidents and situations arisen in these areas to prove their vested points to gain popularity) which ultimately slows down the development processes.

Conclusion

In contemporary corporate sector in India there is a policy of skilling people, re-skilling people in changed scenario, consistently educate people to become and remain useful to the organisation and to be contemporary they consistently train (in rural areas this can be achieved may be through distribution of thin pamphlet literature in vernacular or devenagri and / or, through ½ an hour workshops, may be at panchayat levels as model panchayats in the evening and so on, so that it should be emulated by other panchayats), and retrain and thus retain the masses.

Policies, programmes, processes, products (and services), genuine feedbacks, follow-ups, mid-course corrections etc., are needed to be evolved in response to this changing world.

Another important area to be focused on is to making people self-aware about things and themselves, being backward / having negative traits (problem creator). People needed to be motivated toward attaining social skills especially of 'not at all generating situations / problems' (as it leads to hurdles and obstacles by both the masses and the systems thereby ending into delays, wastage, politics, backwardness, poverty, chaos, mismanagement etc.

Self-regulated / ethical value based daily dealings by the system as well as the masses needed to be evolved; because to make things and population positively long-lasting and sustainable, organized culture is needed to be created through because… "social scientists believe that without values, a society would disintegrate, a risk often present in India." (Bhagat,2012). Self-regulation and Self-organized are characteristics to be adopted by both sides that is, by the system and by the masses as Nation is going to be there for the posterity to come but things may come and go.

References

Barman, Himadri, *"Indian Ethos and Ethics, Values in Modern Management"*. Web. nd. 05th June 2017, himadri.cmsdu.org> documents> Indian

Bhagat, Chetan, *What Young India wants*, 12th ed. Rupa Publications India Pvt Ltd 2012.nd. New Delhi. p. 04. Print.

Chauhan, Abhishek, *"Need of Rural Development in India for Nation Building"*, Web. nd. 05th June 2017, www.asianmirror,in> Need for Rural Development

Dass, Paldeep and Mandal Debraj, *"A Research Paper on Patanjali"*. Web. nd. 04th June 2017, https://tejas.iimb.ac.in>…

Dev, S Mahendra, *India Development Report 2015*. 01st ed. 2015. OUP. New Delhi. p. 81.

Dreze, Jean and Sen Amartya, *India: Development and Participation*. Ed

2002. OUP. New Delhi.

Edelweiss, *"Patanjali Ayurved. Waiting in the wings"*. nd. Web. 04th June 2017, 7:48 pm. Edelresearch.com> PATANJALI

Government of India, Ministry of Finance, *Economic survey 2014-15*, Ed. 01. Vol 02, OUP, New Delhi.

Gupta, KR and Maiti, Prasenjit, *Rural Development in India*, vol 3, nd. Atlantic Publishers & Distributers (P) Ltd. New Delhi. Nice Printing Press. Delhi. p. 14. Print Kalam, APJ Abdul and Rajan, YS, *Beyond 2020 A Vision For Tomorrow's India*, 2014, Viking By Penguin Books India 2014. Delhi. India. p. 57. Print.

Narula, Uma, *Dynamics of Indian Rural Economy Growth Perspective*, nd. Atlantic Publishers & Distributers (P) Ltd. 2010. New Delhi. Nice Printing Press. Delhi. p. 79.

Pandey, Prashoe and Sah, Rahul, *"Growth of Swadeshi- A Case Study on Patanjali Ayurveda Limited"*. July 2016. Web. 04th June 2017, www.ijetmas.com> project> paper

Parikshit, Jayant, *Economic Survey &Budget:2017~ An Analysis*. 01st ed. 2017-18. Eolas Edutech & Publications, New Delhi, India. p. 65.

Sen, Amartya, *Development as Freedom*, 25th ed. OUP, New Delhi 2014. Ram Printograph, New Delhi.

CHAPTER: 9
FIIs & DIIs AND ITS IMPACT ON INDIAN STOCK MARKET

Sahil Mahajan

Abstract

The economic development of any country depends upon existence of well-organized Financial Markets. It is the financial system that supplies the necessary financial inputs for the production of goods and services, which in turn promotes the well-being and standard of living of people. Capital markets are of crucial significance to capital formation as the main function of these markets in mobilization of savings and helps in stimulating capital formation and that to extent accelerating the process of economic growth. Foreign institutional investors have gained a significant role in Indian stock markets. The Foreign Institutional Investors (FIIs) have emerged as important players in the Indian equity market in the recent past. On the other hand, Domestic Institutional Investors refers to the Indian institutional investors who are investing in the financial market of India. The DII activity is also based on capital market segment and it is assembled from trades that are executed by insurance, DFIs, MFs, Banks and New pension system. This study makes an attempt to develop an understanding of the dynamics of the trading behavior and the factors influencing FIIs and DIIs in the Indian equity market by analyzing the secondary data. The dawn of 21st century has shown the real dynamism of stock market and the various benchmarking of Nifty in terms of its highest peaks and sudden falls. The present study is an attempt to determine the impact of Foreign Institutional Investments (FIIs) and Domestic Institutional Investors (DIIs) on Indian stock market as India has emerged as one of the most attractive investment destinations in Asia. Hence, understanding the determinants of FII is very important for any emerging economy as FII exerts a larger impact on the domestic financial markets in the short run and a real impact in the long run. Also attempts to understand the recent trends of FIIs & DIIs during the period of 2010 to 2016 and examine the volatility of NSE due to FIIs & DIIs. The data for the study uses the information obtained from the secondary resources like website of BSE, NSE and SEBI. This paper attempts to study the impact of foreign institutional investment and domestic institutional investments on Indian stock market.

9.1. Introduction

With rapid changes in the economy because of liberal economic policies and fast pace changes due to globalization, Indian market has become a focus point for foreign investors. Organizations tend to target for large volume of trade in this era of globalization. Trade flows are indeed one of the most visible aspects of globalization. International investment is a powerful source in propelling the world toward closure economic integration.FII refers to the investment made by resident of one country in the financial capital and asset of another country It facilitates and persuades large productivity and help in shaping up balance of payments.

FII flows in India have continuously grown in importance and derivatives, easing the norms for FII registration, reducing procedural delays, lowering fees, mandating stricter disclosure norms, improved regulatory standards etc. with a view to improving the scope, coverage and quality of FII flows into India. As a result, India, also supported by her strong economic fundamentals, has become one of the attractive destinations for FII flows in the emerging market space today. The expansionary effect of various reform measures on FII flows over the years can be gauged from the fact that net (i.e., gross purchases minus gross sales) .This increasing dominance of foreign investors in Indian market has necessitated research on the implications of FII flows for the Indian stock market time and again.

Although FII flows help supplement the domestic savings and

augment domestic investments without increasing the foreign debt of the recipient countries, correct current account deficits in the external balance of payments' position, reduce the required rate of return for equity, and enhance stock prices of the host countries, yet there are worries about the vulnerability of recipient countries' capital markets to such flows. FII flows, often referred to as 'hot money' (i.e., short-term and overly speculative), are extremely volatile in character compared to other forms of capital flows. Foreign portfolio investors are regarded as 'fair-weather friends' who come in when there is money to be made and leave at the first sign of impending trouble in the host country thereby destabilizing the domestic economy of the recipient country.

9.1.1. Foreign Institutional Investors Registration

Following entities / funds are eligible to get registered as FII: Pension Funds
1. Mutual Funds
2. Investment Trust
3. Insurance or reinsurance companies
4. Investment Trusts
5. Banks
6. Endowments
7. University Funds
8. Foundations
9. Charitable Trusts or Charitable Societies

9.1.2. Domestic Institutional Investors(DIIs)

Domestics institutional investors are those institutional investors which undertakes investments in securities and other financial assets of the country they are based in institutional investments is defined to be the investment done by institutional or organization such as banks , insurance , companies , mutual fund houses, etc in the financial or real asset of a country . Simplify stated, domestic institutional investors use pooled fund to trade in securities and assets of their country .These investment decisions are influenced by various domestic economic as well as political trends . In addition to the foreign institutional investors, the domestic institutional investors also affect the net investment flow into the economy . Domestic Institutional Investors refers to the Indian institutional investors who are investing in the financial market of India. The DII activity is also based on NSE & BSE on capital market segment and it is assembled from trades that are executed by insurance , DFIs, MFs, Banks and New pension system .

Figure 1

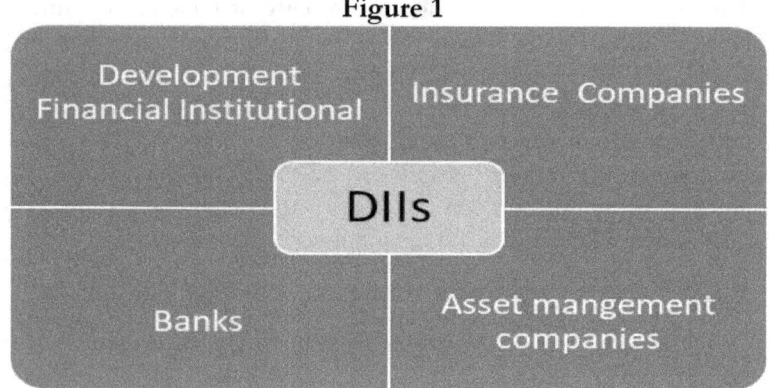

Source : SEBI fact sheet

9.2. Review of Literature

Stanley Morgan (2002) has examined that FIIs have played a very important role in building up India's forex reserves, which have enabled a host of economic reforms. Secondly, FIIs are now important investors in the country's economic growth despite sluggish domestic sentiment. The Morgan Stanley report notes that FII strongly influence short-term market movements during bear markets. However, the correlation between returns and flows reduces during bull markets as other market participants raise their involvement reducing the influence of FIIs. Research by
Morgan Stanley shows that the correlation between foreign inflows and market returns is high during bear and weakens with strengthening equity prices due to increased participation by other players

P. Krishna Prasanna (2013) has examined the contribution of foreign institutional investment particularly among companies included in sensitivity index (Sensex) of Bombay Stock Exchange. Also examined is the relationship between foreign institutional investment and firm specific characteristics in terms of ownership structure, financial performance and stock performance. The promoters' holdings and the foreign investments are inversely related. Foreign investors choose the companies where family shareholding of promoters is not substantial. Among the financial performance variables the share returns and earnings per share are significant factors influencing their investment decision.

9.3. Research Methodology

The present study is of analytical nature and makes use of secondary data. The relevant secondary data are collected from various publications of Government of India; Reserve Bank of India, websites, annual reports, SEBI, Economic Times, World Bank reports, DIPP, research reports etc. Nifty was a natural choice for inclusion in the study, as it is the most popular market indices and widely used by market participants for benchmarking. The present study considers 6 years data starting from 2010 to 2016. To have an empirical idea about the status of FII in India trend analysis has been conducted. The present study has been undertaken with a conduct empirical analysis of status of FIIs and DIIs.

9.4. Objectives of Study

1. To study the pattern and recent trends of FIIs and DIIs flow in India.
2. To study the investment structure of FIIs in different sectors.
3. To study and analysis the relationship between:
    i. FIIs & Nifty (NSE)
    ii. DIIs & Nifty (NSE)
   Independent Variable: FIIs and DIIs
   Dependent Variable: NIFTY (NSE)

9.5. Hypothesis

- **Null Hypothesis (Ho):** There is no relationship between FIIs and Indian Stock Market(Nifty)
- **Alternative Hypothesis (Ha):** There is significance relationship between FIIs and Indian Stock Market(Nifty)
- **Null Hypothesis (Ho):** There is no relationship between DIIs and Indian Stock Market(Nifty)
- **Alternative Hypothesis (Ha):** There is significance relationship between DIIs and Indian Stock Market(Nifty)

9.6. Analytical Tools & Technique

In order to analyze the collected data the statistical tool(SPSS) such as correlation model is used. Correlation coefficient is a statistical measure that determines the degree to which two variable's movements are associated. Correlation coefficient value ranges from -1 to 1. In the current paper attempt is made to study the impact of FII& DII with Indian Stock Market (Nifty) So FII & DII are considered as the independent variable and the dependent variables for model i.e. Nifty.

9.7. Trends of FIIS in Indian Stock Market

The growth of institutional investors in the market is having its own advantages as well as its own share of problems on the brighter side almost always purchase stocks on the basis of fundamentals. And this means that it is essential to have information to evaluate, so research becomes important and this leads to increasing demands on companies to become more transparent and more disclosures. This will lead to reduction in information asymmetries that plagued the Indian markets for quite a while. Also, the increasing presence of this class of investors leads to reform of securities trading and transaction systems, nurturing of securities brokers, and liquid markets. If we see the numbers of FII flows, It is increasing every year expect some of rare years where global factors like slowdown have effected Indian market too.

Table 1: Net Investment by FII (in crore)

Year	Gross Purchase (Cr)	Gross Sale (Cr)	Net Investment (Cr)
2009	624,239.70	540,814.70	83,424.20
2010	766,283.20	633,017.10	133,266.80
2011	611,055.60	613,770.80	-2,714.20
2012	669,184.40	540,823.90	128,360.70
2013	794,231.70	681,264.70	112,968.70
2014	80901.394	73547.95	97,054
2015	92811.089	163417.98	-20,373.69
2016	1111834.7	1068300	43534.76

Source: NSDL
http://www.nsdlindia.com/publications/FIIreports.html

Figure 1

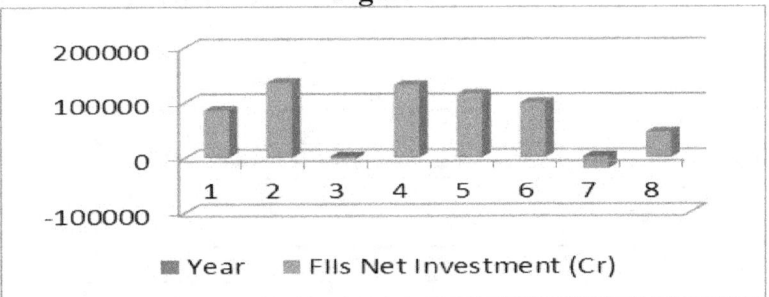

* The data presented above is compiled on the basis of reports submitted to SEBI by custodians and constitutes trades conducted by FIIs on and upto the previous trading day(s).

Table 2: FIIS Inflow

Year	Number of FII
2009	1594
2010	1706
2011	1718
2012	1767
2013	1759
2014	1826
2015	1865
2016	1904

Source: Economic Times

Figure: 2

As above fig. it interpret that in 2009 the no of FII is 1594 and in 2010 it was 1706 and in 2011 it was 1718 and in 2012 it was increase 1767 and in 2013 it was 1759 and increased to 1788 in 2014 and to 1904 in 2016.

9.8. Investment Structure of FIIS in Different Sectors

Table 3

Banks	18.07
FMCG	18.29
Finance	20.77
Information Technology	9.18
Pharmaceuticals	15.32
Infrastructure	8.65
Media & Entertainment	15.18
Miscellaneous	13.25
Telecommunication	11.09
Services	10.04
Petrochemicals	9.24
Engineering	10.13
Manufacturing	10.18
Total stake of FIIs in all the Sectors	11.77

Source: NSE

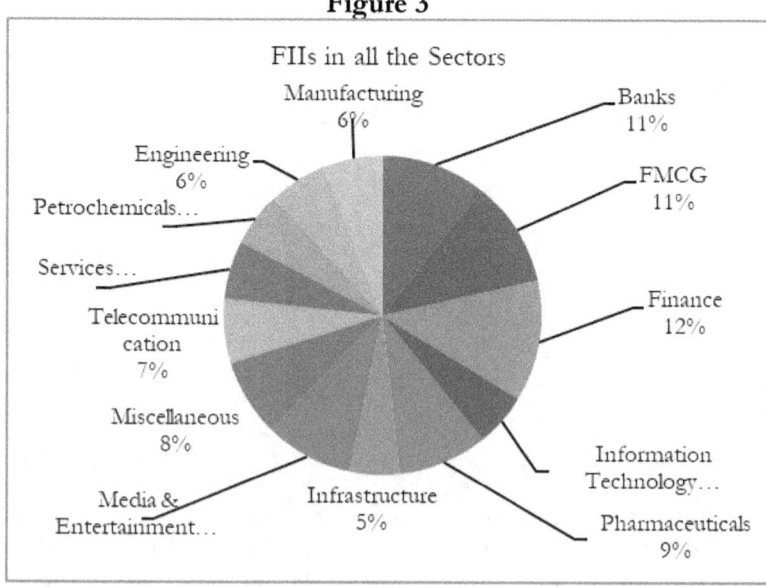

Figure 3

Above Table shows the trend of FII in different sector for the period 2015 in India. The results revealed that maximum contribution (12 percent) of FII inflows in finance sector. After this investors' prefer to invest in FMCG & banks sector i.e (11%). so it interpret that FIIs invested their maximum contribution in finance sector.

9.9. Trend of NIFTY over the Years

Table 4

Year	Close	Percentage change
2009	5249	-
2010	5914	12.669
2011	4787	-19.056
2012	5935	23.981
2013	6251	5.324
2014	8338	33.386
2015	7942	-4.749
2016	8187	3.084

Figure 4

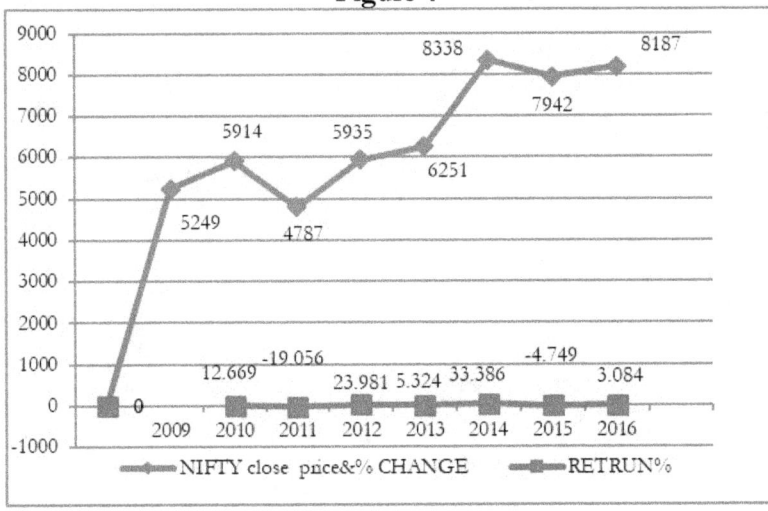

In 2008-09 due to recession the CNX Nifty was lowest. But after that it has increased from 3021 to 5834 in 2010-11 and again decreased to 5296 in 2011-12. After this fall the Nifty indices has again seen a rise to 5683 in 2012-13.and in2014 it was 6704 and in

2015 it was 7834& in 2016 it was 8187.

9.10. Impact of FIIs on Indian Stock Market (NIFTY)

"The term FII is used most commonly in India to refer to outside companies investing in the financial markets of India. "

FII investment is frequently referred to as hot money for the reason that it can leave the country at the same speed at which it comes in. In country like India; statutory agencies like SEBI have prescribed norms to register FIIs and also to regulate such investments flowing in through FIIs.

Table 5

YEAR	CNX NIFTY	NET INVESTMENT FIIS
2009	5249	83,424.20
2010	5914	133,266.80
2011	4787	-2,714.20
2012	5935	128,360.70
2013	6251	112,968.70
2014	8338	97,054
2015	7942	-203,73.69
2016	8187	43534.76

Source: SEBI, NSE fact sheet.

Figure 5

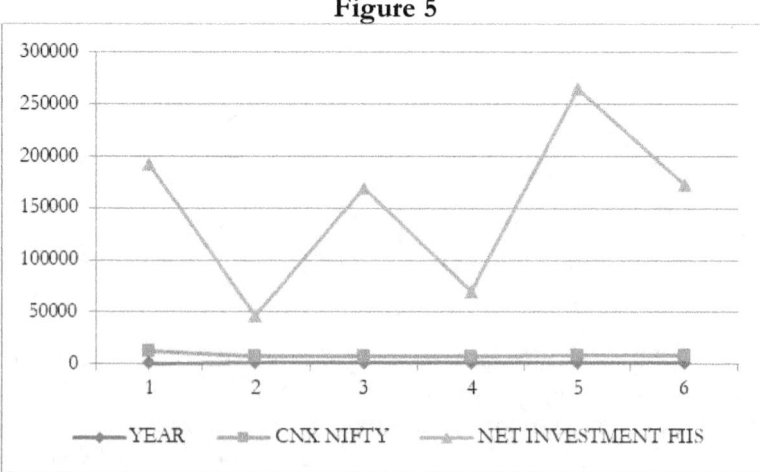

Table 6: Correlation

		NIFTY	FIIS
NIFTY	Pearson Correlation	1	.740
	Sig. (2-tailed)		
	N	8	8
FIIS	Pearson Correlation	.740	1
	Sig. (2-tailed)		
	N	8	8

Above table (two tailed test) clearly analysis that Null hypothesis: (H_0) that there is no relationship between FII and Nifty is rejected and Alternative hypothesis (H_a) is accepted i.e. the positive correlation between these two variables is +.740. So there is positive correlation between FII and Nifty. It means FIIs significantly impacts the Indian Stock market.

9.11. Impact of DIIS on Indian Stock Market (NIFTY)

Nifty is the commonly used name for the Bombay Stock Exchange Sensitive Index – an index Composed of 50 of the largest and most actively traded stocks on the National Stock Exchange (NSE). "The term DII is used most commonly in India to refer to inside companies investing in the financial markets of India

Table 7

YEAR	CNX NIFTY	NET INVESTMENT DIIs
2009	5249	26106.16
2010	5914	18632.06
2011	4787	29482.129
2012	5935	-55800.09
2013	6251	-72370.68
2014	8338	-29648.3
2015	7942	64653.11
2016	8187	40080.69

Source: Moneycontrol.com

Figure 6

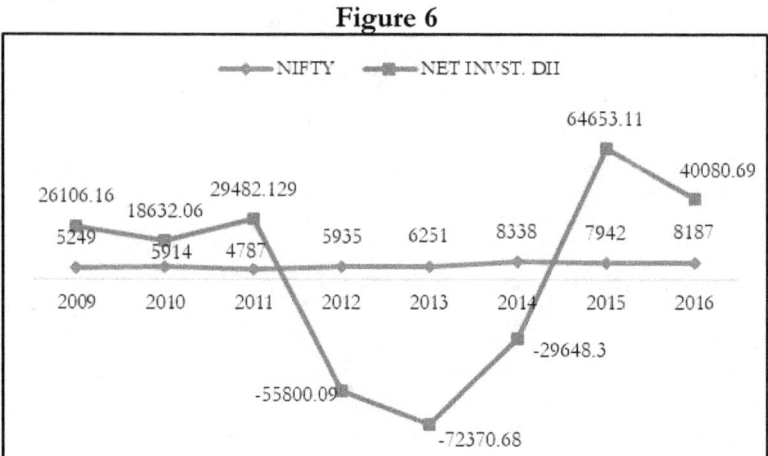

Table 6: Correlation

		NIFTY	FII
NIFTY	Pearson Correlation	1	-.072
	Sig. (2-tailed)		.853
	N	9	9
FII	Pearson Correlation	-.072	1
	Sig. (2-tailed)	.853	
	N	9	9

As above table indicating clearly analysis that Null hypothesis: (H_0) that there is no relationship between DII and Nifty is accepted and Alternative hypothesis (H_a) is rejected i.e. the negative correlation between these two variables is r= -.072. So there is negative correlation between DIIs and Nifty. It implies that DIIs don't impact Indian Stock Market.

Conclusion

The empirical investigation of the direction of causation between FII and DII flows to India and Indian stock market returns over the time period 2010- 2016 has thus revealed that FII flows are caused by rather than causing the national stock market returns. The slight evidence of a reversion of causality running from flows to returns as well has policy implications because of the potential of FII & DII flows to aggravate the crisis already set in the stock market. On the other hand DIIs doesn't impact the Indian stock market as there is negative correlation between both the variables. As the volume of DIIs is quite less as comparison to FIIs.

According to findings and results, it is concluded that FII did have high significant impact on the Indian capital market. Therefore, the alternate hypothesis is accepted. FII's have positive impact on Nifty.

However there are other major factors that influence the bourses in the stock market, but FII is definitely one of the factors. This signifies that market rise with increase in FII's and collapse when FII's are withdrawn from the market. The Pearson correlation values indicate positive correlation between the FII and the movement of Nifty (Karl pearson' correlation value is 0.740) and DII and Nifty (Karl pearson' correlation value is -0.072). Above paper also analyses that there is negative correlation between the DII and the movement of Nifty. That implies flows of DIIs don't significantly effect the movement of Indian Stock market.

So it can be concluded that being India part of BRICS and part of emerging economy FIIs play an important role in the overall growth and sustainable development of Indian economy.

References

Chakraborty tanupa (2007), "Foreign Institutional Investment Flows and Indian Stock Market Returns . A Cause and Effect Relationship Study", Indian Accounting Review, Vol: 11, No: 1, June 2001, pp: 35 – 48.

Samal, C. Kishore (1997), Emerging Equity Market in India: Role of Foreign Institutional Investors, Economic and Political Weekly, Vol. 32, No. 42.

Kumar Saji (2006), FIIs Vs. SENSEX: An Emerging Paradigm, Treasury Management, ICFAI University Press, February.

Ravi Akula, (2014), "An overview of foreign institutional investment in India", Indian journal of Commerce & Management studies, Vol: 2, Issue: 1, January 2014, pp: 100-104.

Stanley Morgan (2002),"FII's influence on Stock Market", Journal: Journal of impact of Institutional Investors on ism. Vol 17. Publisher: Emerald Group Publishing Limited.

Kumar, S. (2001). 'Does the Indian Stock Market Play to the tune of FII Investments? An Empirical Investigation'. ICFAI Journal of Applied Finance 7 (3): 36-44.

Kumar, SSS (2006), "Role of Institutional Investors in Indian Stock Market", Impact, July December, pp.76-80.

Mukherjee, P, Bose, S and Coondoo, D (2008), "Foreign Institutional Investment in the Indian Equity Market", Money and Finance, 3, pp. 21-51.

Websites

www.bseindia.com
www.imf.org
www.rbi.org.in
www.sebi.gov.in

CHAPTER: 10
DEMONETISATION: A MOVE TOWARDS CASHLESS ECONOMY

Dharuv Pal Singh

Abstract

Demonetisation has been the most talked about subject in the last six months and there have been newspapers, magazines, blogs and social media packed with information on this issue. Initially, demonetisation was sold by the Prime Minister of India as a campaign to weed out the evils of black money and to fight against corruption. After six months when remonetisation exercise is almost complete the primary pitch and narrative of the demonetisation drive have taken a major shift to cashless economy. The cashless transaction system is reaching its growth day by day and the growth of banking and financial sector more and more the people moves from cash to cashless system. At this stage India has to overcome numerous obstacles to facilitate the transition towards cashless economy. Issues like infrastructural constraints, internet penetration in rural areas, poor response from rural areas and regulatory hurdles are critical issues need to be addressed. This paper concludes that demonetisation has played an important role in the transition towards cashless economy and has to keep the present momentum sustained and improved through institutions, industry players and supporting regulatory environment.

10.1. Introduction

Demonetisation has been the most discussed and debated subject in the last six months and there have been newspapers, magazines, blogs and social media packed with informative input on demonetisation. Over the past several decades, the Indian economy has been facing the challenges of increasing corruption in the public and private sector, terrorist activities from across the border, fake currency, illegal weapons, militancy, drug and human trafficking popped up in black money. Demonetisation was announced by our Prime Minister Shri Narendra Modi on 8th November, 2016, at 8p.m. in his address to the nation. It is sure to be remembered as a major historic and economic event of 21st century in India. It proved as a historic decision taken by the Prime Minister of India to weed out the evils of black money in the country.3 However, with this move, came up many opinions in favor and also against this revolutionary step. It's important here to have a glance at both the sides of demonetization. Demonetisation is Prime Minister Narendra Modi's attempt to reduce bribery and the black economy so that India may shift towards digitalized money transfer, which is more traceable and taxable.16 Vedanta chairman, Anil Aggarwal firmly believes that Prime Minister Narendra Modi's demonetisation initiative will be good for Indian in long run, arguing that a cashless economy means fewer distractions when it comes to doing business. Aggarwal told Economic Times on 7th December 2016 in an interview. "Cash transactions always slow things down because you have to handle cash. But when you have cashless business, your mindset is only on the business" In the long run this will be good for the country.

10.1.1. Other Face of Demonetisation

As the demonetisation campaign progressed after 8th. November 2016, long queues appeared in the age of 4G and the media anger has been unparalleled. The country, as reflected from the following statements, wasn't prepared to welcome demonetisation for various reasons:

Due to this cash crunch, India ground to a halt. Businesses shut down, farmers couldn't buy seeds, taxi and rickshaw drivers didn't have any way to receive payments, employers had no way to pay their employees, hospitals were refusing patients who only had old banknotes, fishermen watched their catch wither up and rot, some families had difficulty buying food, and weddings throughout the country were canceled.

Supreme Court refuses to stay demonetisation order, asks Government to take immediate steps to ease public inconvenience.

10.1.2. Demonetisation Timeline in India

The decision of the Indian Government to demonetize Rs 500 and Rs 1,000 currency notes is not a new phenomenon. Rs 1,000 and higher denomination notes were first demonetized in January 1946 and again in 1978. The highest denomination note ever printed by the Reserve Bank of India (RBI) was the Rs 10,000 note in 1938. But later on, these notes were demonetized in January 1946 and again in January 1978 as per RBI data. However, this was the first time that Rs 2,000 currency note has been introduced from November 2016 despite giving a new US-Dollar-like look to existing Rs 500 denomination. On the other hand while Rs 1000 note was scrapped.

10.1.3. Objective Behind Demonetisation

The foremost objective behind demonetisation is to motivate masses for cash-less transactions bringing transparency in the economic system and fighting black money. Transparent cashless economic system implemented effectively is sure to bring the desired results of increasing taxation base, thereby raising country's income. On the other hand Nilanjan Bank & Milind Shrikant Padalkar were of the opinion published on 12th January 2016 in "The Diplomat Magazine" that India's demonetization could be the push the country needs to move to digital banking, but it will take more concerted government efforts to promote a long term transition.

10.2. Literature Review

Annamalai, S. and Muthu R. Iiakkuvan (2008) in their article "Retail transaction: Future bright for plastic money" projected the growth of debit and credit cards in the retail transactions. They also mentioned the growth factors, which leads to its popularity, important constraints faced by banks and summarized with bright future and scope of plastic money.

Alvares & Cliford (2009) in their reports "The problem regarding fake currency in India" It is said that the country's battle against fake currency is not getting easier and many fakes go undetected. It is also stated that counterfeiters hitherto had restricted printing facilities which made it easier to discover fakes.

Ashish Das, and Rakhi Agarwal, (2010) in their article "Cashless Payment System in India- A Roadmap" Cash as a mode of payment is an expensive proposition for the Government. The country needs to move away from cash-based towards a cashless (electronic) payment system. This will help reduce currency management cost, track transactions, check tax avoidance / fraud etc. enhance financial inclusion and integrate the parallel economy with main stream.

Grohmann, Antonia, Kouwenberg, Roy and Menkhoff, Lukas, (2014) in their study Financial Literacy and its consequences in the Emerging Middle Class concluded that not only the supply of sophisticated financial products is important for the financial development, but the demand of the financial products also plays the crucial role. Thus, financial literacy is useful to contribute to the financial development and further in the economic growth.

Objective Of The Study

People are always reluctant to go with new things unless it becomes mandatory. The demonetisation has forced people to lessen their dependence on hard money transactions and resort to digital payments. With the implementation of demonetisation recently, it becomes necessary to track progress of this move towards a cashless society, though it is too early to make an assessment. Therefore, the broad objective of the study is to examine the momentum towards digital economy in the wake of India's demonetisation.

10.3. Methodology

The study is based on secondary sources of data input. Sources like different books, journals, newspapers and relevant websites have been consulted in order to make the study an effective one. The pre-requisites of a cashless economy were identified and compared to the digital mechanism in India. This was done by referring to Master Card Advisors cashless journey and database of Reserve Bank of India.

10.4. Concept Of A Cashless Society

The Indian government is also constantly encouraging the people of India to go cashless and reduce dependence on cash transactions adopting digital transactions. A complete cashless society is a society where currency notes or cash money are not used and the entire business runs on digital currency. Cashless societies in the past were based on the barter system where people exchanged their livestock for food crops or other goods. However, the present concept of a cashless society or country is completely a new thing. Here cashless transactions are made with the help of digital currencies. In a truly cashless society, legal tender (money) is exchanged and recorded only in the electronic digital form.

10.5. Cashless Journey at global level

During the 1990's, the growing popularity of electronic banking made the use of non-cash transactions and settlements popular among the residents of some of the most technologically literate nations of the world. Digital payment system was established in countries across the

The cashless journey measures nation's progress toward more modern, efficient electronic payment mechanisms by looking at the current share of cash as compared to non-cash payments. Electronic payments have made substantial aggression among consumers in some developed countries. But even in the most cashless countries on earth, like France and the Netherlands, cash still accounts for 40% or more of all consumer transactions. In many emerging markets, the cashless share of consumer transactions is effectively negligible. Meanwhile, as per table, in most of the countries the cashless journey has only just begun. Looking across the 33 countries, cashless transactions fall into four major categories viz Inception, Transitioning, Tipping Point and Advanced. Each is an indicator of progress towards going cashless. Most inception countries are developing nations while the developed nations fall into an 'Advanced' category. The journey of countries going cashless and their respective stages indicates that developed and developing countries are making great strides to minimize the use of paper currency. Despite the progress at global level, these countries aren't hundred percent cashless. So less-cash countries might be more accurate description at least for now and the global cashless journey is still on the move in many ways.

Table 1: Countries using Non-Cash Mechanism

Rank	Country	Cashless Transactions Percentage	Stage
1	Singapore	61%	ADVANCED
2	Netherlands	60%	
3	France	59%	
4	Sweden	59%	
5	Canada	57%	
6	Belgium	56%	
7	United Kingdom	52%	
8	USA	45%	TIPPING POINT
9	Australia	35%	
10	Germany	33%	
11	South Korea	29%	
12	Spain	16%	TRANSITIONING
13	Brazil	15%	
14	Japan	14%	
15	China	10%	
16	United Arab Emirates	8%	INCEPTION
17	Taiwan	6%	
18	Italy	6%	
19	South Africa	6%	
20	Poland	5%	
21	Russia	4%	
22	Mexico	4%	
23	Greece	2%	
24	Colombia	2%	
25	India	2%	
26	Kenya	2%	
27	Thailand	2%	
28	Malaysia	2%	
29	Saudi Arabia	1%	
30	Peru	1%	
31	Egypt	1%	
32	Nigeria	0%	
33	Indonesia	0%	

Source: Source: Mastercard Advisor's Measuring progress toward a cashless society on 29th December 2016 globe by 2010.

10.6. Digital Journey –An Overview

India is a country where 98 per cent of total financial transactions are done through cash. However, this may no longer be the case in the coming times as the government has already steered the country towards a cash less socio-economy. India has a diversified financial sector undergoing rapid expansion, both in terms of strong growth of existing financial services. The sector comprises of commercial banks, insurance companies, non-banking financial companies, co-operatives, pension funds, mutual funds and other smaller financial entities. The financial sector in

India is predominantly a banking sector with commercial banks accounting for more than 64 per cent of the total assets held by the financial system. The Indian banking system consists of 26 public sector banks, 25 private sector banks, 43 foreign banks, 56 regional rural banks, 1,589 urban cooperative banks and 93,550 rural cooperative banks.13 Banks in the country have added 3.12 Crore new accounts under Pradhan Mantri Jan Dhan Yojna (PMJDY) during the five months after demonetisation. The total number of PMJDY accounts, which stood at 25.51 Crore 10on November 9, increased to 28.63 Crore by May 2017.11

Ritika Mukharjee and Sumit Shekhar of Ambit Capital mentioned in a research paper that India's informal sector accounts for 40 percent of GDP and employs close to 75 percent of the Indian labour force.15 The point is that informal sector forms a significant portion of India's economy and employs three fourths of India's workforce.

Piyush Singh, managing director (financial services group) said that growth in acceptance infrastructure has not been uniform across the country as there is higher concentration of ATMs and POS machines in urban areas and larger towns. According to a JM Financial report, number of POS devices stands at 1.2 million for more than 14 million estimated merchants, which means that over 90% of the outlets are left without a medium to collect payments electronically.5 Furthermore, according to the Bank of America(Akamai report-2016), among top 105 countries, India stands at 104th position so far as the 4G speed is concerned. India needs to improve the internet speed to strengthen digital payment mechanism and infrastructure. Fiber networks, which offer broadband connections, have only reached 76089 17 as on 29th January 2017 of the 2.5 lakh Gram Panchayats targeted by the Information Technology department support poor connectivity in rural areas.

Another facet of infrastructure critically lacking with India is adequate data protection and privacy laws. In October 2016, 3.2 million debit cards belonging to India's premier banks were hacked and unauthorized usage was reported from several locations in China.6 Besides,focusing on connectivity and internet speed issues, security and safety measures also call upon the attention of the Government.

10.7. Digital Payments in India

The digital India programme is a flagship programme of the Government of India with a vision to transform India into a digitally empowered society and knowledge economy. "Faceless", Paperless, cashless" is one of the apparent role of digital India.

Table 2: Digital Payments in India
Volume in million, Value in Billion

Data for the period		Apr-16	May-16	Jun-16	Jul-16	Aug-16	Sep-16	Oct-16	Nov-16	Dec-16	Jan-17	Feb-17	Mar-17	Apr-17
RTGS	volume	8.32	8.7	8.82	8.25	8.50	8.47	9	7.9	8.8	9.3	9.1	12.5	9.5
	value	68411.47	76332.5	83834.9	74919.55	77588.30	86687.3	76473.2	78479.2	84096.5	77486.1	74218.8	123375.8	88512.2
NEFT	volume	111.8	117.5	118.29	113.48	118.56	120.1	133.2	123.0	166.3	164.2	148.2	186.7	143.2
	value	8324.5	7732.54	8815.31	8145.3	8764.14	9880.1	9504.5	8807.8	11537.6	11355.1	10877.9	16294.5	12156.2
IMPS	volume	29.7	31.1	33.4	35.9	38.5	39.8	47.3	40.3	60.5	71.9	65.1	59.6	68.6
	value	224.9	234.6	258.5	271.5	296.5	319.1	378.3	355.0	465.2	549.0	525.1	611.0	600.1
UPI	volume	0	0	0	0	0	0	0.1	0.3	2.0	4.5	4.3	6.2	6.9
	value	0	0	0	0	0	0	0.4	0.9	7.0	16.6	19.0	23.9	22.0
M Wallet	volume	48.8	50.3	58.6	59.5	70.7	75.3	99.6	138.1	213.1	261.7	247.0	307.5	
	value	229.3	243.5	277.4	276	307.4	319.2	338.5	330.5	744.8	835.3	691.1	731.2	
Debit Cards at POS	Volume	118.3	89	118.2	129.1	130.5	125.2	140.6	236.5	415.5	328.6	251.7	271.2	268.0
	Value	148.03	155.15	155	170.92	183.7	159.32	219.41	321.7	580.3	490.0	358.4	357.0	374.8
Credit Cards at POS	volume	72.8	60.1	76.3	79.4	84	77.9	98.9	97.9	116.1	118.8	94.7	106.2	106.5
	value	227.24	249.6	239.55	243.41	257.48	241.97	299.42	265.6	311.5	326.9	284.5	328.9	331.4
PPI	volume	69.3	71	77	77.9	96.3	97.1	126.9	169.3	261.1	295.8	280.0	342.1	344.4
	value	467.2	499.5	534.7	534	564.6	562.8	602.2	507.4	977.0	1100.1	962.8	1067.7	1070.1
Mobile Banking	volume	48.67	61.73	63.17	67.47	71.76	72.6	78.1	87.5	110.6	106.1	95.4	107.3	106.2
	value	524.83	618.13	673.48	809.59	1038.97	1042.6	1139.4	1365.7	1498.2	1383.0	1279.9	1718.5	1612.2

Source: NPCI

Note: RTGS – Real time gross settlement, NEFT- National electronic funds transfer, IMPS- Immediate payment service, UPI-Unified Payment interface, POS- Point of Sale, PPI- Prepaid payment instrument

As part of promoting cashless transactions and converting India into less-cash society, various modes of digital payments are available. In the backdrop of the ongoing intense debate on the benefits of demonetisation, there has been a strong growth in digital payments and transactions in the months since the currency swap was announced. Digital transactions have increased in volume and value across various modes from wallets to cards sharply after demonetisation. Table-2 shows various modes of digital payments available in India for online transfer of funds. These modes are: NEFT- National electronic funds transfer, RTGS – Real time gross settlement ,IMPS- Immediate payment service, UPI-Unified Payment interface, POS- Point of Sale, PPI- Prepaid payment instrument, Mobile Banking, M Wallet, E-Wallets etc

10.7.1. NEFT

The National Electronic Fund Transfer (NEFT) is one of the most commonly-used ways of transferring money online from one bank to another. This system is based on deferred settlement basis.

Figure 1: NEFT

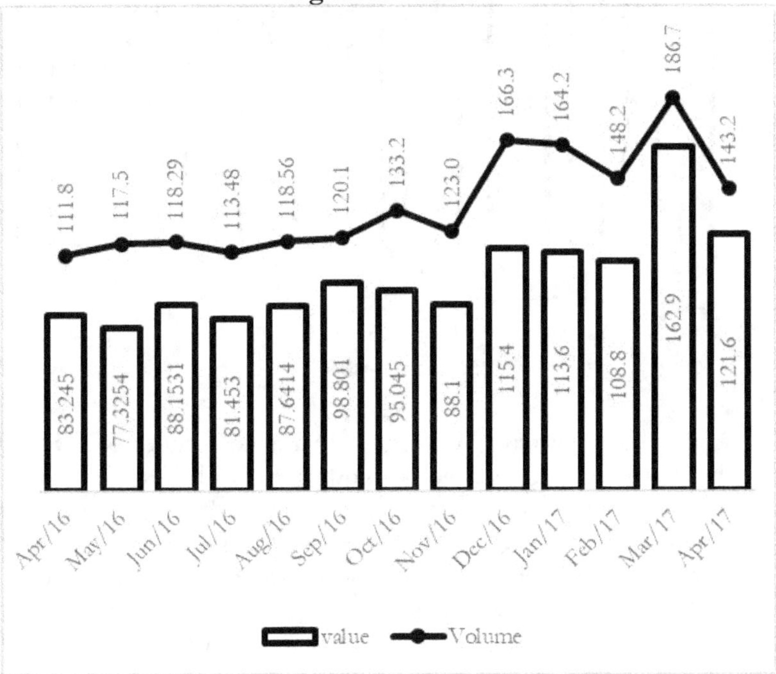

There appears to be a fair degree of correlation between the number of transactions and the amount transacted using NEFT through the period of 13 Months. Number of transactions went up sharply to 186.7 million in March 2017 and falls sharply to 143.2 millions in the beginning of next financial Year.

10.7.2. RTGS

The Real Time Gross Settlement **(RTGS)** is for high value transactions. The transfer happens on real time basis throughout the RTGS business hours.

Figure 2: RTGS

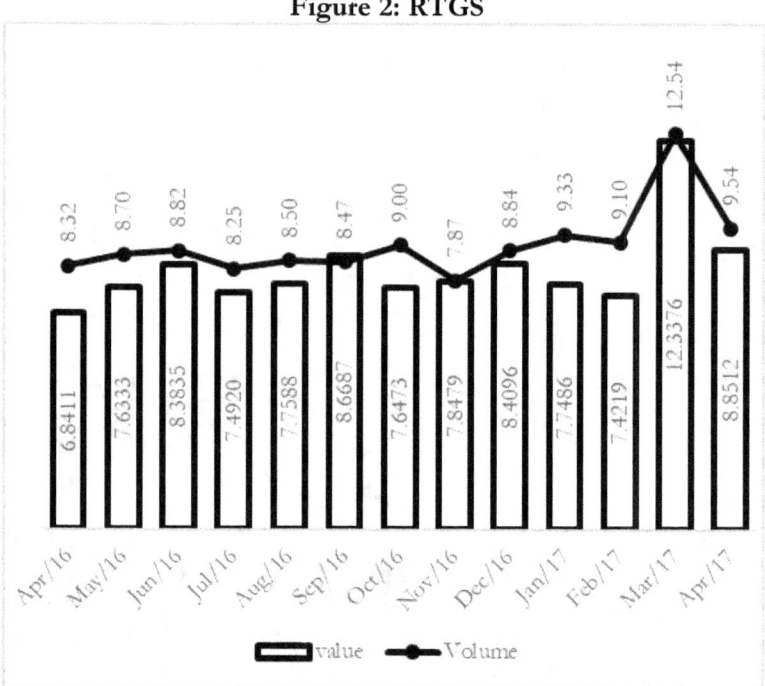

The data shows that electronic transaction under RTGS fell both in value and volume as compared with October 2016. Logically with most of the cash sucked out of the system, cashless transactions should have risen in the month of November 2016. It was the time of little chaos and inconvenience, as to how to go with the digital payment system. However, after November it picked up momentum and went up sharply with Rupees 125.4 million in March 2017. In the month of April 2017, again a sudden fall was witnessed which may be attributed to increase of cash volume in economy.

10.7.3. IMPS

The Immediate Payment Service (IMPS) is an instant fund transfer service available 24×7 during 365 days of the year.

Figure 3: IMPS

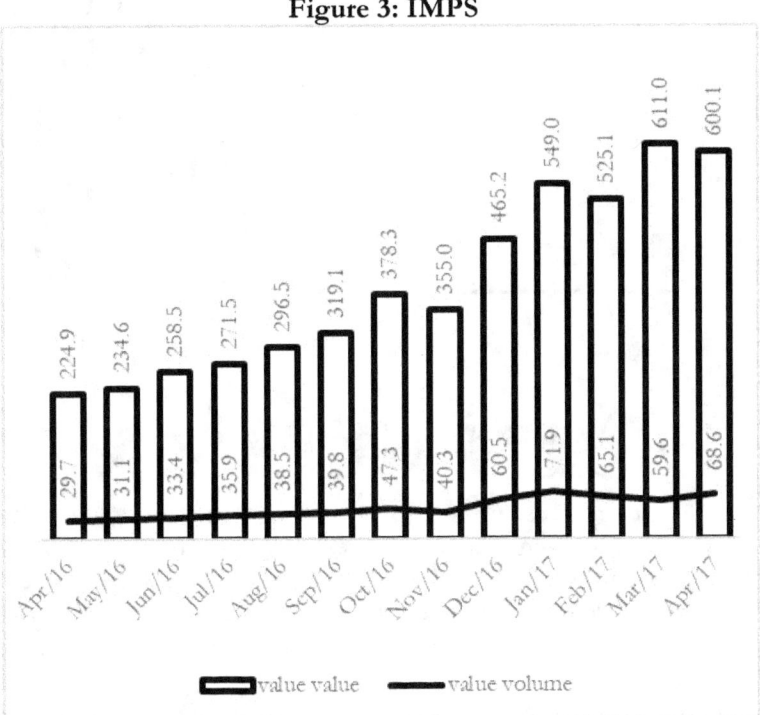

It can be used through mobile as well as internet banking. Transfer through IMPS declined in November 2016 for which the same reason of state of confusion could be assigned but picked up thereafter. Between January and March 2017 number of transactions declined to 59.6 million. But amount transacted increased to 61100 Crore. IMPS volume in terms of transactions and value has more than doubled since April 2016.

10.7.4. UPI

With Jan Dhan Accounts, the **Unified Payment Interface** (UPI) and a greater push towards Aadhaar integration, the foundation had already been laid for cashless economy.

Figure 4: UPI

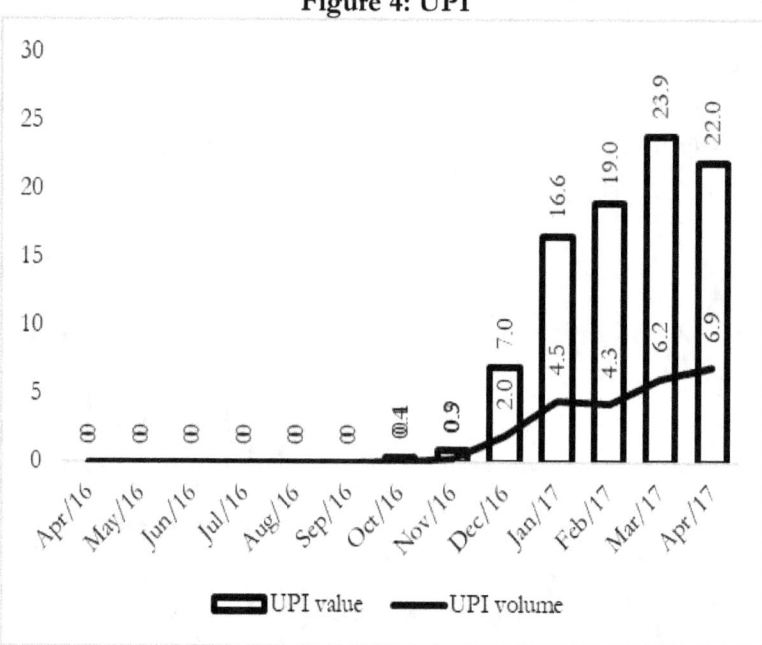

After demonetisation, people began to understand the advantages of going digital. Unified Payment Interface allows transactions to be done through any smart phone using Virtual Payment Address (VPA). The transactions can be done 24/7on a real time basis. UPI went live in August 2016 and got a huge leap following demonetisation. Growth appears to have been impacted by the launch of number of mobile application after demonetisation.

10.7.5. Plastic Money

Plastic money is used to refer to Debit cards, credit cards and form of prepaid cards. Total number of transactions with credit cards jumped to12 percent and amount transacted increased to 16 percent between February and March 2017, Month on Month, the number of credit card transactions triggered by "Apps" grew to 12 million, after a significant 24.11million decline in February 2017.Year on Year, total number of transactions was up by 47 percent.

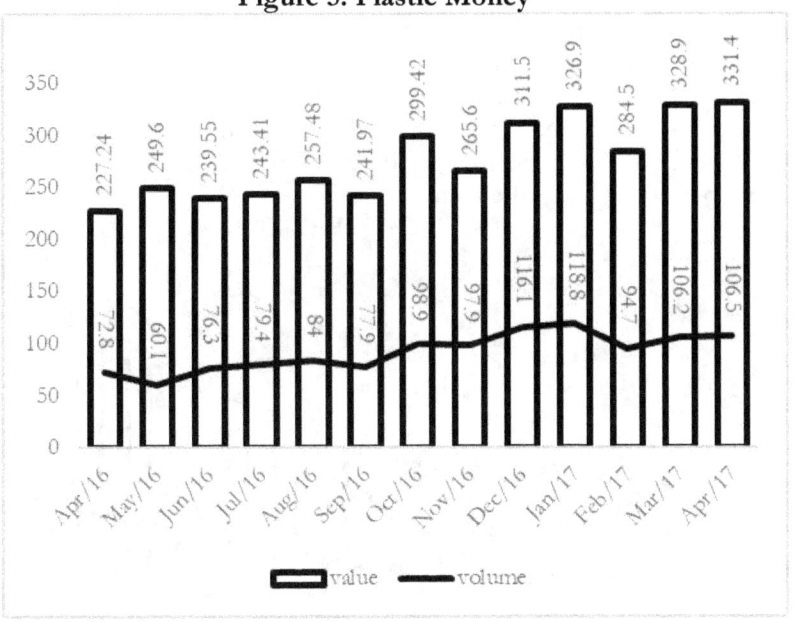

Figure 5: Plastic Money

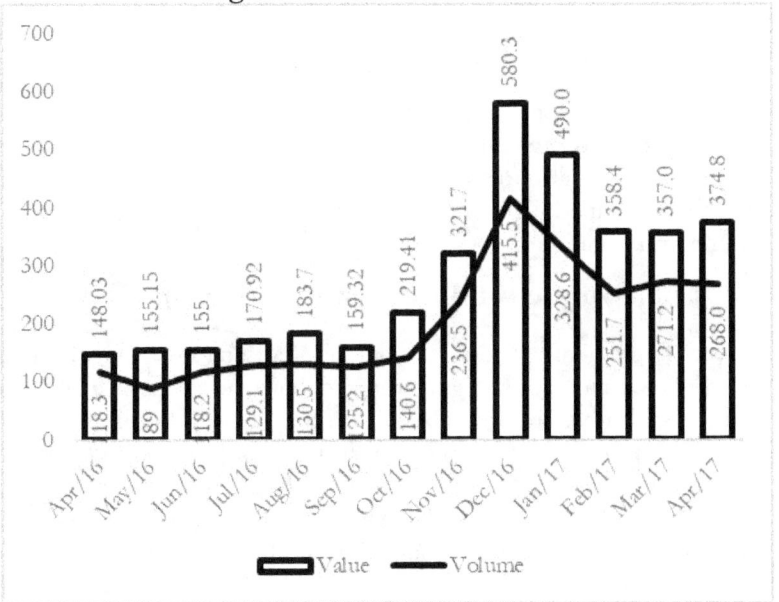

Figure 6: Debit Cards at POS

Total number of transactions 7.7 percent month on month to

268.1 million in April 2017while amount transacted declined slightly in March 2017 and went sharply up to Rs 37480 Crore in April 2017. Between October 2016 and January 2017, there was a jump of over 80 percent in both number of transactions and amount transacted through prepaid payment instruments. However, PPI transfers declined in the month of February 2017, but picked up speed thereafter.

Figure 7: PPI

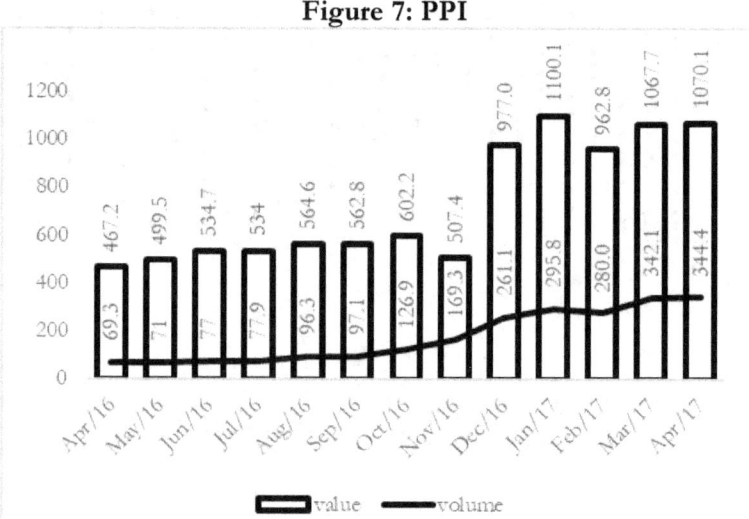

Between October 2016 and January 2017, there was a jump of over 80 percent in both number of transactions and amount transacted through prepaid payment instruments. However, PPI transfers declined in the month of February 2017, but gained momentum thereafter.

10.7.6. Mobile Banking Services (MBS)

Mobile banking refers to banking transactions using mobile phones, including accessing, credit or debit to accounts. An analysis of the data shows the value of Mobile Banking Transactions which recorded increase of 10 percent from Rs. 113.9 million in October 2016 to Rs 138.8 million in January 2017. Between February and April, transactions volume increased by 12 percent to Rs.161.2 million. Money transfer through Mobile Banking Services (MBS) shows an increase of more than 100 percent over 12 months ending April 2017.

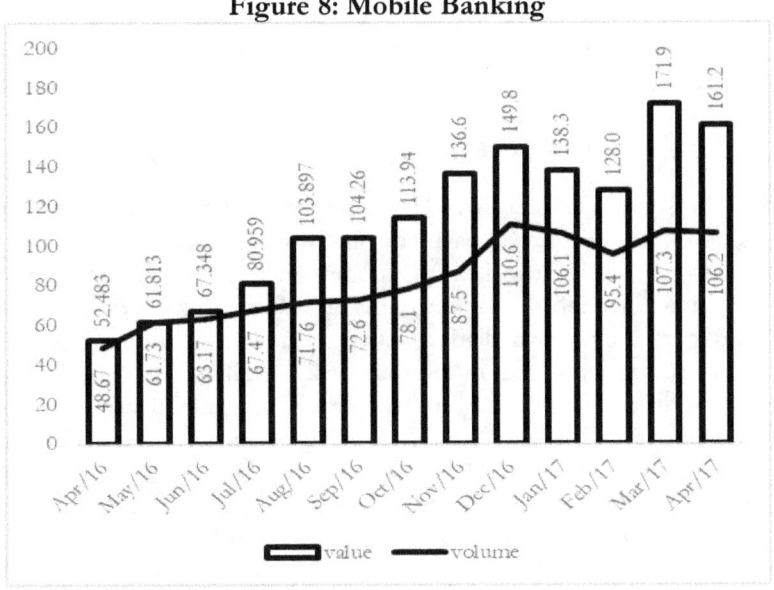

Figure 8: Mobile Banking

10.7.7. M Wallet

A mobile wallet primarily enables an individual to pay as well as to receive payment using a mobile device.

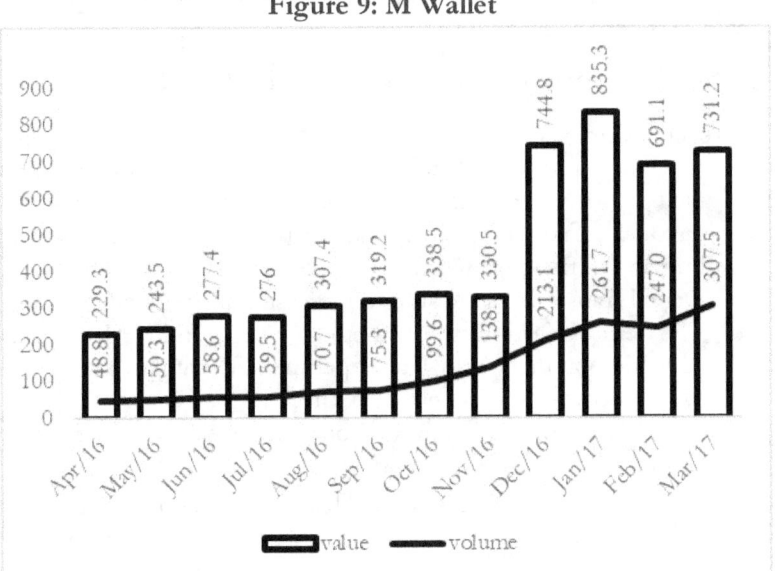

Figure 9: M Wallet

Mobile wallets recorded an increase of 475 percent in year to year comparison and amount transacted growth recorded 207 percent.

10.7.8. E-Wallets

The sudden cash crunch due to demonetisation of Rs 1000 and Rs 500 notes required a payment platform that was used by all. E wallets such as Paytm, Itzcash, money on mobile and MobiKwik were quick to grab this opportunity. E-Wallet means presence of a third party or intermediaries between the payer and the payee. Paytm wallet registered an increase of 218 million users by March 2017. This number is 5.3 times of Paytm's registered user base in March 2015. At present Paytm have five million offline merchants. Paytm's rival MobKwik has also close to 55 million consumers transacting on its platform with a base of 15 lakh active merchants across categories in the month of March 2017. ItzCash, another player in the space has 50,000 franchisees with more than 40 million customers. Money On Mobile is a pre-paid wallet that does not require to be linked with any bank account. Consumers can go to any Money On Mobile supported retail store and load money in the wallet by paying cash to retailer. Currently the company claims over 330000 retail locations in over 700 cities with 190 million customers across the country.

10.8. Summary of Analytical Findings

The salient findings of the study are as follows:
- Over the past several decades, the Indian economy has been facing growing challenges of wide-spread corruption, terrorism, fake currency, illegal weapons, militancy, drug and human trafficking which popped up from black money. Digital transactions are sure to increase transparency.
- The demonetisation isn't something new in India. Many other countries of the world had experimented with it; some met the purposes, while other failed miserably.
- Digital payment methods became well established in countries across the globe by 2010.
- The growth in infrastructure has not been uniform across the country as there is higher concentration in urban areas whereas internet connectivity is poor in rural areas. Another

facet of infrastructure critically lacking is inadequate data protection and privacy laws.
- Traditionally, online transactions were done with limited means but at present various mechanisms have evolved to meet the remittance requirements namely National Electronic Funds Transfer (NEFT), Immediate Payment Service (IMPS) and Unified Payments Interface (UPI) Mobile Banking Services (MBS) etc.
- Digital transactions had been consistently growing over the years, demonetisation gave it an additional leg up as use of plastic money has been recorded in India.

Conclusion

Demonetisation as a campaign to weed out the evils of black money is a daring step towards a cashless economy. Digital transaction system, as apparent from the data on the subject, is becoming robust day by day. However, it's too early to make a complete and final assessment about the impact of demonetisation in such a short span of time as to whether the objective behind it will be met or not, only time will reveal. Issues like infrastructural constraints, internet penetration in rural areas, poor response from rural areas and regulatory hurdles are critical issues which need to be addressed to make digitalisation or cashless system more effective. This paper concludes that demonetisation has played an important role in the transition towards cashless economy and has to keep the present momentum sustained and improved through institutions, industry players and supporting regulatory environment.

References

Asian Voice, *Volume 45, Issue 2*, 19-25 November 2016

TarumBhalla, "https://youstory.com/2017/in the race to be India's next unknown mobikwikclaims steady growth and offline push," 12 May 2017. [Online]

L. Sitaraman, "Demonetisation as an exercise in change management," *The Management Accountant*, pp. 68-70, March 2017.

Salmahsh, "MoneyonMobile transaction value decline to $109 million in Q3FY17," *Medianama*, 21 Feburary 2017.

T. Kishore, "www.livemint.com>money-Personalfinance-why cash

is still king for Indian consumers," 20 April 2016. [Online].
S. S. &. P. Bhakta, "3.2 million debit cardscompromised-SBI,HDFC Bank,ICICI,Yes Bank and AXIS worst hit," *The Economic Times*, 20 October 2016.
S. A. L. R. M. Anamalai, "Retail Transactions:-Futire Bright for Plastic Money," *Facts of You*, pp. 22-28, May,2008.
C. Alvares, "The Problem regarding fake currency in India," *Business Today Vol 18, Issue 5*, pp. 24-24, 03/08/2009.
A. D. A. R. Agarwal, "Cashless payment system in India- A RoadMap," 2010.
"www.thehindubusinessline.com/news/india..pmjdy..accounts-/Article9432465.ece," 17 December 2016. [Online].
"www.pmjdy.gov.in/Account-Beneficaries as on 14062017," [Online].
"www.paybefore.com/ on the wire:itZcash/investsinFintech startup finaly," 2 March 2017. [Online].
"www.humanresources.in/bfsi.php," [Online].
"www.forbes.com,after day 50:the results from India's campaign," 3 January 2017. [Online].
"www.ambitcapital.com/reports/ambit_Economy_Insight_mrtresetstothefora," 18 November 2016. [Online].
"www.adamsmith.org/blog/the very real imact of indias demonetisation," [Online].
"Internet to be available in all Gram Panchayats by 2018," *India Today*, 8 Feburary 2017.
"https://WWW.econstor.eu/bitstrean/10419/100079/1/79166471 6.pdf," [Online].
"https://paytm.com/press.19/06/2017," [Online].

CHAPTER: 11
TRANSFORMING OF HIGHER EDUCATION FOR SUSTAINABLE DEVELOPMENT

Vibha Thakur

Abstract

The role of manufacturing sector in generating employment and accelerating the economic growth is quite discussed in the literature at national level as well as sub-national level for few states of India. Few studies have investigated the growth of manufacturing sector in the context of emerging state economies. Observing the recent economic growth and increasing the importance of the state in the national economy, it is significant to estimate the growth and structure of manufacturing sector of individual state. With this motivation present study has examined the growth and structure of organized manufacturing sector of Himachal Pradesh by using the Annual Survey of Industries (ASI) data from 1981 to 2014. The study has shown that over the period organized manufacturing sector of Himachal Pradesh in term of GVA and employment grow with higher rate against the selected states and national figures especially during the recent period. The resultant employment elasticity in the state is also noted quite high in relation to the national economy and selected states. Most of the industries in the states grew in the range of 8 to 20 percent in term of GVA, while in term of employment 5 industries have achieved more than 10 percent of growth rate during the study period. This extremely high performance of Himachal

Pradesh in organized manufacturing in both GVA and employment has possibly a lot to do with the tax exemptions providing to industrial units set up in the state.

11.1. Introduction

Education is a human right and the primary agent of transformation towards sustainable development by increasing people's capacities to transform their visions for society into reality. To implement education for sustainable development, UNESCO seeks to promote and improve basic education, re-orient existing education programmes at all levels to address sustainable development, develop people awareness and understanding of sustainability and provide training. Sustainable development was defined in the 1987 UN Bruntland Commission Report, our Common Future as development that meets the needs of the present without compromising those of future generations. This simple definition encompasses a complex dynamic that implicates values and value system as well as interdisciplinary knowledge, experience and stresses the inter dependence of the environment, society and the economy.

The role of education for sustainable development (ESD) is to help people develop the attitudes, skills and knowledge to make informed decisions for the benefit of themselves and others, now and for the future and became habitant upon those decisions. In December 2002, the United Nations General Assembly adopted resolution 57/254 to put in place a United Nations Decade of Education for Sustainable Development (DESD), spanning the year 2005 to 2014. UNESCO was designated as the lead agency for the decade. The overall goal of the decade of education for sustainable development is the integration of the principles, values, and practices of sustainable development into all aspects of education and learning like facilitating networking and collaboration among stakeholders in ESD, fostering greater quality of teaching and learning in it, also supporting countries in achieving their development goals through ESD efforts and providing countries with new opportunities to incorporate ESD in education reform efforts. UNESCO major areas of activity in the decade reflect its core responsibilities.

Education is approach to teaching and learning based on the ideals and principles that underlie sustainability human rights, poverty reduction, sustainable livelihood, peace, environmental protection, democracy, health, biological and landscape diversity, climate change, gender equality and protection of indigenous culture. Natural and social sciences promote multi-disciplinary and interdisciplinary approaches to the wise use of natural resources and to the improved understanding of human environment relationships, as well as promoting principles, policies, ethical norms to guide scientific and technological development that is sustainable. Culture is concerned with the identities and values that shape the way people live their responsiveness to educational programmes and degree to which they feel involved in preserving for the future. Communication is virtually instantaneous, serving as a powerful driver of social transformation. In this context, UNSECO acts as a broker for effective sustainable development by increasing the sharing of knowledge, information, expertise and best practices, producing and disseminating scientific knowledge and sensitizing the media to sustainable development issues.

11.2. Barriers and challenges in Education for Sustainable Development

Twelve major issues stymied the advance of ESD during the 1990s and new millennium. By addressing these critical impediments in the planning stage, governments can prevent or reduce delays or derailment of ESD efforts and, ultimately, the attainment of sustainability. In addition to these generic issues, governments at all levels will need to address issues that are specific to local conditions (e.g., the quality of the relationship between the school governors and the teacher union).

11.3. Increasing Awareness: ESD is Essential

The initial step in launching an ESD programme is to develop awareness within the educational community and the public that reorienting education to achieve sustainability is essential. If government officials or school district administrators are unaware of the critical linkages between education and sustainable development, reorienting education to address sustainable development will not occur. When people realize that education can improve the likelihood of implementing national policies, regional land and resource management programs, and local programs, then education is in a position to be reoriented to help achieve sustainability. This awareness form the essential first step in the reorienting process. Fortunately at the international level, ESD is recognized as important and central to the success of sustainable development around the world. At the sixth meeting of the UN commission on sustainable development, delegation from countries worldwide repeatedly mentioned the importance of ESD in achieving goals of sustainability. It was apparent that they were ready to move forward with the next steps; however the importance of ESD must reach beyond the delegation and permeate the educational community and the general public.Inherent in building awareness are efforts to outline important linkages between education and more sustainable societies (e.g increase in females literacy reduces birth-rates and improves family quality of life).

In large part, perceiving a need brings about a corresponding change in educational systems. Unfortunately, the need to achieve sustainable development is not perceived today as sufficiently important to spark a large response in the educational community. If leaders at all levels of governance are to make progress, he recognition and active involvement of the education sector is imperative.

Each country faces a fundamental decision on addressing an ESD strategy. Each country must decide on method of implementation whether to create another "add on" subject,(e.g Sustainable Development, Environment Education, or Population Education) or to reorient entire education programs and practices to address sustainable development. Nation also need to clarify whether their educators are being asked to teach about sustainable development or to change the goals and methods of education to achieve sustainable development. The answer to this question will profoundly affect each nation's course of action. In reality, education related to sustainable development will be implemented in a wide range, inboth depth and breadth. In some communities, ESD will be ignored; in others it will be barely addressed. In some, a new class dedicated to ESD will be created, and in others the entire curriculum will be reoriented to address sustainability. Communities must be aware of the limitations of educating about sustainable development. Teaching about sustainable development is like teaching the theory behind an abstract concept or teaching the principles of sustainability by rote memorization. ESD in its real and effective forms gives students the skills, perspectives, values, and knowledge to live sustainably in their communities. At the same time, true education is not indoctrination or inculcation. Experimentation will determine what level of ESD will be appropriate and successful for communities to meet their sustainability goals. For example, a community may weave a few themes of sustainability into the curriculum, only to find the additions will not achieve sustainability for their community. In cases where schools carry total responsibility for ESD, complete curricular reorientation of education at all levels will probably be necessary. In communities where informal, non-formal, and formal education unite to create an integrated ESD programme for citizens of all ages, a less intense approach in the formal education system might be effective. As programms are developed and implemented, problems will occur. Flaws and questionable practices will need to be addressed as ESD continues to develop and mature

11.4. Linking to existing issues: Educational Reform and Economic Viability

The effectiveness of the world's educational systems is already critically debated in light of the changing needs of society. The current widespread acknowledgment of the need for educational reform may help advance ESD. If it can be linked to one or more priorities of educational reform, ESD could have a good chance for success. However, if promoters try to add another issue to an already over-burdened system, the chances of success are slim. One current global concern that has the potential to drive educational reform in many countries is economic security. Around the world, ministries of education and commerce are asking: What changes will prepare a workforce that will make my country economically viable in the changing economy of the new millennium?

One educational effort that can boost the economic potential of entire nations is educating females. During the last decade, some national leaders have recognized that educating the entire workforce, both male and females, is important for economic viability. In addition, Lawrence Summer of the World Bank says, "Once all the benefits are recognized, investments in the education of girls may well be the highest-return investment available in the developing world" (King and Hill, 1993, p vii). Accordingly, some nations are removing barriers to girls attending schools and have campaigns to actively enroll girls in schools. Further, aligning education with future economic conditions is difficult, because economic and technological forecasting is an art based on imprecise science. Answers are elusive.

11.5. Facing the complexity of Sustainable Development Concept.

Sustainable development is a complex and evolving concept. Many scholars and practioners have invested years in trying to define sustainable development and envisioning how to achieve it on national and local levels. Because sustainable development is hard to define and implement, it is also difficult to teach. Even more challenging is the task of totally reorienting an entire education system to achieve sustainability. When we examine successful national education campaigns, we find they often have simple messages. For example, messages that encourage us to vaccinate our children and boil our water, or discourage us from driving drunk and taking drugs, are simple concepts compared to the complex range of environmental, economic, and social issues that sustainable development encompasses. Success in ESD will take much longer and be more costly than single-message public-education campaigns. Rather than being clear, simple, and unambiguous, the concepts involved in ESD are complex. Their complexity stems from the intricate and complicated interactions of natural and human systems. The challenge to educators is to derive messages that illustrate such complexity, without overwhelming or confusing the learner.

11.6. Developing an ESD Program with Community Participation

Perhaps the greatest obstacle to reorienting the world's educational systems is the lack of clarity regarding goals. In simple terms, those who will be called upon to educate differently (e.g., the world's 59,000,000 teachers or agricultural instructors or water-treatment trainers) eventually will ask, "What am I to do differently ?" "What should I do or say now that I didn't say before?" These simple questions leave most "experts" in a quandary and the questioner without an adequate response. Education for sustainable development remains an enigma to many governments and schools. Governments, ministries of education, school districts, and educators have expressed a willingness to adopt ESD programs; however, no successful working models currently exist. Without models to adapt and adopt, governments and schools must create a process to define what education for sustainability is with respect to the local context. Such a process is challenging. It calls for a public participation process in which all of the stakeholders in a community carefully examine what they want their children to know, do, and value when they leave the formal education system. This means that the community must try to predict the environmental, economic, and social conditions of the near and distant future.

Public participation processes whereby stakeholders examine the needs and desires of a community and identify essential elements of basic and secondary education can be adapted and implemented in many types of communities. Seeking the opinions of parents and workers to shape the education of their children will be a totally new idea in some cultures. Although community consolation and other forms of public participation can be effective tools, they should be introduced slowly and in accordance with local traditions and cultures where they have not been used previously. However valuable, the community consultation process is not without pitfalls. For example, an organized, educated, and articulate few might dominate the process.

11.7. Engaging Traditional Disciplines in a Trans disciplinary Framework

ESD by nature is holistic and interdisciplinary and depends on concepts and analytical tools from a variety of disciplines. As a result, ESD is difficult to teach in traditional schools settings where studies are divided and taught in a disciplinary framework. In countries where national curriculums describe in detail the content and sequence of study in each discipline, ESD will be challenging to implement. In other countries where content is described generally, ESD will be more easily implemented, although doing so will require creative teaches who are comfortable and skilled at teaching across disciplines.

11.8. Sharing the Responsibility

Popular thinking promotes the myth that an informed society is solely the responsibility of the ministry of education. In reality, however, the ministries of environment, commerce, state, and health also have a stake in ESD, just as they have a stake in sustainable development. By combining expertise, resources, and funding from many ministries, the possibility of building a high-quality, successful education program increases. Every sector of the government that is touched by sustainable development (i.e., every ministry and department) can play a role in ESD and the reorienting process. At the UN meeting of the Commission on Sustainable Development, ministries of the environment have taken the lead in stating that education, awareness, and training are essential tools in bringing about sustainable development. Ministries of the environment need to work with both formal and non-formal sectors of the education community to implement ESD. In addition, it is absolutely essential for teachers to be involved in the process of building consensus concerning ESD.

11.9. Building Human Capacity

The successful implementation of a new educational trend will require responsible, accountable leadership and expertise in both systemic educational change and sustainable development. We must develop realistic strategies to quickly create knowledgeable and capable leadership. It is unrealistic to expect nations to retrain 59,000,000 teachers and thousands of administrators in either – or both– ESD and educational change. We must find ways, such as employing the strengths model, to use existing skills. Two models of human resources development currently exist – in-service training and preserve training. In the first, experienced professionals are provided with additional training. Then, they reshape existing programs by drawing on their new knowledge, previous expertise, understanding of national and local systems, and network of contacts. In pre-service training, concepts, principles, and methodologies are provided during initial training.

11.10. Developing Financial and Material Resources

Perhaps one of the greatest expenses of implementing ESD will come with providing appropriate basic education. Basic goals, which were established at Jontiem and reaffirmed at Dakar, include educating more children and increasing the universal average minimum of schooling to six years. Meeting these goals will require hiring many more teachers. These new teachers must be trained, and current teachers must be retrained, to reorient their curriculums to address sustainability.The good news is that many countries are spending a larger percentage of their gross national product (GNP) on education. Two-thirds of the 123 countries listed in the UNESCO World Education Report 2000 that reported public expenditures on education as a percentage of GNP in both 1990 and 1996, reported spending more in 1996 than in 1990. Although governments are prioritizing education in terms of funding, how much of this funding is going to reorient education to address sustainability? As we pointed out in the "Education: Promise and Paradox" section, simply providing more education does not reduce the threat high resource consumption poses to sustainability. In addition, many countries are evaluating new educational technologies (e.g., distance learning, computers, Internet, TV) and strategies to implement them. ESD is already woven into many of these technologies. For example, many free sources of environmental data are available on the World Wide Web as are other teaching resources such as lesion plans. Governments and school districts investing in these technologies will offset expenditures with access to free ESD information and materials.

11.11. Developing Policy

To succeed, ESD must have an authoritative impetus from national or regional governments that will drive policy development. The omission of such an impetus proved to be the downfall of the 1970s global effort to infuse environmental education into the elementary and secondary curriculums. This same fate could befall the ESD effort. The reality of any educational reform is that success depends on both "top down" and "bottom up" efforts. Administrators at the top echelons of ministries are in a position to create the policies that will make reform occur. Together, administrators, teachers, and community leaders at the local level must interpret what the policy should "look like" locally.

11.12. Developing a Creative, Innovative, and Risk-Taking Climate

In order to bring about the major changes required by ESD, we need to nurture a climate of safety. Policymakers, administrators, and teachers will need to make changes, experiment, and take risks to accomplish new educational and sustainability goals. They need to have the authority and support of the educational community to change the status quo. Teachers must feel that the administration will support their efforts if parents or vested interest groups in the community question or criticize their initiatives. We need to develop and implement policy to ensure administrators and educators at all level s have the right to introduce new or controversial topics and pedagogical methods. Of course, an overzealous few could abuse these rights; therefore, a system of checks and balances within professional guidelines and cultural context should also be in place.

Summary & Conclusion

Education is a process of providing learning experience to obtain knowledge understanding skills and awareness with desirable attitudinal changes about man's relationship with his natural and man-made surrounding which includes the relation of population, pollution, resource allocation, transportation technology and urban & rural planning to the human activities. It is a life long process and must be promoted among the society as a whole the key to development is transformation complete change. Development is a process of revealing creative potential of people. Change is not without pain or discomfort. The more the intensity of change the greater will be the pain. A part from eco degradation that has taken place owing to poverty, it may be recalled that during the British rule India's natural resources were only exploited in order to sustain industrial development. We also need transformation at the local national, regional and global levels, together with an abundant measure of economic and social transformation at the level of individuals, communities and nationalities. Transformation of individuals is very necessary because a society or government is but an extension of the individual. To successfully implement ESD, governments and schools districts must plan ahead and develop strategies to address the issues above. These issues should be addressed at every level, especially the national level, to ensure consistent implementation of ESD across the country. Purposeful deliberation and planning around these issues as well as issues particular to each region will increase the likelihood of successfully implementing ESD programs and reorienting curriculum to achieve sustainability.

References & Bibliography

McKeown, R. (2002) "Education or Sustainable Development Toolkit", retrieved 7/7/10.

Dernback, J.C. (2002) Stumbling toward sustainability. Environmental Law Institute. P. 608.

Huckle, J. and Sterling, S.R. (2006) Education for sustainability. Earthscan. P. 139.

Tilbury, D. and Wortman, D. (2004). Engaging People in Sustainability. IUCN, Gland, Switzerland.

"The UN Decade of Education for Sustainable Development 2005-2014", UNESCO. Retrieved 7/7/10.

"National Project for Excellence in Environmental Education". North American Association for Environmental Education. Retrieved 7/7/10.

"Sustainable Packaging Scorecard". Retrieved 7/7/10.

Jones, P., Selby, D., sterling, S. (2010) Sustainability Education: Perspectives and Practice Across Higher Education. Renout Publishing.

Sims, G.D. (2007) Sustainability Education : where does it belong? Minnesota State University. Li, Z., and Williams, M. (2006) Environmental and Geographical Education for Sustainability: Cultural contexts. Nova Publishers.

Lang, J. (2007) How to Succeed with Education for Sustainability. Curriculum corporation. Principles of Sustainability – University of Idaho – Washington State University 50-Part HD/Surround Sound Doculecture Open Course.

United Nations Decade of Education for Sustainable Development (EfSD)2005-2014 by North East Centre for Transformative Education and Research (aka RCE North East) Education for Sustainability at the Global Sustainability Institute.

CHAPTER: 12
ROLE OF PRADHAN MANTRI JAN DHAN YOJANA IN FINANCIAL INCLUSION: AN EVALUATION STUDY

Baljeet Jamwal

Abstract

Financial inclusion enables improved and better sustainable economic and social development of the country. It helps in the empowerment of the underprivileged, poor and women of the society with the mission of making them self-sufficient and well informed to take better financial decisions. Financial inclusion takes into account the participation of vulnerable groups such as weaker sections of the society and low income groups, based on the extent of their access to financial services such as savings and payment account, credit insurance, pensions etc. Present study is an attempt to Analyze the Respondents Opinion Regarding Benefits Available under PMJDY.

12.1. Introduction

The Pradhan Mantri Jan Dhan Yojana is an ambitious scheme that will provide a host of benefits including a bank account, insurance and a debit card for all. It is a mega financial inclusion plan under which bank accounts and RuPay debit cards with inbuilt insurance cover of Rs 1 lakh will be provided to crores of persons with no access to formal banking facilities. The ambitious scheme aims to bring poor people into the ambit of the Government's financial programme. It will cover both urban and rural areas and those who open account would get Domestic Debit Card (Ru-pay card). The long term vision of the Jan Dhan Yojana is to lay the foundation of a cashless economy and is complementary to Narendra Modi's Digital India Scheme. Aim of the Jan Dhan Yojana: The scheme intends to accomplish the objective of housing for all by providing basic banking accounts with a debit card with inbuilt accident insurance. The government aims to open as many as 1 crore bank accounts on the first day itself.

The main features of the PMJDY scheme include Rs 5,000 overdraft facility for Aadhar-linked accounts. RuPay Debit Card with inbuilt Rs 1 lakh accident insurance cover. One of the salient features of this scheme is that after remaining active for 6 months the account holder will become eligible for an overdraft of up to Rs 2,500. This will further be enhanced by the bank to Rs 5000 over time. The PMJDY has set an ambitious target of bringing in more than 7.5 crore un-banked families into India's banking system by opening more than 15 Crore bank accounts (two bank accounts per household). Pradhan Mantri Jan Dhan Yojana will be launched nationally in the capital by the Prime Minister himself. The major cities where the functions will be held on August 28 for the launch of the scheme include Dehradun, Port Blair, Guwahati, Patna, Muzaffarpur, Vizag, Panjim, Mumbai, Gandhinagar, Surat, Bharuch, Bilaspur and Raipur. As many as 76 functions will be held across the country. Besides this, over 60,000 enrolment camps in rural areas will also be set up with a view to make people aware of the importance of bank accounts. Two phases of the scheme, the first phase of the mission, starting this month, would end in August next year. Phase-1 of PMJDY begins on the August 28, 2014 and will last until August 14, 2015. The first phase will be focused on opening a bank account and providing credit facilities to those who are outside the banking system in urban and rural India. The second phase will start from 2015 till 2018. It will cover aspects such as micro insurance and pension schemes like 'Swavalamban'. Why this Yojana? "We want to integrate the poorest of the poor with bank accounts with Pradhan Mantri Jan Dhan Yojana.

Today, there are crores of families which have mobile phones but no bank accounts. We have to change this. The economic development must benefit poor and it should start from here." Under the Jan Dhan Yojana, he said, "The person who opens a bank account will get a debit card and the family will get Rs 1 lakh insurance cover. This will help the family to deal with any unforeseen eventuality.

Financial inclusion enables improved and better sustainable economic and social development of the country. It helps in the empowerment of the underprivileged, poor and women of the society with the mission of making them self-sufficient and well informed to take better financial decisions. Financial inclusion takes into account the participation of vulnerable groups such as weaker sections of the society and low income groups, based on the extent of their access to financial services such as savings and payment account, credit insurance, pensions etc. Also the objective of financial inclusion exercise is easy availability of financial services which allows maximum investment in business opportunities, education, save for retirement, insurance against risks, etc. by the rural individuals and firms.

Planning Commission (2009), financial inclusion refers to universal access to a wide range of financial services at a reasonable cost. These include not only banking products but also other financial services such as insurance and equity products. The household access to financial services includes access to contingency planning, credit and wealth creation. Access to contingency planning would help for future savings such as retirement savings, buffer savings and insurable contingencies and access to credit includes emergency loans, housing loans and consumption loans. On the other hand, access to wealth creation includes savings and investment based on household's level of financial literacy and risk perception.

12.2. Review of Literature

The achievement of objectives of the seminar, the related literature has been reviewed because no research can be completed in itself without its scientific analysis of literature. The review of concerned literature has been completed by taking the help of journals, abstracts, books, web-sites and reports etc. the number of studies related to the PMJDY have been analyzed to identify main gaps in literature.

A group of studies undertaken by **Rajnikanta (2014), Harpreet and Nain (2014), Achala and Getanjali (2015), Shanti (2015) and Bijoyata (2016),** concluded that the PMJDY was a National Mission on financial inclusion which was concentrated on individual household with an aim to provide formal financial support through the organized financial system.

12.3. Objectives of the Study

The main objectives of the study as under:
1. To Analyze the Respondents Opinion Regarding Benefits Available under PMJDY.
2. To find out the problems faced by the beneficiaries of the PMJDY and advanced suggestions overcome such problems.

12.4. Methodology adopted

In order to study the performance of PMJDY and to know the accrued benefits, a sample of 100 customers have been taken. Since the study is based on Hamirpur district of Himachal Pradesh, the sample for the study has taken from the customers who have opened their accounts under the PMJDY scheme in different branches consisting of five commercial banks and one cooperative bank operating in the district. In all, a sample of 100 customers has taken with the help of convenience sampling from the banks selected for study. While selecting the sample, an utmost care was taken that the respondents of all ages, qualifications, sex and occupation were taken into consideration and regional and geographical variations are also duly represented. Consistent with the objective of the study, different techniques like the simple percentage, mean, standard deviation, skewness, kurtosis and chi-square have been used for the analysis of the collected data.

12.5. Result and Discussion

12.5.1. Benefits Available to Account Holders under PMJDY- Interest on Deposit

Table 2 shows that there are 62 percent respondents replied 'yes' about the benefits available to account holder under PMJDY – interest on deposit, out of which, 72.7 percent respondents are qualified up to matric, 54.5 percent respondents are graduate and above and 50 percent respondents are illiterate. It shows that majority of the respondents are of the opinion that they know that account holder under PMJDY will get benefit in the form of interest on deposit amount. While, 22.7 percent respondents comes under the group of graduation and above, Nearly 18.2 percent respondents of up to matric, about 16.7 percent respondents among the illiterate did not know about the PMJDY that the benefits available to account holder under PMJDY – interest on deposit account. Almost 33.3 percent respondent's are illiterate, nearly 22.7 percent respondents come under graduation and above and 9.1 respondents under up to matric are replied don't know about it. The values of mean, skewness and kurtosis also support the above analysis.

Table 2: Benefits Available to Account Holders under PMJDY- Interest on Deposit

Education level	Responses			Total	Mean	σ	SKW	Kurtosis
	Yes	No	Do not know					
Illiterate	6 (50.0)	2 (16.7)	4 (33.3)	12 (100.0)	2.167	0.938	-0.383	-1.931
Up to Matric	32 (72.7)	8 (18.2)	4 (9.1)	44 (100.0)	2.636	0.650	-1.599	1.348
Graduation and Above	24 (54.5)	10 (22.7)	10 (22.7)	44 (100.0)	2.318	0.829	-0.668	-1.212
Total	62 (62.0)	20 (20.0)	18 (18.0)	100 (100.0)	2.440	0.608	-0.590	-0.557

Chi – Square (d.f = 4) Value = 5.847 Table Value = 9.48 P Value = .211

Source: Field Survey

Note: Figure in brackets shows percentage

The computed value of chi-square is 5.847 at and table value is 9.48 which have found less than table value therefore null hypothesis is accepted and there is found insignificant relationship at 5% level of significance. So it is concluded that there is found insignificant relationship between the education level of respondents and their awareness about PMJDY that the benefits available to account holder under PMJDY – interest on deposit account.

12.5.2. Benefits under PMJDY to Account Holders - Accidental Insurance of Rs 1 Lakh

Table 3 observed that 74 percent of respondents are aware to PMJDY, out of which, majority of respondents 81.8 percent come under the group of up to matric followed by 72.7 percent from graduation and above, 50 percent among illiterate are aware about the benefits available to account holders under PMJDY – accidental insurance of Rs.1 lakh. While 18.2 percent of respondents under graduation and above, 13.6 percent of respondents up to matric, are not aware about that benefits available to account holders under PMJDY – accidental insurance of Rs.1 lakh. Almost 50 percent of the respondents' among illiterate, 9.1 percent respondents among graduate and above, 4.5 percent respondents among up to matric are replied don't know. The mean scores of the respondents of each qualification level shows that it is above the mean standard score. The negative values of skewness also point out that the majority majority of the opinions of the respondents are highly concentrated towards the higher side on the three point scale.

Table 3
Benefits Available to Account Holders under PMJDY- Accidental Insurance of Rs 1 Lakh

Education level	Responses			Total	Mean	σ	SKW	Kurtosis
	Yes	No	Do not know					
Illiterate	6 (50.0)	0 (0.0)	6 (50.0)	12 (100.0)	2.000	1.044	0.000	-2.444
Up to Matric	36 (81.8)	6 (13.6)	2 (4.5)	44 (100.0)	2.770	5.522	-2.307	4.683
Graduation and Above	32 (72.7)	8 (18.2)	4 (9.1)	44 (100.0)	2.636	0.650	-1.599	1.348
Total	74 (74.0)	14 (14.0)	12 (12.0)	100 (100.0)	2.262	0.693	-1.557	0.918

Chi – Square (d.f = 4) Value = 20.329 Table Value = 9.48 P Value = .000
Source: Field Survey
Note: Figure in brackets shows percentage

The values of mean, skewness, standard deviation and kurtosis also support the above analysis. On application of chi-square test it has been found to be 20.329 at corresponding P-value 0.000 is less than the 0.050. It is significant at 5% level of significance. So it is concluded that there is significant relationship between the education level of respondents and their awareness about the benefits available to account holders under PMJDY – accidental insurance of Rs.1 lakh.

Suggestions

By inference from the study, the following recommendations and suggestions are made with regard to the improvement and development of the PMJDY:

- ➢ Benefits of the scheme should be explained to every person in the country. Pradhan Mantri Jan Dhan Yojana through entitles of an accidental insurance of Rs. 1 lakh, life insurance of Rs. 30000/- and overdraft limit up to Rs. 5000/- after 6 months.
- ➢ Financial literacy, awareness should be created about use of RuPay card at least once in 90 days, to get benefits of accidental insurance cover.
- ➢ Survey shows that some people still have no bank account. So there is needed to make efforts through government agencies and also through banks for 100% financial inclusion.
- ➢ BC's are not fully involved because of less compensation. Being scattered area, BC found difficult to locate customers to earn lively hood so, BCs should be suitably compensated to work whole heartedly.
- ➢ Rate of interest on deposit should be increased gradually and rate of interest on loans should be decreased gradually.
- ➢ Life insurance coverage to be implemented to all account holders irrespective of family head or earning hand of the family under the scheme. Accidental insurance coverage of 1 lakh and life insurance coverage of Rs. 30000/- should be increased, speedy settlement and less condition at the time of claim settlement be applicable.
- ➢ Majority of the respondents are of opinion that Pradhan Mantri Jan Dhan Yojana put an additional pressure on banks account of overdraft facility in the accounts especially when banks are already reeling under rising NPAs, so for availment of overdraft limit of 5000/- in the account under the scheme, seeding of Aadhaar card number and linking of DBT should be compulsory to avoid account becoming NPA and inoperative.

➤ Proper mechanism should be developed for controlling overlapping of accounts and seeding of Aadhaar card number should be compulsory in each account for availment of benefits of the scheme, which will help government for keeping proper control and for transparent data for future planning.

References

Ashish, Amrita, B.P, and A.B (2014), *"Pradhan Mantri Jan Dhan Yojana for weaker section – An evaluation"*, Shabd Brahan – International research journal of Indian languages, Vol.2, Issue-12.Oct, PP.69-70.

Brij (2014), *"Pradhan Mantri Jan-Dhan Yojana: Features Needs and Challenges"*, International Journal of Marketing, Financial Services, Vol. 3 (12), PP. 111-117.

itender and Rashmi (2015), *"Pradhan Mantri Jan Dhan Yojana (PMJDY): An innovative scheme for financial inclusion in India"*, TIJ's research journal of social science, Vol.4, Issue-9.Jan.

Kumar Divyesh, Venkatesha H R (2014), *"Financial Inclusion Using Pradhan Mantri Jan- Dhan Yojana- A Conceptual Study"*, A Peer Reviewed International Journal, Vol.1, Issue.XX.Dec, PP.38-39.

Pathak Ashish, Soni Amrita, Agrwal .B.P, Vajpayee A.B.(2014). *"Pradhan Mantri Jan Dhan Yojana for weaker section – An Evaluation,"* Shabd Braham – International Research Journal of Indian Languages, Vol.2, Issue12. Oct, PP.69-70.

CHAPTER: 13
FOREIGN DIRECT INVESTMENT IN INDIA: A STUDY OF GROWTH AND INSTABILITY IN TELECOMMUNICATIONS SECTOR

Manoj Sharma and Ritu Rana

Abstract

Foreign Direct Investment plays a significant role in the overall growth and development of the economy of a nation. It provides non- debt creating foreign resources, technology up- gradation, new employment, skill enhancement and a wide range of other benefits which are crucial for the multi- dimensional development of a country's economy. For this purpose, it becomes extremely important for a developing country to monitor the trends and the stability of the inward flows of FDI and making some analytical interpretations to further predict the future of the inflows of FDI and thus the development of that country's economy. Foreign Direct Investment (FDI) has been looked upon as a tool to transform under developed countries into advanced nations and almost every government has encouraged the expansion of FDI. When the Indian government opened up cellular telephony to private industry, several foreign investors were ready to enter India's telecom sector. Telecom is a highly Capital intensive sector. With the advent of FDI in this sector, the companies are accessing foreign capital markets and serving the hinterland by bringing affordable telecom services. Through FDI more funds are flowing into telecom sector, apart from increasing the flexibility of the operators. Increasing FDI limits in telecom sector has allowed telecom players to raise fresh capital for the growth and development of telecom infrastructure. The present paper is an attempt, 1] to study the FDI inflows in India in general and telecommunications sector in particular, and 2] to analyse the growth and instability in the FDI inflows in the Indian economy as well as in telecommunications sector. The data for the study is sourced from various fact sheets published by Department of Industrial Policy and Promotion (DIPP), Ministry of Commerce and Industry, Govt. of India. The amount is in US$ million throughout the study. The magnitude of FDI inflows is analyzed for a period of 16 years i.e. since the financial year 2000-01 till 2015-2016, whereas, to study about the FDI equity inflows in Indian telecom sector, the period of study is from the financial year 2002-03 to 2015-16 i.e. for 14 years. Time series analysis is the basic form of analysis adopted in this paper as the data collected is in the form of time series. Trend analysis (in excel) with the trend-line graphical representation, Compounded Annual Growth Rate and the Instability Index are used to analyse the time series.

13.1. Introduction

The main motive behind all the economic activities of a developing country is its multidimensional economic development and growth. FDI (Foreign Direct Investment) plays a vital role in improving the economic status of any country, especially, a developing country as it brings a number of benefits like technology transfer and up-gradation, increasing skills and standards of labour, employment opportunities, export markets exposure, quality products, increased standards of living, optimal utilization of natural and other resources and many more, apart from just providing financial assistance or generating capital sources. Investment inflows in India coming from developed economies help boost its GDP per capita and hence a robust growth rate. Foreign direct investment has been one of the major contributors in the growth of the Indian economy, and therefore, the need for higher FDI is felt across different sectors in the Indian economy. The telecommunications sector has played a crucial role in attracting FDI in India. Today, telecommunications sector is the fourth major sector attracting FDI inflows after services sector, infrastructure sector and computer software & hardware sector. As far as the share of telecommunications sector is concerned, it is accumulating an FDI equity inflow of about 7% of total inflows of FDI into India as per the information provided in the recent Fact Sheet i.e., Quarterly Fact Sheet on Foreign Direct investment (upto Sep., 2016) of Department of Industrial policy and Promotion (DIPP), Government of India, Ministry of Commerce and Industry. Telecommunications relates to many other economic and industrial sectors like entertainment, manufacture, and communication sectors (Bansal & Gupta, 2013). Mobile based Internet is a key component of Indian Internet usage, with seven out of eight users accessing internet from their mobile phones. Availability of affordable smartphones and lower rates are expected to drive growth in the Indian telecom industry (www.ibef.org). It, therefore, becomes crucial to understand the trends of foreign investment inflows in India in this competitive, ever-changing and ever-growing era and that too in the telecommunications sector, to be very particular. There is also a need to analytically evaluate these trends to monitor the overall and sector-specific growth and stability in these investment inflows so that a futuristic view can be obtained. This paper is aimed to do a descriptive analysis of Total FDI inflows and FDI Equity inflows since the beginning of the 21st century i.e. since the year 2000. The focus of the paper is also on understanding the trends of these foreign investment inflows in the telecommunications sector so that the implementation of a liberalized telecommunication investment can produce considerable benefits not only within the country's telecom sector but also for the national economy as a whole.

13.2. Objectives of the Study

This study is based on the following objectives:
1) To study the trends of FDI inflows in India
2) To analyse the growth and instability in the FDI inflows in the Indian economy
3) To study the trends of FDI equity in telecom sector in India
4) To analyse the growth and instability in the FDI equity inflows in telecom sector in Indian economy

13.3. Methodology

In this paper, the data collected to analyse the FDI inflows in India is based on secondary sources, i.e., various fact sheets published by Department of Industrial Policy and Promotion (DIPP), Ministry of Commerce and Industry, Govt. of India. The amount is in US$ million throughout the study. The magnitude of FDI inflows is analyzed for a period of 16 years i.e. since the financial year 2000-01 till 2015-2016, whereas, to study about the FDI equity inflows in Indian telecom sector, the period of study is from the financial year 2002-03 to 2015-16 i.e. for 14 years. Time series analysis is the basic form of analysis adopted in this paper as the data collected is in the form of time series. Trend analysis (in excel) with the trend-line graphical representation, Compound Growth Rate and the Instability Index are used to analyse the time series. The compound growth rates and instability indexes have been measured by using following tools and techniques.

13.3.1. Estimation of Growth Rate

Analysis of growth of FDI presents difficulties because of wide year to year fluctuations and the absence of smooth trend. One of the technique used to form judgement on the growth rates, i.e., a study of end point of the series is wrong in procedure, not only because thereby the measure of growth rate is unduly affected by the incidental or accidental circumstances of the end of the years but also because, on principle measurement of growth over period should take into account the entire series of the observations over the period. The use of linear function for estimating growth rate into compound one is considered inappropriate (Parthasarthy, 1984).

The compound growth rate will be worked out by an exponential function of the form:

$Log Y = A + BT$

Where:
  Y = FDI inflows
   T = years (time).
r = [(antilog B-1) × 100] = compound growth rate (in per cent)

13.3.2. Measuring Instability

When FDI shows irregular changes during a year (apart from seasonal variations) or over a period of years, that are considered as a form of economic instability. Issues relating to fluctuations in foreign investment inflows are important for several reasons. There are various methods used to measure the extent of instability. The most common of these is to fit a trend line to the raw data, obtain the residuals, and then derive either the 'standard deviation' or the 'root mean square error' of these residuals. The problem with such measure is that they are scale dependent and hence cannot readily be used for cross comparisons (Sen, 1989). Some different measures result in different numerical values for the same data series; however, there is disagreement in the literature not only on the proper index that should be used to measure instability but also on whether the selection of the certain index makes any difference to the results of the analysis. As a measure of instability, this analysis utilizes an exponential index (IXEXP). IXEXP are defined as the coefficient of "unexplained" variations observed from the estimated time trend. The equation of the exponential trend is written as:

$$X_t = a + eb_t + u_t$$

$$\text{Log}(X_t) = \log a + b_t + \log u_t \quad (t = 1, 2, \text{-------}, n)$$

Where (X_t) is the FDI inflows in India in time 't', 't' represents time and 'u' is the disturbance term, Ordinary Least Square is then used to estimate the equations. IXEXP measures deviations from constant growth rate trend line.

$$\text{IXEXP} = \frac{100}{\overline{X}} \left[\frac{\sum_{t=1}^{n}\left(X_t - \hat{a}e^{\hat{b}_t}\right)^2}{n-2} \right]^{\frac{1}{2}}$$

$\overline{X}$ being the mean of X_i.

13.4. FDI in India

The importance of FDI in Indian economy has grown considerably over the past decade. Flows of FDI have witnessed manifold growth since the liberalisation period. According to

Akhtar (2013), after mid 1990 the political disturbances along with other economic problems gave rise to severe financial crisis in the Indian economy. The high rate of inflation, fiscal deficit and political instability downgraded the international credit of the country. Compared to most industrialising economies, India followed a fairly restrictive foreign private investment policy until 1991 - relying more on bilateral and multilateral loans with long maturities (Nagaraj, 2003). As per Nagaraj (2003), all this changed since 1991 as foreign investment was now seen as a source of scarce capital, technology and managerial skills that were considered necessary in an open, competitive, world economy. India sought to consciously 'benchmark' its policies against those of the rapidly growing south-east Asian economies to attract a greater share of the world's FDI inflows. This led to attract foreign investors to enter Indian markets and to give and take the benefits of flows of not just finances but also the technologies, skills, trainings, quality products etc. To understand how these changes in foreign investment policy have influenced the Indian economy, some quantitative information is needed on the inflow of foreign investments in India. For this purpose, the quantitative data has been collected from the different fact sheets of Department of Industrial Policy and Promotion, Ministry of Commerce and Industry, Government of India.

13.5. Trends of FDI Inflows in India since 2000-01

The amounts of total FDI inflows in India (as per International Best Practices) since the year 2000 are given in Annexure 1. The amounts given show how year by year the inflows of foreign investments have grown significantly to a lot more than 10 times of the amount of inflows in the year 2000-01 i.e., from the amount of 4029 million USD in the financial year 2000-01 to 55457 million USD in 2015-16. The data also depicts that the total FDI inflows in India have witnessed several ups and downs.

Similarly, the amounts of FDI equity inflows in India (as per DIPP's FDI Data Base) since the year 2000 are given in Annexure 2. These amounts depict that the share of FDI equity inflows in the total FDI inflows has also grown significantly each year since the year 2000-01, except for a few years, i.e., from the amount of 2463 million USD in the financial year 2000-01 to 40001 million USD in

2015-16. Thus, FDI equity inflows in India also have witnessed several ups and downs.

A graphical representation of the amount of Total FDI inflows and the amount of FDI Equity inflows since the year 2000-01 till 2015-16 and the trend line that represents the trend of FDI equity inflows in India since 2000-01 is shown in Fig.1. The data was plotted on the graph and a trend line was drawn to study the trend of FDI equity inflows since the financial year 2000-01 till 2015-16. The trend line in the figure is moving upwards to the right representing an upward trend in the equity inflows of FDI in India since the year 2000-01 till 2015-16. Although the trend line is moving with a slow pace but it depicts that the FDI equity inflows have an increasing trend over the past 16 years i.e., since 2000-01 till 2015-16.

Also the trends in total FDI inflows and FDI equity inflows since the year 2000-01 till 2015-16 are shown separately with the help of graphical representation in Annexure 5. This graphical representation is done to see both the trends in inflows separately.

Figure 1: Trend of FDI inflows in India: Total FDI vs. FDI Equity

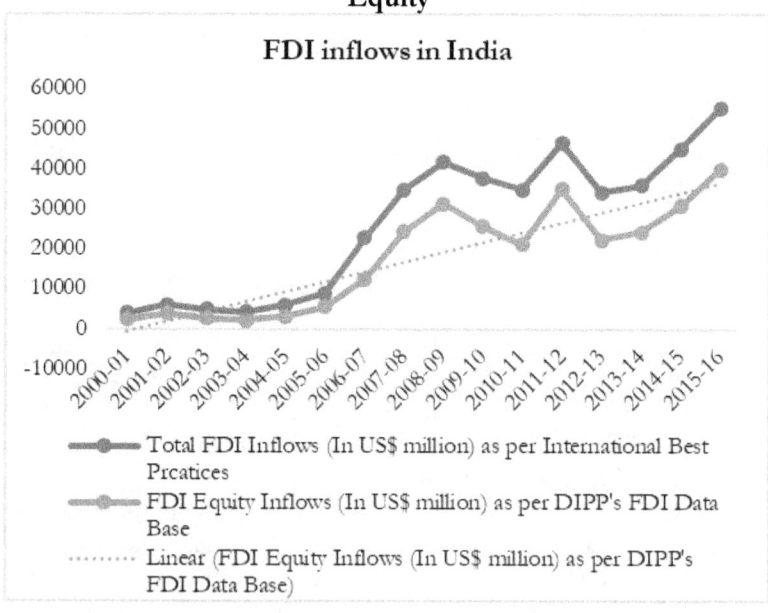

The percentage share of equity inflows in total FDI inflows

since the year 2000-01 till 2015-16 was also calculated to get a clear picture of the share of fresh foreign investments in total FDI each year. Annexure 3 shows the calculated percentage share of FDI equity inflows in total FDI inflows since 2000-01 till 2015-16, which shows it has tremendously increased cumulatively.

13.6. Growth and Instability in FDI Inflows in India

For analytical purposes and to understand the Compounded Annual Growth Rate as well as the Instability in the inflows of foreign investments in India since the year 2000, the whole data on Total FDI inflows and FDI equity inflows was divided into 2 equal periods of 8 years each i.e., Period I, starting from the financial year 2000-01 to 2007-08 and Period II, starting from the year 2008-09 till 2015-16. Also, the growth rate and instability in the FDI inflows for Period III i.e., for the entire period of 16 years starting from the financial year 2000-01 to 2015-16 was calculated to see the overall growth and instability in these inflows. The growth rate and the instability index in the Total FDI inflows and FDI Equity Inflows for the said periods is given below in Table 4 and Table 5, respectively.

The tables 1 and 2 clearly state that the growth rate in the FDI inflows, either total FDI or FDI equity, was more during Period I as compared to Period II. The growth rate of total FDI inflows during Period I was 32.66, which is much higher than the growth rate of 3.21 during Period II. Similarly, the growth rate of FDI equity inflows during Period I was 33.47, which is much higher than the growth rate of 3.05 during Period II. Thus, it becomes clear that India has witnessed a very high growth rate in the initial years of 21st century i.e., from 2000-01 to 2007-08 as compared to the period after that till 2015-16.

But, at the same time, there had been a very high instability in the total FDI inflows during Period I, i.e. 4.79 as compared to the instability index of Period II i.e., 1.52. Also, the instability index for FDI equity inflows show that these inflows were highly unstable during Period I than that during Period II.

If we look at the overall growth and instability in the total FDI inflows and FDI equity inflows during these 16 years i.e., during Period III, we may observe that there had been a slow growth in the inflows i.e., 20.77 and 22.71, respectively. But at the same time the instability index shows that these inflows had been highly unstable over these years as the instability index during Period III for total FDI inflows was 4.48 and for FDI equity inflows was 5.42. It is definitely an unacceptable situation for a developing nation like India as the growth with high instability does not guarantee a nation of its future growth with full assurance.

Table 1: Growth and Instability of Total FDI Inflows

	Period I	Period II	Period III
Growth	32.66	3.21	20.77
Instability	4.79	1.52	4.48

Table 2: Growth and Instability of FDI Equity Inflows

	Period I	Period II	Period III
Growth	33.47	3.05	22.71
Instability	6.22	2.22	5.42

13.7. Trends of FDI in Indian Telecommunications Sector

Earlier the amount of FDI in India was low conforming to some selected sectors, but now the inflow of FDI has grown tremendously and almost in all the sectors of the economy (Akhtar, 2013). The Indian Telecom Sector has emerged as one of the critical components of economic growth required for overall socio-economic development of the country as there is a positive correlation between the penetration of mobile services and internet on the growth of GDP of a country (Baruah & Baruah, 2014). Indian telecom sector, nowadays, is an attracting marketplace for foreign investments as telecom subscriber base in India has expanded substantially (www.ibef.org) and:

- India is currently the second-largest telecommunication market and has the third highest number of internet users in the world
- India's telephone subscriber base expanded at a CAGR of 19.96 per cent, reaching 1058.86 million during FY07–16
- In March 2016, total telephone subscription stood at 1,058.86 million, while tele-density was at 83.36 percent

The amount of FDI equity inflows in India since the year 2002-03 till 2015-16 is given in Table 6 (Annexure 4). The data on FDI inflows in Indian telecom sector shows that this sector has really emerged as one of the top most choice for investment by foreign investors with an FDI of 223 USD million in 2002-03 to 1324 USD million in 2015-16.

Fig. 2 is the graphical representation of FDI equity inflows particularly in the telecom sector in India since 2002-03 till 2015-16. A trend line was also generated to see the trends in the foreign investments inflows in the telecom sector of India. This trend line reveals that Indian telecom sector has witnessed an extreme and substantially high growth since these past years and has really emerged as one of the most favourite and attractive sector to foreign investors.

13.8. Growth and Instability in FDI Inflows in Indian Telecom Sector

To analyse the growth and instability in the FDI equity inflows in Indian telecom sector, the available time series data was, again, divided into two equal periods i.e., Period I and Period II, of 7 years each. Thus, period I starts from the financial year 2002-03 till 2008-09 and Period II starts from the year 2009-10 to 2015-16. Similarly, the overall growth and instability over these past 14 years in the FDI equity inflows in Indian telecom sector was calculated for the whole period from the year 2002-03 till 2015-16 as Period III. Table 7 provides the growth rates and instability indexes of FDI inflows in Indian telecom sector for the said 3 periods.

Figure 2: Trend of FDI Equity Inflows in Indian Telecommunications Sector

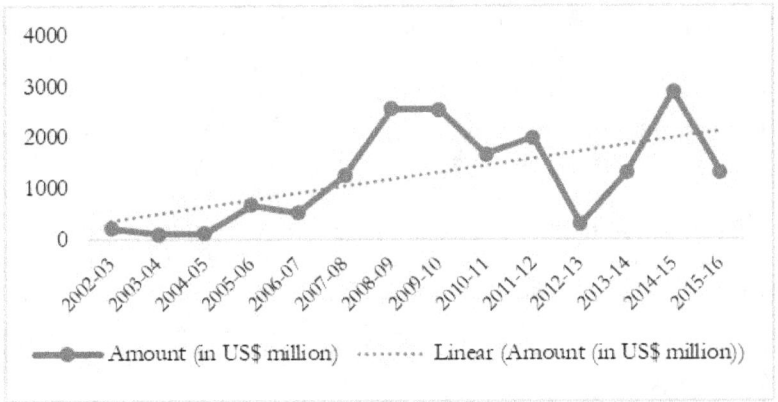

Table 3: Growth and Instability of FDI Equity Inflows in Indian Telecom Sector

	Period I	Period II	Period III
Growth	9.16	-4.5	19.56
Instability	1.14	11.2	12.94

As per the table, the growth in the FDI inflows in Indian telecom sector was higher during Period I as compared to the growth during Period II. The growth during Period I was 9.16 which is much higher than that during Period II which was -4.5. A negative sign of the growth rate in Period II indicates a decline in the rate of inflows of foreign investment in this sector during said years. At the same time, the instability indexes show that there had been a smaller instability in these inflows during Period I (1.14) as compared to Period II (11.2) which again is an indication that Period II encountered a low rate of growth and stability as compared to Period I.

If we look at the overall growth in FDI equity inflows in Indian telecom sector since 2002-03 till 2015-16, there had been a moderate growth in these inflows i.e. 19.56, but the instability of 12.94 was very high which, again, is highly unacceptable for Indian economy which is still in its developing phase. So, India needs a trend in the FDI inflows which can assure it of a sustainable growth rate with lower instability.

Conclusion and Suggestions

The analyses and discussions made above provide a view of all the time series data of FDI inflows in India since the financial year 2000-01 till the year 2015-16. These analysis and interpretations show that India has witnessed a higher rate of growth in the FDI inflows, may it be total FDI inflows or FDI equity inflows, during the initial years of the 21st century (i.e., Period I), or we can say, between the years 2000-01 and 2007-08 as compared to the years after that (i.e., Period II), or we can say, between the years 2008-09 and 2015-16. Also, the overall growth during these 16 years comes to be moderate and not much high. At the same time, the instability indexes show that there had been a high rate of instability in these inflows, may it be Periods I, II or III. Similar is the case with the FDI inflows in the Indian telecom sector.

Thus, India needs to focus on an investment policy that may attract foreign investors in such a way that can help grow its foreign investments on a steady basis with lower instability indexes. The foreign investment policy of India should be such that helps grow these inflows year by year and with lesser unstable chances so that India, being a developing country, can assure of a growing economy in future too.

References

Akhtar, G. (2013). Inflows of FDI in India: Pre and Post Reform Period. *International Journal of Humanities and Social Science Invention*, Vol. 2 Issue 2, pp. 1-11.

Bansal, Dr. S., & Gupta, Dr. S. K. (2013). FDI's in India- A Study of Telecommunication Industry. *International Journal of Advanced Research in Management and Social Sciences*, Vol. 2 Issue 3, pp. 189-201.

3] Baruah, Dr. P., & Baruah, R. (2014). Telecom Sector in India: Past, Present and Future. *International Journal of Humanities and Social Science Studies*, Vol. 1 Issue 3, pp. 147-156.

Nagaraj, R. (2003). Foreign Direct Investment in India in the 1990s: Trends and Issues. *Economic and Political Weekly*, Vol. 38 Issue 17, pp. 1701-1712.

Parthasarthy, G. (1984). Growth Rates and Fluctuations of Agriculture Production: A District-wise Analysis in Andhra Pradesh. *Economic and Political Weekly*, Vol. 19 Issue 26, p. A-74.

Sen, P. (1989). Growth and Instability of Indian Exports to the USSR. *Economic and Political Weekly*, Vol. 24 Issue 13, p. 688.

www.ibef.org

www.dipp.nic.in

Annexure: 1

Total FDI Inflows in India

Year	Total FDI Inflows in India (in US$ million)
2000-01	4029
2001-02	6130
2002-03	5035
2003-04	4322
2004-05	6051
2005-06	8961
2006-07	22826
2007-08	34843
2008-09	41873
2009-10	37745
2010-11	34847
2011-12	46556
2012-13	34298
2013-14	36046
2014-15	45148
2015-16	55457

Note: As per International Best Practices
Source: Quarterly fact sheet on foreign direct investment (FDI) from April, 2000 to March, 2016, http://dipp.nic.in/English/Publications/FDI_Statistics/2016/FDI_FactSheet_JanuaryFebruaryMarch2016.pdf

Annexure: 2

FDI Equity Inflows in India

Year	FDI Equity Inflows in India (in US$ million)
2000-01	2463
2001-02	4065
2002-03	2705
2003-04	2188
2004-05	3219
2005-06	5540
2006-07	12492
2007-08	24575
2008-09	31396
2009-10	25834
2010-11	21383
2011-12	35121
2012-13	22423
2013-14	24299
2014-15	30931
2015-16	40001

Note: As per DIPP's FDI Data Base
Source: Quarterly fact sheet on foreign direct investment (FDI) from April, 2000 to March, 2016
http://dipp.nic.in/English/Publications/FDI_Statistics/2016/FDI_FactSheet_JanuaryFebruaryMarch2016.pdf

Annexure: 3

Percentage Share of Equity Inflows in Total FDI Inflows

Year	Percentage Share of Equity Inflows in Total FDI Inflows
2000-01	61.13
2001-02	66.31
2002-03	53.72
2003-04	50.62
2004-05	53.20
2005-06	61.82
2006-07	54.73
2007-08	70.53
2008-09	74.98
2009-10	68.44
2010-11	61.36
2011-12	75.44
2012-13	65.38
2013-14	67.41
2014-15	68.51
2015-16	72.13

Annexure: 4

FDI Equity Inflows in Indian Telecommunications Sector

Year	Amount (in US$ million)
2002-03	223
2003-04	116
2004-05	129
2005-06	680
2006-07	521
2007-08	1261
2008-09	2558
2009-10	2554
2010-11	1665
2011-12	1997
2012-13	304
2013-14	1307
2014-15	2895
2015-16	1324

Annexure: 5

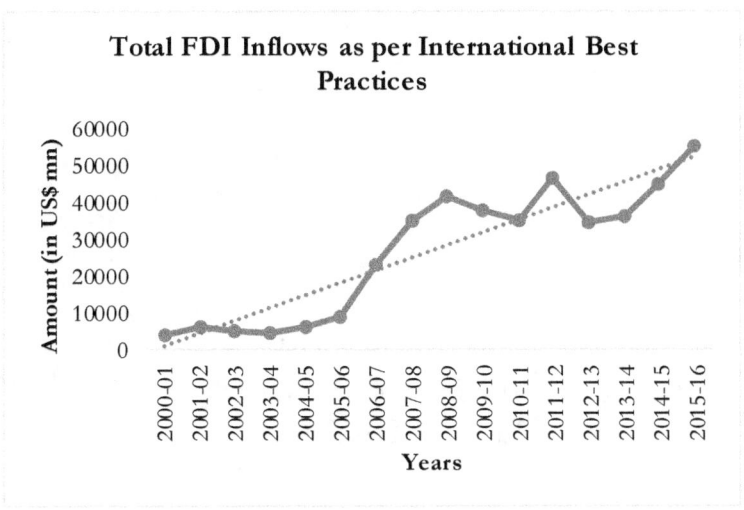

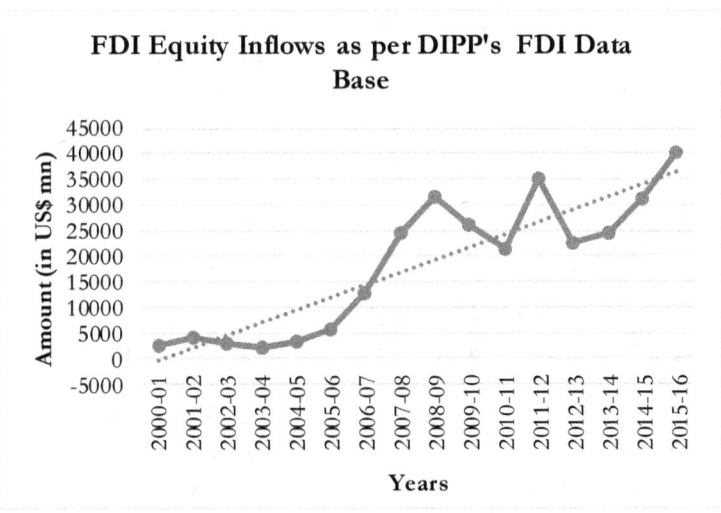

CHAPTER: 14
MICROFINANCE IN INDIA: A SUCCINCT LITERATURE REVIEW

Aman Sharma

Abstract

Microfinance has turned out to be a compelling and effective instrument for destitution diminishment. From now onwards, it is considered as an innovative idea that has enormous future implications. Around the globe, the area of microfinance has evidenced to be an effective plan of action that settles various difficulties confronted by the financial services. In Indian scenario, this eventually brightens the role of a microfinance programme in alleviating poverty and exhibits inquisitive probes like what constitutes empowerment and how best it can be achieved. The primary objective of the study is to discuss what has happened to the deprived section of the society in India during the last two decades. Many micro, as well as macro-level studies, have been undertaken so far by various scholars, institutions, non-government organisations (NGOs) and microfinance institutions (MFIs) that highlight its strengths and weaknesses at national and regional levels. The present research has been prepared with the help of extensive literature available on Indian microfinance that discloses the contemporary debates at the theoretical level. The study has employed content analysis for empirical examination. The trends of microfinance programme remained positive for achieving desired results since its inception and it has impacted all the sections of the society. Lastly, it can be inferred that the long-run restructuring process of the micro-financial system has resulted in nationwide alleviation of poverty, augmented empowerment and initiation of financial inclusion, which further leads to developmental consequences.

14.1. Introduction

Microfinance as a deliberated tool for poverty alleviation has become progressively prevalent in all areas for enabling the poor to raise their income levels and improve living standards. During the last two decades, generous work has been done in developing and experimenting with different ideas and approaches to reach financial services to the poor.

Microfinance in the world has revealed an efficacious development model to resolve several challenges confronted by financial services to deliver services to the low-income population. Around the world, it has shown to be positively correlated with reducing poverty and improving welfare by allowing the rural people to increase their sources of income **(Gemalto, 2008)**. Microfinance is budding as a powerful technique for poverty alleviation around the globe. In India, microfinance prospect is dominated by self-help group – bank linkage programme (SBLP), aimed at providing a cost-effective mechanism for delivering financial services to the 'unreached poor'. Based on the idea of peer pressure and group savings as collateral substitute, the SHG programme has been successful in not only designing financial products meeting atypical needs of the rural poor, but also in strengthening collective self-help capacities of the poor at the local level, leading to their empowerment **(Krishnamurthy & Ratnaparkhi, 2002)**.

Simultaneously, women empowerment, as a basic parameter in measuring social development index, is gaining broader interests among economies today. Numerous studies at micro and macro levels, both in developed and developing nations, bear witness to this.

14.1.1. The Background of Microfinance

The word microfinance is relatively a new term in the field of development, first coming to eminence in the 1970s. The concept is, however, not new – more like "*old wine in a new bottle.*" It is a successful model that developed gradually over a period of time. It is a product of a trial and error approach adopted and nurtured centuries ago. Informal credit and saving institutions for the poor have been, around for decades, providing for the clients who were traditionally neglected by the formal financial system.

The credit for identifying the prospective benefits of microfinance and the subsequent popularization of the same goes to Prof. Muhammad Yunus who launched an Action Research Project known as "*Grameen* Bank" in Bangladesh to examine the possibility of designing a credit delivery system to provide banking services to the rural poor in 1976. His efforts established that poor are not only bankable but are also a profitable business and the project was formally recognized as a bank through an ordinance issued by the Government in 1983. The focus was on the delivery of credit and mobilize the savings to poor, especially women.

Microfinance in India can trace its geneses back to the early 1970s when the Self Employed Women's Association (SEWA) formed an urban cooperative bank, called the Shri Mahila SEWA Sahakari Bank. The bank was formed to provide banking services to poor women employed in the unorganized sector in Ahmedabad city of the Gujarat state.

The microfinance sector went on to grow in the 1980s around the concept of SHGs that provided their clients with much-needed savings and credit services. From modest starts, the sector has grown significantly over the years to become a multi-billion worth industry with bigger bodies such as the Small Industries Development Bank of India (SIDBI) and the National Bank for Agriculture and Rural Development (NABARD) devoting substantial financial resources to microfinance. At present, the top five private sector MFIs have reached more than 20 million clients in nearly every state in India and many Indian MFIs have been recognized as global leaders in the industry **(Legatum Ventures, 2011).**

The foremost apprehension about development minded MFIs, however, was that many of them did not attach importance to their financial soundness and sustainability within a reasonable timeperiod and thus became subsidy dependent. This made the continuous funding very difficult for donors and funders. Thus, in the 1990s, the emphasis was on ensuring that MFIs were financially sound. There was little hope for reaching the large numbers of poor households without self-sufficient financial institutions **(Nair & Tankha, 2015)**.

14.1.2. The Concept of Microfinance

Often, the term microfinance is restricted to the narrow definition of 'microcredit for microenterprise'. However, both in theory and in practice, microfinance includes a wider range of financial services that target low-income clients, particularly women. Broadly, microfinance refers to permanent access to a range of high quality and affordable financial services such as savings, credit, insurance, remittances, and payments, and others by low-income households.

The term microfinance, according to **Ledgerwood (1999)** refers to *"the provision of financial services to low-income clients, including the self-employed. Financial services generally include savings and credit; however, some microfinance organizations also provide insurance and payment services"*. The Task Force on Supportive Policy and Regulatory Framework for Micro Finance in India by **NABARD (1998)** defines microfinance as *"provision of thrift, credit and other financial services and products of very small amounts to the poor in rural, semi-urban or urban areas for enabling them to raise their income levels and improve living standards"*.

While there are many definitions of microfinance, but is generally taken to refer to the provision of financial services, primarily savings and credit but also covers other financial services like insurance, leasing, money transfers, etc. to poor and low-income households that do not have access to formal financial institutions.

14.1.3. The Core of Microfinance Ecosystem

Ledgerwood *et al.* (2013) explain that the heart of the market systems approach is to understand the demand side and support customer-focused development and innovation driving the supply side. The key players in the core of the market are clients and financial service providers, connected to each other by-products.

14.1.4. Demand Side: The Clients

The demand or need for microfinance comes from the

disadvantaged sections of the society, who are without access to services of formal sector financial intermediaries and are typically excluded from the formal banking system for lack of collaterals. In short, they are the poor and poorest of the poor. Poor households are in dire need of financial tools to improve their productivity and secure the best possible consumption and investment choices, all the while managing potential or existing risks.

The effective financial services for the poor should entail mechanisms to turn savings into lump sums for a wide variety of uses. There has been a growing consensus among microfinance practitioners that, in addition to credit, the poor need an entire range of financial services including savings, insurance, and fund transfers **(Rutherford, 1999)**.

14.1.5. Supply Side: The Providers

There are several Microfinance Institutions (MFI), Non-Governmental Organizations (NGOs), Self-help Groups (SHGs), Banks and other institutions, which are actively engaged in microfinancing activities with innovative methods **(Khandelwal, 2007)**.

While most of the first microfinance institutions were established as NGOs, the sector has evolved to include many types of providers. Specialized commercial banks providing a range of financial services have proven that the poor are bankable, while member-based community groups have shown that financial services can be provided directly by the community on a sustainable basis. While financial service providers are often characterized as formal, semi-formal, or informal, traditionally referring to their regulatory status, they can be classified as either community-based (generally informal with no legal status) or institutional (generally more formal and in some cases regulated).

The MFIs have started to move beyond microcredit, micro-enterprise loans, and savings products to insurance, housing, infrastructure and micro-leasing loans. The demand is high for finance for purchase of land, infrastructure, and housing loan finance for shelter-related investments that are rarely made available for the poor households from the formal commercial sector (Mitlin, 2003).

14.2. Methodology

The study aims at establishing a theoretical and methodological framework for the concept of microfinance. The theoretical arguments give an idea about the research conducted in the past in the field of microfinance in India. Secondary data has been collected from various sources including journals, magazines, books, internet sources, official reports, etc. Content analysis has been applied for a comprehensive exploration of the past research from scholarly papers/articles, which includes the current knowledge including substantive findings as well as theoretical and methodological contributions to the field of microfinance in India. Collected data has been analysed, synthesized and interpreted with a focus to derive important conclusions.

14.3. Discussion

The basic idea of microfinance is to provide credit to the poor who otherwise would not have an access to financial services. Microfinance programme extends small loans to the very poor for self-employment projects that generate income and allows them to take care of themselves and their families. This programme is well received in many developing countries. Since conceptualization and initiation by Prof. Mohammed Yunus, microfinance and its attendant microcredit have come a long way and financial inclusion and microfinance are widely discussed and researched topics today. As such, there is no dearth of literature related to microfinance and a review of earlier studies is essential for new and underdeveloped areas to be identified and examined.

A comprehensive literature review has been done that covers most of the perspectives of Indian microfinance sector since its inception. The reviewed literature shows a mix of positive results with some negative impacts of microfinance programme in India. The contemporary study starts with a study of **Puhazhendhi & Satyasai (2000)** and ends with the study of **Baland et al. (2017)**. The reviewed literature has been presented in chronological order for a few, yet important, studies that covers the comprehensive literature on Indian microfinance for a period of two decades up until the present time.

17.3.1. Analysis & Synthesis

The literature has been analysed extensively, and further, synthesized in terms of key issues/findings/results. The briefly analysed literature on microfinance in India has been presented as follows:

Table 1: Review of Literature

Sr. No.	Year	Author(s)	Key Issues / Findings / Results
1	2000	Puhazhendhi & Satyasai	*Impact of Microfinance in Post-SHG situation.* • Self-help group - bank linkage programme (SBLP) was instrumental in improving economic and social conditions of beneficiary households • Average annual income increased • Employment days per household increased • Reduction in number of families living below poverty line was observed • Social empowerment of SHG members, in terms of self-confidence, decision-making, better communication, etc., improved significantly
2	2001	Singh	*Impact of Microfinance in Post-SHG situation.* • Simple & quick credit delivery with lower interest rates of SHGs replaced the money-lenders • Loans taken were used mainly for income generating purposes • Increased average value of assets and the annual income per household was noted • Compulsory savings were initiated, even by cutting necessary expenditures • Very high recovery rate, between 95 to 100 percent, was recorded

3	2002 Harper	***Comparison between SHG and Grameen Bank Mechanisms.***
		• Both the systems are best suited to their specific environments:
		  – SHG-Bank Linkage Mechanism to Indian context
		  – *Grameen* Banking Mechanism to Bangladesh
		• SHGs were less likely to include the poor than *Grameen* Bank groups but neither mechanism actually reached the poorest
		• SHG members were free to manage the group's financial affairs
		• Grameen groups were better protected against internal and external threats

4	2002 Kropp & Suran	***Performance of SHG-Bank Linkage Programme (SBLP).*** • Supply-side multiple initiatives led by capacity building programmes have made tremendous inroads into conventional 'banker mindsets' • Represents new dimension of the quality portfolio with very low risks and with a marginal increase in operating costs • First step towards feminization of (micro) banking portfolio of Indian banks • Stimulating self-help among poor sparks off entrepreneurial enthusiasm and risk mitigation mechanisms in low-income households • Helps in overcoming the poverty and addresses crucial social issues

5	2002 Puhazhendhi &	***Comparison of New & Older SHGs.***
		• Members of the older groups were more socioeconomically benefited
		• In Post-SHG situation:
		  – most of the sample households registered a rise in annual income and asset ownership
		  – bank loans were largely used for income

#	Year	Author	Content
			generating purposes − estimated employment days per household increased − higher activity & percentage share for non-farm activities followed by off-farm activities and farm activities − improvement in social empowerment of group members
6	2004	Singh	***Role of Microfinance in Development.*** • Microfinance programme was playing an important role in the process of development • However, − government-implemented rural development programmes have failed because they were centrally invented and politically motivated − microfinance showed diversified growth and a multiplicity of impacts in its initial age
7	2005	Basu & Srivastava	***Issues of Microfinance in Rural Economy.*** • Rural banks primarily serve the richer rural borrowers while rural poor faced severe difficulties in accessing savings and credit from the formal sector • Marginal/landless farmers had a bank account but no access to credit from a formal source • Informal loans were availed largely to meet familial emergencies and social expenditures • Poorest borrowers availed loans for consumption • Poor borrowers often lack technical/business skills and market information to make their businesses viable • Transaction costs of rural loans were higher due to small loan amounts

8	2007 Kumar & Sharma	***Performance of Self-Help Group – Bank Linkage Programme (SBLP).***
		• The number of SHGs linked with banks got increased
		• Share of all states in total disbursements remained stagnant
		• Two Northern states, namely Himachal Pradesh and Uttaranchal, accounted for the largest share of SHGs linked to banks and the highest loan disbursements
		• Within the North-Eastern Region, Assam dominated microfinance activities and credit per SHG
		• Bank linked groups were more active in the districts with low poverty in Himachal Pradesh
		• It was found out that there was need:
		   – to make microfinancing operations broad-based for all states
		   – to strengthen bank linkage programme in districts with relatively high levels of poverty

9	2007 Sarangi	***Comparison of Participant & Non-participant Households in Microfinance Programme.***
		• Significant positive effect on income & consumption of the participant households revealed that:
		   – income of the households, reporting self-employment in off-farm activities, was much higher for the participant households
		   – indicators of consumption items showed high average values for the participant households
		• Without other corroborative mechanisms, credit was not a plausible poverty alleviation instrument

			• Location factors contribute to the creation of opportunities for diversification of economic portfolio & employment choices • Exclusion of very poor households from participation in the group-based credit programme • Increase in the share of off-farm earnings was directly proportional to the size of landholding • Among participants, gains were mostly observed for the better-off

10	2007	Swain	***Differences between the SHG Participants and the Control Group.***
			• SHG participants showed:
			   – better levels of mobility, confidence, exposure and communication skills
			   – increased self-confidence was reported by participants as compared to control households
			   – greater involvement of SHG participants in decision-making
			• Small increase in family violence was observed in participant households

11	2008	Karmakar	***Impact of SHG-based microfinance nurtured and aided by NGOs.***
			• NGOs aided SHGs:
			   – became an accepted part of the rural finance
			   – lending to groups of poor women without collateral
			   – an important alternative to traditional lending
			• Government and NABARD have emphasized the need of working with NGOs and SHGs
			• Microfinance was too small to create a massive impact on poverty alleviation

12	2008 Kumar et al.	***Impact of Microfinance.*** • Microfinance did make a significant 'first-round impact' on income, employment, and poverty of member households • Credit alone is enough to successfully move rural households out of poverty • Structural constraints needed redressal on priority to make microfinance an effective instrument to combat unemployment and poverty
13	2008 Rangarajan Committee	***Comments on Microfinance Programme.*** • Recommendations focus on the need to modify credit delivery system of the banks and other related institutions • Banks and other financial institutions encouraged to make some efforts on their own to improve the absorptive capacity of clients • Governments actions at various levels needed to enhance the earning capacity of the poorer sections of society

14	2009
	Venkataramany & Bhasin
		The success of linkage between Commercial Banks and SHGs.
		• Public Sector Banks and Regional Rural Banks offer financial services to nearly 80 percent and credit facilities to nearly 90 percent SHGs
		• Outstanding loan of an individual member of an SHG was 200 times lower than average loan per group
		• Out of four million savings accounts opened for SHGs by the Commercial Banks:
		  – only about 2.9 million had obtained credit from the banks
		  – 85 percent of savings accounts opened were exclusively by women SHGs.

15	Samapti 2010	***Results of SHG Membership through Microfinance Programme.***
		• Members experienced a higher level of independence in economic decision-making
		• Overall development of the socio-economic status of the members documented
		• Increased
		  – members' understanding towards contemporary social issues was established
		  – participation of SHG members in the local political process was also recorded

16	Parida & Sinha 2010	***Sustainability of SHGs.*** • Since income-generating activities and other characteristics varied with the gender composition of SHGs, their performance and sustainability also differ • Performance analysis revealed that all-female SHGs performed best • Only all-female SHGs were sustainable

17	Maurya 2011	***Microfinance through Financial Inclusion.***
		• Microfinance is a powerful tool to:
		  –remedy the poverty
		  –achieve women's empowerment through access to financial services
		• The opening of no-frills accounts would ensure the safety of savings
		• Access to affordable credit would encourage the individual to access different financial products and services
		• Financial inclusion approach needs to:
		  –be comprehensive and holistic
		  –adopt a collaborative strategy to ensure its success

18	2011 Rizvi & Rizvi	**Need to Strengthen the Microfinance Institutions.** • Social impact was not assessed by MFIs due to difficulty and cost considerations • MFIs need to be brought to par with NBFC • RBIs regulatory environment regarded unfavourable for the growth and proliferation of microfinance • Mere one-fifth of the country's poor reached despite being one the largest emerging markets in microfinance • There is imperative need: −to work out efficient mechanisms involving external entities to cater the under-serviced areas and rural poor −to redefine activities financed by microfinance to qualify as 'micro'
19	2012 Nishanka & Subudhi	**Performance of Microfinance Programme.** • Banks treat microfinance as a general credit on the basis of costs of borrowing without the cooperation and coordination of officials • India is the best performing microfinance country • There is a need to give equal importance to non-monetary issues recognized • Tribal Bank was suggested as the best option for tribal areas throughout India
20	2013 Choudhary	**Issues and Needs of Tribal Microfinance.** • The issue of indebtedness was major; as tribal population largely depends on friends, relatives and local informal source of money lending • Women's empowerment is possible through microfinance by constituting SHGs • MFIs must link employees' incentives to profit and enhancement in the number of groups per square kilometre must be attempted

			• Positive changes were claimed in economic empowerment, reduction of poverty and social empowerment of beneficiary households • NGOs should act as a facilitator and motivator to microfinance • Microfinance acts as a catalyst in the livelihood diversification among the tribal
21	2013	Wagh	***The pattern of Growth of Microfinance.*** • SHGs had savings accounts with private and cooperative banks • NABARD and SIDBI use SHG-Bank Linkage Programme for women's empowerment • Loan repayments were very slow and it was suggested that such loans should be given special consideration and special lending rates
22	2014	Bhattacharjee	***Sustainability of Microfinance Industry.*** • Heavy amounts borrowed as a loan from the informal sector for meeting requirements • Borrowers habitually parked their investable surplus funds in the unorganized sectors with the expectation of earning more profit within a short period • Most unorganized operators are devious and try to grab investible surplus by providing various schemes • Financial literacy and financial awareness need to be promoted with GoI and RBI taking the lead
23	2014	Rather & Lone	***Financial Inclusion and Tribal Microfinance.*** • Institutions interested in financial inclusion have made significant progress • Despite large rapid growth and effectiveness of microfinance institutions, there were still large tribal areas where microfinance was still absent

			• Only those poor, who had access to formal sources of finance in these areas, were SHG members • Microfinance can contribute to solving the problem of inadequate housing and urban services • MFIs, NGOs and Post Offices, by performing the role of Business Facilitators and Correspondents, could make banks reach the previously excluded groups

24	2015	Pathrose et al.	**Impact of Microfinance on Income, Savings and Employment.**
			• The impact on the income, saving and employment was hopeful
			• The factors impeding the use of financial services were identified
			• Microfinance:
			  – acts as a catalyst in the livelihood diversification among the tribal
			  – promotes women's empowerment through microfinance by forming SHGs
			  – must link the employees' incentives to profits to enhance the number of groups

25	2016	Demont	**Impact of Microfinance Institutions.**
			• Entry of a microfinance sector in local credit markets triggers an increase in the equilibrium informal interest rate
			• Group lending institutions, typically:
			  – increased the utility of safe borrowers
			  – attracted a share of constrained safe borrowers back to the market
			• Policy makers and practitioners need to be aware of potential negative spillover
			• Development of microfinance:
			  – lessen the local credit constraints
			  – trigger an increase in the equilibrium informal interest rate
			• Distributional consequences of the creation

26	2017 Baland *et al.*	of MFIs: – transfers welfare from borrowers with no access to microfinance to microfinance users – reduces inequality among borrowers **Effect of Group Activities on Repayment Behavior and Group Attrition.** • Investigated the relationship between loan size and the value of ancillary group activities to highlight their importance in encouraging compliance in credit contracts • Identified repayment equilibria with and without exclusion – exclusionary equilibria are most likely when debt burdens are large – there is significant heterogeneity across members in the benefits from group activities • Members with the largest gains from group activities contributed more often to loan repayment and exclusion was used as an effective disciplinary device • Collective activities undertaken by microfinance groups were not incidental and could be directly linked to their performance • Development of alternative activities by microfinance groups should be encouraged as a way to increase their ability to sanction defecting members

Source: Reviewed, Analysed & Synthesized by the Author.

17.3.2. Interpretation

A detailed analysis has been synthesized in the previous section. Most of the studies focus on the impact assessment of the microfinance programme. It is evident from the reviewed studies that the overall empowerment - including social, economic, political and psychological upliftment - has been made possible through the initiation of the microfinance programme. The vulnerable groups, *e.g.* poor and women, have been benefitted to a large extent. Participation of the women in the local politics has increased with improved decision-making power.

The sustainability of the microfinance programme has also been addressed by some researchers. The role of self-help group–bank linkage programme (SBLP) and microfinance institutions (MFIs) has been exemplary in the field of microfinance. The growth of the microfinance institutions has been recorded by few researchers. The new initiatives by the Government of India have also accelerated the progress of microfinance sector. Microfinance combined with financial inclusion ensured a more formal approach to the vulnerable groups due to reduced financial risk. After reviewing the available literature on microfinance, it is found that most of the studies addressed the demand-side issues only and the counterpart supply-side dynamics have been discussed narrowly.

Conclusion

Microfinance is one of those small ideas which in turn has enormous implications. Microfinance is considered as a vital tool for the alleviation of poverty around the globe. In order to realize its full potential, microfinance must be sustainable and capable of expansion beyond the restrictions imposed by a dependence on development assistance. Both developing and developed nations are key players in this regard. Although most of the studies belong to the demand-side research, supply-side dynamics should be brought into the ambit of research on microfinance sector. It's no secret that microfinance is the most innovative technique which can truly address the problems of global poverty if mapped properly with policy measures.

References

Baland, J. M., Gangadharan, L., Maitra, P., & Somanathan, R. (2017). Repayment and exclusion in a microfinance experiment. *Journal of Economic Behavior & Organization, 137*, 176-190.

Basu, P., & Srivastava, P. (2005). Scaling-up microfinance for India's rural poor. *Policy Research Working Paper, World Bank, Washington, DC,* (3646).

Bhattacharjee, N. (2014). Financial inclusion of the identified slum dwellers in Assam. *Reviews of Literature, 1*(12), 1-9.

Choudhary, M. (2013). A detailed study of micro finance as a tool for tribal transformation in areas of Madhya Pradesh. *International Journal of Business and Management Invention*, *2*(3), 72-76.

Demont, T. (2016). Microfinance spillovers: A model of competition in informal credit markets with an application to Indian villages. *European Economic Review*, *89*, 21-41.

Gemalto. (2008). *Micro Finance: Accelerating micro banking for the under banked people to benefit from simplified access to financial services* [PDF document]. Retrieved from: http://www.gemalto.com/brochures-site/download-site/Documents/micro_finance.pdf

Harper, M. (2002). Self-help groups and Grameen Bank groups: What are the differences? In T. Fisher and M.S. Sriram (Eds.), *Beyond micro-credit: Putting development back into micro-finance* (pp. 169-198). New Delhi: Vistaar.

Karmakar, A. (2008). Indian Microfinance – An Avenue towards Human Capital Development. *The Management Accountant*, *43*(11), 827-834.

Khandelwal, A. K. (2007). Microfinance development strategy for India. *Economic & Political Weekly*, *42*(13), 1127–1135.

Krishnamurthy, R., & Ratnaparkhi, M. (2002, May). Micro-Finance in the new economy-India's Experience. In *International Association of Official Statistics Conference on Official Statistics and the New Economy*. London: ISI.

Kropp, E. W., & Suran, B. S. (2002, September). Linking banks and (financial) self help groups in India - An assessment. In *Seminar on SHG bank linkage programme at New Delhi, Micro Credit Innovations Department, NABARD, Mumbai.*

Kumar, V., & Sharma, H. R. (2007). Micro-Finance in Mountainous States (Disparities in Outreach). *Journal of Man & Development*, June, 81-95.

Kumar, V., Sharma, R. K., & Sharma, H. R. (2008). Impact of Microfinancing on employment, income and empowerment - Micro evidence from Himachal Pradesh. *Financing Agriculture*, *40*, 3-8.

Ledgerwood, J. (1999). *Microfinance handbook: An institutional and financial perspective*. Washington, DC: World Bank.

Ledgerwood, J., Earne, J., & Nelson, C. (Eds.). (2013). *The new microfinance handbook: A financial market system perspective*. Washington, DC: World Bank.

Legatum Ventures. (2011). Microfinance in India: A Crisis at the Bottom of the Pyramid. *Dubai, UAE: Legatum Group.*
Maurya, R. (2011). Women, microfinance and financial inclusion in India. *International Journal of Business Economics and Management Research, 2*(7), 61-72.
Mitlin, D. (2003). Finance for shelter: recent history, future perspectives. *Small Enterprise Development, 14*(1), 11-20.
NABARD. (1998). *Task force on Supportive Policy and Regulatory Framework for Micro Finance in India.* Mumbai, India: National Bank for Agriculture and Rural Development.
Nair, T. S., & Tankha, A. (2015). *Inclusive Finance India Report 2014.* New Delhi: Oxford University Press.
Nishanka, A. K., & Subudhi, M. (2012). *Organisational structure of 'Tribal Bank': A new banking operating system in Odisha towards a best financial inclusion* [PDF document]. Retrieved from: http://ssrn.com/abstract=2017553
Parida, P. C., & Sinha, A. (2010). Performance and sustainability of self-help groups in India: A gender perspective. *Asian Development Review, 27*(1), 80-103.
Pathrose, E. P., Baby, A., & Maheshwari, U. (2015). A Study on the challenges faced by customers in financial inclusion. *International Journal of Scientific Research and Management, 3*(1), 1989-1995.
Puhazhendhi, V., & Satyasai, K. J. S. (2000). *Microfinance for rural people: An impact evaluation.* Department of Economic Analysis and Research. Mumbai: NABARD.
Puhazhendi, V., & Badatya, K. C. (2002, November). SHG-Bank linkage programme for rural poor–An impact assessment. In *Seminar on SHG bank linkage programme at New Delhi, Micro Credit Innovations Department, NABARD, Mumbai.*
Rangarajan Committee. (2008). *Report of the Committee on Financial Inclusion.* Ministry of Finance, Government of India.
Rather, N. A., & Lone, P. A. (2014). Addressing financial exclusion through micro finance: Lessons from the state of Jammu and Kashmir. *International Journal of Management Research and Business Strategy, 3*(2), 72-79.
Rizvi, H. S., & Rizvi, S. A. M. (2011). *Microfinance amongst Tribals in India.* Manuscript in preparation.
Rutherford, S. (1999, January). *The poor and their money: An essay about financial services for poor people.* Institute for Development Policy

and Management, University of Manchester, UK.

Samapti, G. (2010). Microfinance for micro enterprises: an impact evaluation of self help groups. *Occasional Paper, National Bank for Agriculture and Rural Development, Mumbai,* (55).

Sarangi, N. (2007). *Microfinance and the rural poor: A study of group-based credit programmes in Madhya Pradesh, India* (Doctoral dissertation). Jawaharlal Nehru University, New Delhi. Retrieved from: http://hdl.handle.net/10603/17649

Singh, D. K. (2001). Impact of self-help groups on the economy of marginalised farmers of Kanpar Dehat District of Uttar Pradesh (A case study). *Indian Journal of Agricultural Economics, 56*(3), 463.

Singh, N. (2004). *Building social capital through micro-finance: A perspective on the growth of micro-finance sector with special reference to India.* Retrieved from: http://www.sasnet.lu.se/EASASpapers/20NareshSingh.pdf

Swain, R. B. (2007). Can microfinance empower women? Self-help groups in India. *Microfinance and Gender: New Contributions to an Old Issue (ADA Dialogue), 37,* 61–82.

Venkataramany, S., & Bhasin, B. B. (2009). Path to financial inclusion: The success of self-help groups-bank linkage programme in India. *The International Business & Economics Research Journal, 8*(11), 11-19.

Wagh, Y. (2013). A study on various dimensions of problems and prospects of MFI's in Udaipur city. *Asia Pacific Journal of Marketing & Management Review, 2*(2), 161-171.

ABOUT THE EDITORS

Dr Manoj Sharma is presently working as Assistant Professor, Department of Management & Humanities, National Institute of Technology Hamirpur, Himachal Pradesh [INDIA]. During twelve years of research and teaching, the editor has published more than twenty research papers in National and International Journals. Dr. Sharma has also served to various universities and institutes in different capacities. He is also the life time member of Indian Economic Association and Indian Commerce Association

Dr. Yogesh Gupta is working as Associate Professor and Head of Department of Management & Humanities, National Institute of Technology Hamirpur, Himachal Pradesh [INDIA]. He has teaching and research experience of thirty years. He has served in different capacity in various institutes and organizations.

Aman Sharma holds an M.Phil. (Economics) degree along with M.A. (Business Economics) [Gold Medalist] and P.G. Diploma (Population Studies) [Gold Medalist]. He has also qualified the UGC-NET in the subjects of Economics and Management. He has a research experience over 3 years as Research Assistant/Investigator with the reputed institutions like Population Research Centre, Shimla (India); Himachal Pradesh Institute of Public Administration (HIPA), Shimla (India); National Institute of Rural Development & Panchayati Raj (NIRDPR), Hyderabad (India); and Lakehead University, Ontario (Canada).

www.ingramcontent.com/pod-product-compliance
Lightning Source LLC
Chambersburg PA
CBHW071206240526
45470CB00018B/1522